If you have a home computer with Internet access you may:
- request an item to be placed on hold.
- renew an item that is not overdue or on hold.
- view titles and due dates checked out on your card.
- view and/or pay your outstanding fines online (over $5).

To view your patron record from your home computer click on Patchogue-Medford Library's homepage: www.pmlib.org

HITLER'S ITALIAN ALLIES

This book tries to understand *why* the Italian armed forces and Fascist regime were so remarkably ineffectual at an activity – war – that was central to their existence. Military-economic weakness, Mussolini's ideological fantasies and strategic megalomania, and Hitler's failure in the wider war made Italian defeat inevitable. But those factors do not wholly account for the peculiarly undignified character of Fascist Italy's final ruin. The book offers an innovative analytical cross-section of the Italian war effort, from society and culture, through politics and war production, to strategy, operations, and tactics, and demonstrates the extent to which Italian *military culture* – a concept with applications far beyond Fascist Italy or its last war – and the blinkered approach of Italy's major industrial enterprises made humiliation inescapable. The result is a striking portrait of the military institutions and regime whose most significant – if temporary – conquest in 1940–43 was a dusty and useless corner of Africa, British Somaliland. The armed forces proved unable to imagine modern war, much less prepare or fight it. The industrialists, with the connivance of generals, admirals, and dictator, produced the least effective, least numerous, and most overpriced weapons of the Second World War. The regime failed miserably in mobilizing the nation's resources. *Hitler's Italian Allies* analyzes the resulting disasters, and explains why the Italian armed forces dissolved prematurely and almost without resistance, in stark contrast to the grim fight to the last cartridge of Hitler's army or the fanatical faithfulness unto death of the troops of Imperial Japan.

MacGregor Knox is Stevenson Professor of International History at the London School of Economics and Political Science. His other works on Fascist and National Socialist foreign and military policies include *Mussolini Unleashed, 1939–1941: Politics and Strategy in Fascist Italy's Last War* and *Common Destiny: Dictatorship, Foreign Policy, and War in Fascist Italy and Nazi Germany*.

HITLER'S ITALIAN ALLIES

Royal Armed Forces, Fascist Regime, and
the War of 1940–1943

MacGregor Knox

The London School of Economics and Political Science

CAMBRIDGE
UNIVERSITY PRESS

PUBLISHED BY THE PRESS SYNDICATE OF THE UNIVERSITY OF CAMBRIDGE
The Pitt Building, Trumpington Street, Cambridge CB2 1RP, United Kingdom

CAMBRIDGE UNIVERSITY PRESS
The Edinburgh Building, Cambridge CB2 2RU, UK   http://www.cup.cam.ac.uk
40 West 20th Street, New York, NY 10011-4211, USA   http://www.cup.org
10 Stamford Road, Oakleigh, Melbourne 3166, Australia
Ruiz do Alarcón 13, 28014 Madrid, Spain

First published 2000

Printed in the United States of America

Typeface Janson 10.5/15 pt.   System 3b2 6.03d [ADVENT]

A catalogue record for this book is available from the British Library

Library of Congress Cataloging-in-Publication Data

Knox, MacGregor.
    Hitler's Italian allies : Royal Armed Forces, Fascist regime, and the war of 1940–1943
MacGregor Knox.
    p. cm.
Includes bibliographical references.
ISBN 0-521-79047-6
    1. World War, 1939–1945—Italy. 2. Italy—History—1922–1945. 3. Fascism—Italy. I.
Title.

D763.18 K57 2000
940.54′1245--dc21   00-023706

ISBN 0 521 79047 6   hardback

per Tina, anche questa volta e sempre

CONTENTS

ACKNOWLEDGMENTS

This short book is in one sense an accident. It emerged from the rewriting of an old essay on Italian "military effectiveness" in the Second World War to fit within a book, *Common Destiny: Dictatorship, Foreign Policy, and War in Fascist Italy and Nazi Germany*, that sought to provide a comprehensive comparative analysis of the Italian and German dictatorships. The new questions that purpose imposed – about the underlying causes of the striking contrast in wartime performance between Fascist Italy and Nazi Germany – soon cracked open the narrowly military-technical framework of the original essay. The mass of new primary sources and often excellent Italian secondary material on many aspects of Italy's war that have appeared since the late 1980s likewise opened up entirely new questions, especially about the performance of the war economy. I pursued those questions obstinately, suppressing the guilty realization that I was writing an essay so long and complex that it would inevitably destroy the symmetry of the book for which I had intended it. When I had finished, I found I had written a novella-length piece that could and should stand on its own. Conversely, its sections on army operations and tactics, once equipped with an appropriate introduction and conclusion, fit well within the original collection as counterpart to a chapter on the unique synthesis between Prusso-German military tradition and Nazi revolution that propelled the *Wehrmacht*'s fight to the last cartridge in 1943–45.

In a broader sense this book, whatever its immediate origins, is nevertheless no accident. It derives from more than two decades of research and thought about Fascist Italy, Nazi Germany, and their last war. It covers material and issues largely unfamiliar to the English-speaking public within an analytical framework or frameworks often viewed as eccentric in Italy. It exploits German as well as Italian sources, a quality still relatively rare in the Italian literature, although happily less unknown now than in earlier decades.

The book's analytical purpose dictates only brief chronological narrative of the military events, and rules out treatment of many aspects of Italy's war. The internal politics of the regime and the dissolution of the home front in 1942–43 are best understood through the readings suggested in the bibliographical note. The wartime travails of Italian society, a subject of great fascination and some recent work in Italian, appear only briefly; however bizarre it may seem to an academic discipline under the domination of social and cultural microhistory, the conduct of war is subject to autonomous laws. Fascist Italy's *military* failure, like that of France in 1940, was first and foremost a failure of Italy's *military culture* and *military institutions.*

But by way of compensation, the book offers a large-scale analytical cross-section of the armed forces, Fascist regime, and their political and social roots that seeks to clarify the much-debated causes of Italy's humiliation in the great war that Mussolini sought for twenty years and finally found. At its deepest level, and despite an occasional note of perhaps misdirected irony, the book is in its peculiar way an expression of a profound and enduring affection for Italy acquired in childhood along with – and through – the language itself. The critical analysis that Clausewitz taught, the unblinking search for the causes of things, is the fittest commemoration of the immense suffering that *guerra fascista* in alliance with Hitler inflicted upon Italy and its neighbors.

Many friends and acquaintances have helped me over the years, but three in particular have been indispensable to the writing of this book. Giorgio Rochat, with whom I have sometimes cordially disagreed, has been ever generous with copies of his own works, which are vital to understanding the subject, and with works by others. Brian R. Sullivan supplied me, as he has for many years, with far-ranging bibliographical counsel and encouragement, and with documents turned up during his extensive archival explorations. And Lucio Ceva, whose work on the Italian armed forces and military-industrial complex in the interwar period and Second World War defines the field, has been tireless in keeping me up-to-date bibliographically and in offering incisive criticism and encouragement in equal measure. I also thank Allen R. Millett and Williamson Murray for permission to adapt parts of the essay from which this book ultimately derives, "The Italian Armed Forces, 1940–1943," which appeared under their editorship in *Military Effectiveness*, vol. 3 (Boston: Allen & Unwin, 1988), pp. 136–79.

I remain above all immeasurably beholden to my wife, Tina Isaacs, and I dedicate this book to her in love and gratitude. The faults of commission or omission it may yet contain are nevertheless my responsibility alone.

MacGregor Knox
London, December 1999

ABBREVIATIONS

AAR: after-action report.

ACS: Archivio Centrale dello Stato (Central State Archive, Rome).

ADAP: *Akten zur deutschen auswärtigen Politik* (Baden-Baden, Frankfurt, Göttingen, 1950–) (cited as series/volume/document).

Africa: Mario Montanari, *Le operazioni in Africa settentrionale*, 4 vols. (Rome, 1984–93).

Bottai: Giuseppe Bottai, *Diario 1935–1944*, ed. Giordano Bruno Guerri (Milan, 1982).

Ciano: Galeazzo Ciano, *Diario 1937–1943* (Milan, 1980).

DDI: *I documenti diplomatici italiani* (Rome 1952–) (cited as series/ volume/document).

Direttive Superaereo: Francesco Mattesini and Mario Cermelli, eds., *Le direttive tecnico-operative di Superaereo*, 2 vols. (Rome, 1992).

DRZW: *Das Deutsche Reich und der Zweite Weltkrieg*, 6 vols. to date (Stuttgart, 1979–).

NARA: National Archives and Records Administration, Washington, DC (cited as microcopy/roll/frame, microcopy/serial/frame or record group/box/folder).

OO: Benito Mussolini, *Opera omnia* (Florence and Rome, 1951–78).

USE: Stato Maggiore dell'Esercito, Ufficio Storico (Italian Army Historical Office, Rome).

USMM: Ufficio Storico della Marina Militare (Italian Navy Historical Office, Rome).

VCSMG 1939–43: Antonello Biagini and Fernando Frattolillo, eds., *Verbali delle riunioni tenute dal capo di Stato Maggiore Generale*, 4 vols. (Rome, 1983–85).

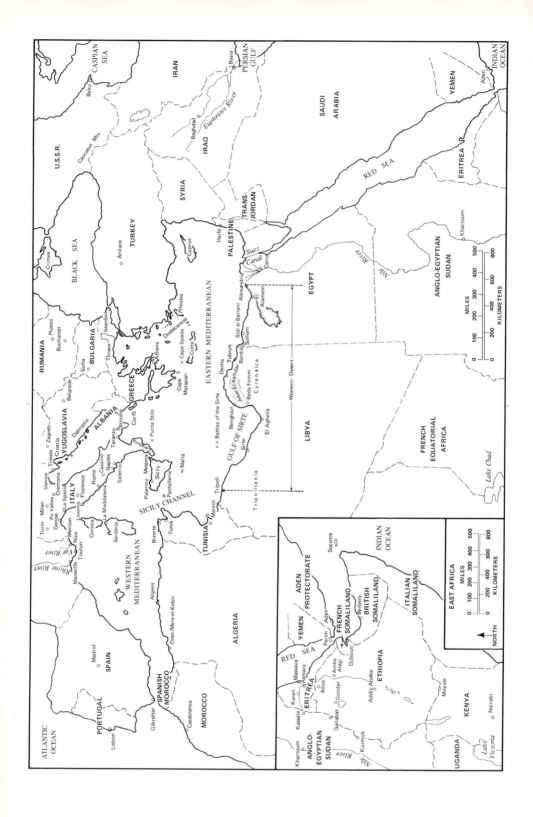

INTRODUCTION:
DEFEAT – AND HUMILIATION

Defeat was inescapable. Mussolini's associate and senior partner, Adolf Hitler, challenged by December 1941 the same world of enemies that had destroyed his royal predecessor, the Emperor Wilhelm II. For all its operational-tactical brilliance, stunning initial victories, and plunder, the Axis coalition of National Socialist Germany, Fascist Italy, and Imperial Japan possessed less than half the economic power of its enemies. Barring improbable levels of incompetence or irresolution in Britain and the United States, that crushing imbalance doomed the Axis in the intercontinental war of attrition that emerged from Hitler's failure to destroy Soviet Russia, Imperial Japan's attack on Pearl Harbor, and the Führer's immediately following and wholly eccentric declaration of war on the United States.[1]

In that global struggle, Hitler's Fascist allies were a pygmy among giants. The fatal consequences of the miscarriage of Nazi Germany's

---

1. Even a renewal of his 1939–41 alliance with Stalin might not have saved Hitler, for after mid-1945 the Americans could destroy cities – or point targets such as Reich Chancellery and Führer headquarters – with nuclear weapons. For a brilliant but ultimately unpersuasive effort to locate the war's turning point far later than December 1941, and in part at the operational-tactical level, see Richard Overy, *Why the Allies Won* (London, 1995).

Opposite: The Mediterranean and Africa, 1940–43.

1

"global Blitzkrieg" would have destroyed them whatever their level of military and military-economic effectiveness.[2] Yet Italy's record of defeat in 1940–43 was peculiarly humiliating. It had little in common with the heroic disasters of Benito Mussolini's German ally, whose *Götterdämmerung* was worthy in its pitiless and gleeful destructiveness of the Wagnerian myth its leader so admired. And Italy tasted defeat from the beginning; no years of striking victories delayed and cushioned its sting.

The sources of the military misadventures that destroyed Fascism's prestige and internal cohesion, determined its bloodless collapse in July 1943, and foreshadowed the disintegration of the Italian armed forces that September have largely escaped comprehensive analysis. Partial answers, such as Italy's dependence on foreign energy and raw materials, the dictator's sovereign fecklessness, and the alleged absence of popular support for war, still dominate the field. What follows is an attempt to do justice to the complexity and interrelatedness of the causation and the sheer bulk of the accumulated evidence. The result emphasizes above all the cultural and organizational failings of Italian society and especially of its military institutions. However great the contribution of other factors, it was Italy's *military culture* that largely determined the technological imagination, force structure, and operational-tactical expertise of the armed forces with which Fascism sought to realize its wide-ranging ideological aspirations, both foreign and domestic. That insight – and the wide variety of military pathologies evident in the Italian armed forces at war – have a direct bearing on states and military institutions in other times and places. For regardless of the technological ingenuity

2.   For details, see Mark Harrison, "The Economics of World War II: An Overview," Table 1.3, p. 10, in Harrison, ed. *The Economics of World War II* (Cambridge, 1998), and Chapter 2, Table 2.3 of this work ("total industrial potential," 1938: USA + Britain + Soviet Russia = 861; Germany + Italy + Japan = 348). "Weltblitzkrieg": Andreas Hillgruber, *Hitlers Strategie: Politik und Kriegführung 1940–41* (Frankfurt a. M., 1965), p. 16.

or economic brute force at a power's command, effectiveness in war ultimately depends upon the culture, command style, and professional ethos of its armed forces. That law is as true and as merciless in its consequences in the purported new era of "battlespace information dominance" as it was in the age of mass armies in which Fascist Italy fought and failed.[3]

The book's purpose has dictated a topical structure. The first chapter seeks to explain how and why Italy entered the Second World War as Hitler's ally, and the stages through which it descended into defeat and humiliation; a chronology at the book's end likewise offers narrative detail useful in situating events described in the topical sections. Chapter 2 analyzes the social and cultural bases of the Italian war effort, the regime's capacity to direct that effort, and the contributions of Italian industry. Chapter 3 sketches the three armed forces' visions of modern war. Chapter 4 investigates the enduring characteristics of Italian strategy. And the two final chapters chart the operational and tactical performance of the armed forces, the chief determinants of whether the Italian state would retain a measure of dignity in defeat.

---

3. For the contemporary implications of that insight, and trenchant application to the armed forces of the United States, see especially Williamson Murray, "Does Military Culture Matter?," *Orbis* (Winter 1999), pp. 27–42.

1

FASCIST ITALY'S LAST WAR

War, a very great war, was from the beginning the essence of Mussolini's program. His final effort, the war of 1940–43, to his mortification destroyed the Fascist regime. But from the very beginning of his trajectory from 1914 to 1943, from Socialist fanatic to deposed Duce of Fascism, he had unhesitatingly invoked "that fearful and enthralling word: war." Only war, he insisted in October–November 1914, could produce the genuine national integration missed during Italy's territorial unification in 1859–70. Only war could confirm Italy's membership in the charmed circle of dominant nations: "Either war, or let's end this *commedia* of [claiming to be] a great power."[1] The war of 1915–18 that Mussolini and a motley coalition of *interventisti* helped to force upon parliament and nation through oratorical passion and street violence did not disappoint. The Great War "completed the *Risorgimento*" through the conquest of Trento, Trieste, and the Brenner frontier. It abolished Austria-Hungary, bled France white, and gave Italy far greater latitude to entertain the ambitions of Mediterranean domination long-current among its

1.   OO 7:7, 197, 147; see also in general MacGregor Knox, *Common Destiny: Dictatorship, Foreign Policy and War in Fascist Italy and Nazi Germany* (Cambridge, 2000), Chapter 2.

The eve of disaster: a voluble Mussolini receives Hitler in Florence as Italian troops attack Greece, 28 October 1940 (U.S. National Archives 242-JRB-43-6).

5

governing elite. Above all, the Great War by delayed action made Mussolini himself Duce of Fascism and chief of government.

He had preached war in 1914–15 as a revolutionary conflict that would overthrow "this Italy of priests, pro-Austrians, and monarchists."[2] The 650,000 deaths, bitter defeats, and innumerable privations along the road to a victory bought too dearly, and Liberal Italy's predictable failure to achieve its inflated war aims in 1918–19 so unhinged the Italian establishment that in 1919–20 it lost command of government.[3] War had indeed become a sort of revolution. Italy's socialists, under the impulse of the Soviet example but without Lenin's disciplined organization or ruthless drive, bid inchoately for power in the factories and countryside. By autumn 1920 they had failed. As their power receded, the paramilitary gangs of the *fasci di combattimento*, which Mussolini had founded in spring 1919 from shock-troop veterans, ex-socialist apostates, and nationalist university students, took the offensive with the complicity, open or tacit, of the Liberal governing class, police, and army. By summer 1922 Fascist violence throughout north Italy had destroyed both the rural and municipal "baronies" of the Socialist Party and the power-position of the Liberal state itself. At the center, in Rome, Mussolini's alternation of threats and blandishments paralyzed his Liberal and Catholic rivals. In the end, in October 1922, he forced the monarchy to choose between making him prime minister or fighting him in the streets.

Yet the "March on Rome" by the blackshirted gangs that gave force to his claim to rule Italy only produced a peculiar condominium, a regime based on precarious compromises between Fascism and the monarchy, the royal army behind it, and the Italian establishment. The March on Rome, Mussolini conceded privately in 1924 to Party leaders, was "a revolutionary deed and a victorious insurrection, [but] not a revolution.

---

2.   OO 6:429 (10 November 1914); war as revolution: 7:139–41, 182, 251, 393–95.
3.   For a comparative analysis of the path to dictatorship in Italy and Germany (1919–22/33), see Knox, *Common Destiny*, Chapter 1.

The revolution comes later."[4] The nature of that revolution emerged most eloquently from a December 1924 report assembled from conversations with Mussolini and members of his entourage by the German ambassador in Rome, Constantin von Neurath:

> [Mussolini] was attempting to make the Mediterranean a *mare italiano*. In that effort France stood in the way, and he had begun to prepare for battle with that adversary. Hence ... the reversal in his attitude toward Germany. For that [change], as Mussolini has remarked both to his entourage and to me personally, his conviction of Germany's vitality and swift revival was decisive. On the other hand he also believed that the situation in Europe created by the Versailles Treaty was untenable. In the new war between France and Germany that would therefore break out, Italy, led by Mussolini, would place itself at Germany's side in order to crush France jointly. If that endeavor succeeded, Mussolini would claim as his booty the entire French North African coast and create a great "imperium latinum" in the Mediterranean. Then he might also judge the moment had come to have himself acclaimed emperor, and to push aside easily the unwarlike king.

World war had made Mussolini head of government. It had flattened the Socialists, as he had foretold when they had expelled him in November 1914. Yet war had not decapitated the state, as it had in Germany; the travails of 1915–18 had merely shaken rather than destroyed an establishment that retained under its hesitant master, King Victor Emanuel III, a degree of cohesion sufficient to block the claims of Fascist Party and Duce to total power. Fascism for its part fell far shorter than its German counterpart and eventual ally in its attempt to create an all-embracing and all-explanatory system of belief, a militant ideology that linked the dictator's goals to the historical process and inspired fanatical commitment. And as in Germany, despite valiant Mussolinian efforts at the indoctrination of the young and the

4.   OO 44:10 (emphasis added).

"fascistization" of the masses "so that tomorrow Italian and Fascist, more or less like Italian and Catholic, will be the same thing," only another great war could make the regime total. Demography – another vital ideological ingredient in the Duce's program – likewise demanded and made possible violent expansion: "numbers are strength." And only war could achieve for Italy the true great-power status grasped at but demonstrably missed in 1915–18.[5]

Geography predetermined Fascist Italy's enemies: Britain's command of the distant choke points at Gibraltar and Suez, and the threat of close blockade from British and French naval and air bases – Malta, Bizerte, Corsica, Toulon – almost within sight of Italy, galled the Italian navy. Its foremost Great War leader and Mussolini's navy minister in 1922–25, Grand Admiral Paolo Thaon di Revel, trumpeted repeatedly in parliament that Italy "instead of dominating [it], would remain a prisoner in the Mediterranean" unless the navy rather than the army secured priority in armaments.[6] Mussolini made this doctrine his own, and by 1926–27 had enunciated a geopolitical dogma that fused navalist geopolitics with the Italian establishment's post-*Risorgimento* aspiration to great-power status:

5. "Italian and Catholic": OO 21:362 (22 June 1925). For an effort to understand the disparate natures and differences in motivational force of the ideologies of the Italian and German dictatorships, see Knox, *Common Destiny*, pp. 59–78, 231–32, which also includes discussion of Mussolini's demographic fantasies (see also Carl Ipsen, *Dictating Demography: The Problem of Population in Fascist Italy* [Cambridge, 1996]).

6. *Atti del Parlamento Italiano, Camera dei Deputati*, 1925, vol. 3, pp. 3151, 3171 (30 March 1925); for other Di Revel sallies, ibid., *Senato*, 1921–22, vol. 3, pp. 3833–34 (14 August 1922), vol. 4, p. 4651 (16 February 1923); 1924, vol. 1, pp. 915–16 (20 December 1924); also Thaon di Revel to Mussolini, 28 March 1925, in Giovanni Bernardi, *Il disarmo navale fra le due guerre mondiali (1919–1939)* (Rome, 1975), p. 217.

A nation that has no free access to the sea cannot be considered a free nation; a nation that has no free access to the oceans cannot be considered a great power.[7]

In July 1927 – scarcely a year before the Kellogg-Briand Pact through which the guileless Americans sought to "outlaw" war – he informed his principal military advisers with evident satisfaction that war was inevitable: "soon or perhaps less soon, but it will certainly come." War against Yugoslavia for a start – "the attack must be aggressive, unexpected."[8] But war must ultimately also embrace France and Britain, Italy's "jailers" in the Mediterranean.

Geography and the alignments and resentments of the European powers also determined Fascist Italy's choice of allies. Only one great power – potentially the very greatest – opposed France and Britain: Germany. It had already bid for European and world mastery in 1914–18, and had failed narrowly; only its strategic lunacy in challenging the United States and in refusing in winter 1917–18 to trade Belgium and northern France for a peace that gave it mastery of eastern Europe to the Urals and Caucasus had brought it down. But abortive attempts to enlist the German army and Right in the 1920s led to nothing: Germany, Mussolini confided to his undersecretary for war in 1929, was "disarmed – we cannot negotiate for possible cooperation against France." The coming to power of the German Right, Mussolini foresaw, would nevertheless make Germany a fit ally for Fascist Italy by the mid-1930s and open the road for the "revolutionary

---

7. Mussolini, speech to military leaders, autumn 1926–early 1927 (source: General Arturo Vacca-Maggiolini, quoted in Emilio Canevari, *La guerra italiana* [Rome, 1948–49], vol. 2, p. 211). Giorgio Rochat, *Badoglio* (Turin, 1974), pp. 557–58, places the speech in autumn 1926; see also OO 40:51–52.

8. Antonello Biagini and Alessandro Gionfrida, eds., *Lo Stato Maggiore Generale tra le due guerre (verbali delle riunioni presiedute da Badoglio dal 1925 al 1937)* (Rome, 1997), p. 105.

foreign policy" (in the dismayed words of Mussolini's foreign minister in 1929–32, Count Dino Grandi) that the Duce sought.[9]

The advent of Adolf Hitler – whom Mussolini secretly commended to the Grand Council of Fascism in spring 1932 and whose conquest of power he supported noisily in the Italian press – indeed gave Italy much additional freedom. But Mussolini's efforts in winter 1932–33 to persuade his military advisers and the king that the time had come to attack Yugoslavia predictably failed. France would turn on Italy and – in the words of Mussolini's then minister of war, General Pietro Gàzzera – "give us a lesson that would last us for a century."[10] The quarrel with Germany that erupted in 1933–34 over Hitler's ambition to annex his native Austria forthwith in the wake of the Nazi *Machtergreifung* in Germany temporarily wrecked Mussolini's hopes of the ideological alliance with a resurgent nationalist Germany that his foreign policy program required. But the Italo-German quarrel over Austria brought dividends: France renewed the implicit offers of backing for Italian expansion in East Africa that it had made in 1932 in a futile effort to lure Mussolini away from Germany. And Ethiopia at least proved a victim that Mussolini's military advisers and their royal master were willing – grudgingly and on condition of great-power acquiescence – to allow him to conquer.

In the event only French acquiescence was forthcoming; London proved initially puzzled, then sought to bribe Mussolini with scraps of Ethiopia, and at last deployed its naval might to the Mediterranean in a diffident effort at deterrence. The Duce's military advisers and the monarch quailed – war with Britain would reduce Italy "to a Balkan level."[11] But

9. Mussolini, in notes by General Pietro Gàzzera (undersecretary, then minister of war, 1928–33), 11 June, 7 August 1929; 30 June 1930; 27 January 1931, Gàzzera papers microfilm; see also Knox, *Common Destiny*, pp. 125–26.

10. Gàzzera notes, 8 and 9 January 1933, Gàzzera papers microfilm.

11. Badoglio to Mussolini, September 1935, in Rochat, *Militari e politici nella preparazione della campagna d'Etiopia* (Milan, 1971), p. 229.

Mussolini had by then committed over 200,000 troops and the regime's prestige to war in Africa; London's craven private protestations that it wished to avoid a Mediterranean war allowed him to hold his course.[12] King, generals, and admirals swallowed their doubts: Mussolini faced them, as before and later, with the unpalatable choice of removing him by violence and thus opening the road to Communist and Socialist resurgence, or of accepting the risks that his foreign and military policies entailed.

Fascist Italy attacked Ethiopia on 3 October 1935 and by May 1936 had overwhelmed Haile Selassie's armies through massive logistical effort, immensely superior fire-power, total command of the air, and prodigal use of mustard gas. The resulting estrangement from the Western powers was far from unwelcome to Mussolini. The economic sanctions they imposed on Italy in autumn 1935 were severe enough to rally all patriotic forces to support the regime and its war – from the Roman Catholic Church to tacit anti-Fascists such as the philosopher and *Senatore* Benedetto Croce. Yet sanctions were too feeble to force Italy to desist. Hitler was happy to assist; Germany's contribution to the coal imports that powered Italy's industry and railroads rose swiftly from 23 percent in 1933 to almost 64 percent in 1936.[13] Mussolini greeted the collapse of Anglo-French efforts at an eleventh-hour compromise – the Hoare-Laval plan of December 1935 – with ill-disguised glee. And in January–March 1936 he clinched the long-sought alignment with Germany by proposing to the German ambassador that Germany make Austria its "satellite," and by giving Hitler advance approval to

12. See especially the abject remarks of Sir Samuel Hoare in *Documents on British Foreign Policy*, Second Series, vol. 14 (London, 1976), document 620 (and the resulting Italian assessment of British resolve, 653); likewise ibid., vol. 15, documents 93, 98, 105; and DDI 8/2/166, 181, 189, 202, 218, 224, 250, 284, 376 (further astonishing assurances by Hoare), 388.

13. Figures: Elizabeth Wiskemann, *The Rome-Berlin Axis* (London, 1966), p. 76.

Germany's remilitarization of the Rhineland and the consequent destruction of the Locarno security treaty which had linked Germany, France,
Belgium, Britain, and Italy.[14]

Mussolini's subsequent course – in popular wisdom ("if only he had
stopped after Ethiopia") and in the interpretations of many historians –
resulted above all from a loss of all sense of proportion, an *involuzione*
deriving from African victory: Mussolini ostensibly became the first
and greatest victim of his own propaganda. The reality is simpler.
The founding of the new Italian empire in 1936 at last gave the
dictator the domestic prestige to implement both the "revolutionary
foreign policy" to which he had aspired since the 1920s and its domestic complement. The time for the real Fascist revolution had at last
come.

Germany's growing preponderance in armaments and visibly
increasing dynamism so cowed the Western powers that they were
prepared to pay for Italy's friendship. But Mussolini showed little
interest, despite bizarre efforts by Grandi – whom Mussolini had exiled
to the London embassy – to bring Mussolini and the British prime
minister, Neville Chamberlain, together by stealth and duplicity.[15]
Mussolini had already chosen a new war – in Spain after July 1936 –
along with ever-closer alignment with Germany in foreign policy. At
home he stepped up his efforts to supplant the monarchy. War made
Fascists and was the principal element of Mussolini's "permanent revolution": "When Spain is over, I'll think of something else: the character
of the Italians must be [re-]created through battle." The Rome-Berlin
"Axis," which Mussolini proclaimed in November 1936, led inexorably

---

14. Renato Mori, *Mussolini e la conquista dell'Etiopia* (Florence, 1978), Chapter 5;
    ADAP C/4/485, 579; Knox, *Common Destiny*, pp. 141–43.

15. See especially William C. Mills, "The Chamberlain-Grandi Conversations of
    July–August 1937 and the Appeasement of Italy," *International History Review*
    19:3 (1997), pp. 594–619.

to a triumphant visit by the Duce to Germany in 1937 and to Italy's accession that November to the German-Japanese Anti-Comintern Pact, "the most formidable politico-military bloc that has ever existed." The Italo-German alignment, noted Count Galeazzo Ciano, Mussolini's son-in-law, foreign minister, and putative successor from mid-1936 until his dismissal in early 1943, was "based above all upon the identity of political regimes, which determines a common destiny."[16]

Mussolini plunged into Spain without consulting the king, and despite the misgivings of both the army and navy leaderships. Yet for the moment the Duce had acquired the power to override such constraints: he replaced the army chief of staff of the Ethiopian war, General Federico Baistrocchi, with a less contentious figure, Alberto Pariani. And in March 1938 he organized his own elevation – and the king's demotion – to the newly invented rank of "First Marshal of the Empire."[17] Yet growing discontent with the regime's course could still restrain Mussolini. His acquiescence to the logical outcome of his Austrian policy – German annexation in March 1938 – notably sapped his personal ascendancy over elite and popular opinion. In the eyes of the sophisticated public the regime had for its own ideological reasons – or out of weakness – surrendered the key element of Italy's 1918 triumph, the Austrian buffer state.[18]

Hitler's ensuing visit to Rome, Naples, and Florence in May 1938 therefore did not produce the military alliance that the Germans offered and at which Mussolini still aimed. Ciano, avid for the British recognition of Italy's conquest of Ethiopia that Chamberlain had promised, sought

---

16. Ciano, 23 September, 13 and 6 November, 27 October 1937.
17. Navy opposition: Ciano, 14 November 1937; Renzo De Felice, "Mussolini e Vittorio Emanuele III Primi Marescialli dell'Impero," in Università degli Studi di Messina, *Scritti in onore di Vittorio De Caprariis* (Rome, n.d.), pp. 347–68.
18. See especially Ciano, 12 and 15 March 1938.

delay, and Mussolini recognized the need to "prepare a wide basis of popularity" for the coming alliance.[19] What he nevertheless could do was to place Fascist Italy squarely at the side of National Socialist Germany in the swiftly escalating crisis that Hitler provoked over Czechoslovakia in summer–autumn 1938. Only Hitler's own loss of nerve and belated willingness to accept Bohemia-Moravia by installments saved Mussolini from the consequences of his bellicose speeches in support of Germany, and of his private conviction that the Axis would "liquidate" the decadent Western powers if war came.[20]

Nor did Mussolini relish the popularity as savior of peace that his unsought role as go-between at the Munich conference had brought.[21] In the aftermath he intensified his war on Italy's own upper middle classes, "the revolting craven bourgeoisie." Hitler, affected by a similar post-Munich sense that his own far more compact and ideologically aligned intelligentsia had wavered ("unfortunately, we need them; otherwise one could – who knows – exterminate them or whatever") merely commanded that his propaganda apparatus infuse the public with blind faith in his leadership and conviction that National Socialism and Germany were identical.[22] Italy's campaign rested on a far different premise – the notion that ridicule and coercion could produce fanatical

19. Ciano, 5 May and 11 July 1938.

20. OO 29:146, 153, 158, 161, 163–64; Ciano, 25, 27, 28 September 1938.

21. Chamberlain's last-minute appeal for Mussolini's mediation diverted Italian policy from its warlike course by implicitly and unintentionally threatening Mussolini with universal opprobrium and with disaffection on the home front if he refused his cooperation and war resulted: see Mussolini's concession to Ciano (28 September 1938) that it was "impossible" to refuse the British request.

22. Hitler secret speech, in Wilhelm Treue, ed. "Die Rede Hitlers vor dem deutschen Presse (10. November 1938)," *Vierteljahrshefte für Zeitgeschichte* 6:2 (1958), pp. 186, 188.

loyalty. It culminated in the formal adoption of Nuremberg-style anti-Semitic laws in October–November 1938 against opposition even from within the Fascist Party. The Church manifested legalistic displeasure at the law's discrimination against Catholic converts in mixed marriages. But the autocratic Pope Pius XI, although he had consistently denounced the "pagan state idolatry" of the regime and its German ally, shrank from provoking an open quarrel. A generalized disquiet, tempered by an upsurge of the mockery that had long served as a safety valve for popular discontent, nevertheless surrounded the regime.[23]

Not content with infuriating or unsettling the very educated classes upon whom he relied to organize Italian expansion, Mussolini openly claimed French territory – "Tunis, Corsica, Nice, Savoy" rang the cries in the Chamber of *Fasci* and Corporations – in November 1938. In the following months, he toyed with ideas of a single-handed war against France. Conflict with France would give a Rome-Berlin-Tokyo alliance, to which he gave the green light in January 1939, some degree of public support. Even the king, "who viewed the French with loathing and scorn," was pleased at the prospect of German military support.[24] In the event, Japanese evasiveness, Italian consternation at Hitler's sudden and unannounced seizure of Prague in March 1939, and Mussolini and Ciano's own answering invasion in April of Italy's de facto colony, Albania, delayed the proceedings.[25] But on 22 May 1939 Ciano and his German counterpart, Joachim von Ribbentrop, solemnly signed the "Pact of Steel," which bound the two regimes irrevocably to fight as allies should either find itself "involved in warlike complications" – whether

23. See particularly De Felice, *Storia degli ebrei sotto il fascismo* (Turin, 1972), pp. 285–88.

24. Ciano, 5 January 1939.

25. Despite its narrow diplomatic focus, Mario Toscano, *The Origins of the Pact of Steel* (Baltimore, 1967) still provides the best account of the alliance negotiations.

through defense or aggression – with a third power or powers. Mussolini personally removed what little residual ambiguity existed about the alliance's purposes by inserting into the preamble a statement of intent: Fascist Italy and Nazi Germany sought through the Pact "to secure their living space." The Duce's embarrassed postscript, a missive conveyed to Berlin by General Ugo Cavallero, a high military figure with a unique reputation for ingenuity and deviousness, spelled out the subtext the Italians had pressed upon a complaisant – but characteristically mendacious – Ribbentrop. Italy desired to postpone the "inevitable" war with the Western democracies until 1943, by which time Italy's armed forces would have fully rearmed. Hitler replied that "he was generally in full agreement" with the Italian position.[26]

Increasingly urgent warnings that Hitler was in actuality bent upon war with Poland that autumn even at the price of a conflict with the Western powers belatedly roused Ciano to visit Hitler and Ribbentrop at Salzburg in mid-August. There he discovered, not for the last time, that "they have tricked us and lied to us." Mussolini's instincts nevertheless counseled war, especially once the announcement of the Nazi-Soviet pact on 22–23 August appeared to have nullified the Western powers' sharpest weapon, the British blockade. But in the end, Italy's dependence on seaborne coal, oil, and food; its exposed strategic position facing the combined naval might of Britain and France; the desperate unpreparedness of its armed forces; the anguish with which Italian opinion regarded war; and – last but decidedly not least – the king's veto forced the Duce to declare Italy's "nonbelligerence" on 1 September, as Germany attacked. To save face, Mussolini had presented Hitler with a list "that would kill a bull, if a bull could read" (as Ciano put it) of the raw materials the Italian armed forces and economy required if Italy were to fight. Hitler had in turn graciously released Mussolini from his obligations.[27]

26.   ADAP D/6/386, 426; DDI 8/12/59, 130.

27.   The most vivid, if inevitably selective, account of these events remains Ciano, 11 August–3 September 1939; see also the summary in Knox, *Mussolini*

In the nine months that followed, Mussolini strove singlemindedly to redeem himself as the leader of a warrior people. And as in 1933–36 and the Spanish war, it was the growth of German power that in the end freed him to act. When the tightening British blockade of German exports threatened to deprive Italy of Ruhr coal and force the nation and the regime into dependence on the West, Hitler offered in March 1940 to supply Italy's entire requirement – 1,000,000 tons a month – by rail through Switzerland and Austria.[28] Then the immense Nazi victories in Scandinavia in April and in France and the Low Countries in May dissolved the opposition to war of the king, the generals and admirals, and the Italian public. The Mediterranean hegemony to which the educated classes had long aspired seemed momentarily within Italy's grasp; perhaps Mussolini had been right after all. The Duce himself reiterated in his war speech of 10 June the aim he had held since the mid-1920s. Italy took up arms "to resolve . . . the question of [its] maritime frontiers; we seek to break the territorial and military chains that suffocate us in our sea, for a people of forty-five million souls cannot be truly free unless it has free access to the oceans."[29]

Within six months the independent Italian war "parallel" to that of Germany that Mussolini had projected from January 1940 onward was in ruins. A fleet encounter off Calabria in July and the sinking of three Italian battleships at anchor at Taranto in November confirmed the British Royal Navy's tactical and operational superiority – a lesson driven home by the destruction in night action of three heavy cruisers, the pride of the fleet, at the battle of Cape Matapan in March 1941. On land, Italy's long-delayed thrust into Egypt in September 1940 turned into

---

Unleashed, 1939–1941: Politics and Strategy in Fascist Italy's Last War (Cambridge, 1982), pp. 42–43.

28. See Knox, *Mussolini*, pp. 69–74, 82–84.

29. OO 29:404–05; Knox, *Mussolini*, Chapters 2 and 3, offers comprehensive treatment of Italy's nonbelligerence and intervention.

disaster when Britain counterattacked in December. And the greatest humiliation of all was the steady retreat into Albania in November–December 1940 of the Italian forces that had attacked Greece and of the reinforcements that army and regime rushed in disorder across the Adriatic.[30]

Defeat, as Hitler sardonically put it on 5 December, "has had the healthy effect of once more compressing Italian claims to within the natural boundaries of Italian capabilities."[31] Mussolini's efforts to ensure exclusive ownership of Mediterranean victory by barring German forces from Italy's theater gave way between December 1940 and February 1941 to ever more urgent entreaties for aid. Luftwaffe forces based on Sicily and North Africa, the dispatch of a small German armored force to Tripoli, and Hitler's descent on Greece and Yugoslavia in spring 1941 temporarily saved Libya and rescued Mussolini from Balkan humiliation. Only the Italian empire Mussolini had created in East Africa remained beyond the range of German help, and the British rolled it up expeditiously. Defeat on all fronts destroyed any hope of realizing through war the Fascist revolution Mussolini had sought; the regime henceforth concealed with increasing embarrassment its own ideological demise.

And the *guerra subalterna* under German tutelage which succeeded the collapse of Mussolini's "parallel war" proved as perilous and humiliating as its predecessor.[32] Germans such as General Erwin Rommel – whose first encounter with Italy dated from 1917, when he had led a mountain

30. For the course and end of the "parallel war," see ibid., Chapters 4–6.

31. Franz Halder, *Kriegstagebuch: Tägliche Aufzeichnungen des Chefs des Generalstabes des Heeres 1939–1942*, 3 vols. (Stuttgart, 1962–64), vol. 2, p. 212.

32. Lucio Ceva, *La condotta italiana della guerra: Cavallero e il Comando Supremo 1941/ 1942* (Milan, 1975), offers a penetrating overview of the *guerra subalterna*; Sir William Deakin, *The Brutal Friendship: Mussolini, Hitler and the Fall of Italian Fascism* (London, 1962) remains vital for its later phases.

battalion with ruthless élan in the Austro-German offensive that had cracked Italy's front at Caporetto – often lacked tact toward their allies and nominal superiors. More humiliating still, the extent of German commitment – whether of aircraft, armored units, or U-boats – inexorably determined thenceforth the ebb and flow of the Mediterranean and North African war. Between January and June 1941 German airpower and armor reduced Britain's forces to desperate straits. Then the invasion of Soviet Russia – which in the German view, then and later, took absolute priority over all other undertakings – absorbed the Luftwaffe. Malta's striking power grew radically, as British surface forces joined submarines and aircraft. In November 1941 the Axis forces in North Africa received less than 40 percent of the supply tonnage shipped from Italy. The British army correspondingly revived, and briefly drove the Axis from Cyrenaica in December.

The return that winter from Russia of *Luftflotte* 2 under that jovial war criminal, Field Marshal Albert Kesselring, then reduced much of Malta to rubble and reestablished the Axis supply position in North Africa – which was never so prosperous as in the first half of 1942. Italian navy frogmen took revenge for Taranto, temporarily sinking Britain's last two Mediterranean fleet battleships at Alexandria a bare week after Japanese aircraft had destroyed the *Prince of Wales* and *Repulse* off Malaya. Rommel, his fuel, ammunition, and armored vehicles replenished, struck British 8th Army a series of terrifying blows, seizing Tobruk, the key port in eastern Cyrenaica, and preempting any discussion of strategic alternatives such as a landing on Malta by dashing for the Nile delta. Then the drawdown of Luftwaffe forces in favor of the Russian front as well as the increasing strength of the British – now backed by the staggering industrial power of the United States – imposed stalemate along the final British defense line at El Alamein. The other major theaters in which Italian forces operated confirmed the subordinate character of the Italian effort. In the Balkans the army found itself committed to ineffectual anti-guerrilla operations under ever-closer German supervision. In Russia, a theater to which Mussolini had perversely demanded admission, a small

Italian force sent in 1941 grew by mid-1942 into an army screening part of the northern flank of Hitler's great offensive toward Stalingrad and the Caucasus oilfields.

The culminating point of Rommel's attack marked that of the Axis alliance as a whole: from the Western Desert to the Don Steppes to the seas around Midway Island, German and Japanese forces advanced and suffered defeat either immediate or briefly delayed. The triple catastrophe of winter–spring 1942–43 that followed struck Italy with particular force; the disastrous early course of the war the regime had claimed in its propaganda for its very own – *la guerra fascista* – prevented Mussolini from summoning up fanatical crowds to welcome total war in the manner of Goebbels's famous Berlin speech of February 1943. The British, having accumulated the two to one or better superiority needed to make sure of Rommel, attacked at El Alamein on 23 October 1942. As the Axis line crumbled and the Germans retreated, leaving much of the footbound Italian infantry behind, an immense Anglo-American armada descended on French Morocco and Algeria: the United States had entered the Mediterranean theater in force. And in November–December Soviet counteroffensives encircled German 6th Army in Stalingrad, destroyed Italian 8th Army as a fighting force, and drove the remaining Germans and their allies back in confusion. By January 1943 Italy had lost Tripolitania for good; its remaining forces fought on in Tunisia as guests of the Germans until the final African surrender in May.

The Anglo-American forces scarcely paused; they seized Pantelleria in June and Sicily in July–August, while deluging Italy's ports, airfields, railroads, and cities with an ever-greater weight of bombs. In Rome, the king at last mastered his terror of ending in a cage at Dachau, and dismissed Mussolini as prime minister after the majority of the Party's inner circle, led by Grandi and Ciano, had voted that the Duce should relinquish command of the armed forces. The regime crumbled without resistance. Then the king and generals so mismanaged Italy's exit from the war that the armed forces – with the exception of the fleet – collapsed in the face of preemptive action by small, well-armed, and vengeful German units. Italy, occupied and divided, ceased to exist as a power, while the armed forces and people of the Greater German Reich fought on for their Führer until over 7 million of them had died – at least three times the already huge German losses of 1914-18. Fascist and monarchical Italy, by contrast, had shattered after only 205,000 military and 25,000 civilian dead – slightly over a third of the death toll that Liberal Italy had withstood in the First World War.[33]

33. Italian war dead after 9 September 1943 amounted to another 225,000, in the majority prisoners of the Germans or noncombatants. Italian data from Rochat, "Una ricerca impossibile: le perdite italiane nella seconda guerra mondiale," *Italia contemporanea* 201 (1995), pp. 691–94, 698, 687 (1915–18 dead: 500,000 killed in action or died of wounds or illness with the units; a further 100,000 deceased while POWs; grand total, all causes, 650,000). For Germany's roughly 5.3 million military and 2 million civilian dead in 1939–45 (1938 population: 76 million), see Rüdiger Overmans, *Deutsche militärische Verluste im Zweiten Weltkrieg* (Munich, 1999), pp. 219, 228, 299 (civilian casualties from air bombardment from Overmans, "Die Toten des Zweiten Weltkriegs in Deutschland," in Wolfgang Michalka, ed., *Der Zweite Weltkrieg* [Munich, 1989], p. 859). For more on the sources of Germany's fight to the bitter end, see Knox, *Common Destiny*, Conclusion and Chapter 5, and "1 October 1942: Adolf Hitler, *Wehrmacht* Officer Policy, and Social Revolution," *The Historical Journal* 43:3 (2000).

2

SOCIETY, POLITICS, REGIME, INDUSTRY

Hitler's doomed allies were poor both in relative terms and in the aggregate. By the 1930s Italy was still thirty to fifty years behind Germany in becoming an industrial society – a gap overcome only in the long peace after 1945. Whereas illiteracy in Germany had virtually vanished by 1900, Italy's 1931 census registered an illiteracy rate of 20.9 percent among those over six years of age: roughly 10 percent in the North, 21 percent in the Center, and 39 percent in the South and islands. But those figures understate the gravity of the situation in the 1940s: the first postwar census, in 1951, listed 12.9 percent of Italy's population as illiterate, but also disclosed that a further 17.9 percent of the population had not completed elementary school. Almost a third (and a decade earlier, probably two-fifths) of the population was thus either illiterate or semiliterate.[1] And by the late 1930s slightly less than a third of Italy's workforce was industrial, and about half agricultural; the corresponding German figures were 42 percent for industry and 26 percent for agriculture (1939). But German industry's share of the national product had passed that of agriculture in 1889–90, whereas Italy only

1. SVIMEZ, *Un secolo di statistiche italiane*, p. 795; Daniele Marchesini, "Città e campagna nello specchio dell'alfabetismo (1921–1951)," in Simonetta Soldani and Gabriele Turi, eds., *Fare gli italiani: Scuola e cultura nell'Italia contemporanea* (Bologna, 1993), vol. 2, pp. 9–10.

The end of Italy's air war: Macchi MC 202 fighters, Tunis, 1943 (U.S. National Archives 208-N-12303-FA).

reached that decisive benchmark in 1935–40, and slipped backward in 1941 and after.[2] Italy's aggregate social and economic position with respect to its allies and enemies, as suggested by Tables 2.1–2.3, firmly established its claim to be "the least of the great powers".[3] Its "total industrial potential," the primary measure of latent military-economic might, amounted by 1938 to scarcely more than a fifth of that of its German ally, and a bit over half the swiftly rising potential of Imperial Japan.

Table 2.1. *Per capita gross national product*
(in 1960s US dollars and prices)

	1913	1929	1933	1938
Italy	**441**	**517**	**492**	**551**
Germany	757	770	716	1126
France	695	982	846	936
Britain	996	1038	995	1181
Russia/USSR	326	293	340	458

Table 2.2. *Per capita levels of industrialization*
(as a percentage of Britain in 1900)

	1913	1928	1938
Italy	**26**	**39**	**44**
Germany	85	101	128
Japan	20	30	51
France	59	82	73
Britain	115	122	157
Russia/USSR	20	20	38
USA	126	182	167

2.   B. R. Mitchell, *European Historical Statistics, 1750–1975* (New York, 2nd rev. ed., 1981), pp. 164, 166.

3.   For the phrase, and much trenchant commentary, see Richard J. B. Bosworth, *Italy, the Least of the Great Powers: Italian Foreign Policy before the First World War* (Cambridge, 1979).

Table 2.3. *Total industrial potential*
(as a percentage of Britain in 1900)

	1913	1928	1938
Italy	**23**	**37**	**46**
Germany	138	158	214
Japan	25	45	88
France	57	82	74
Britain	127	135	181
Russia/USSR	77	72	152
USA	298	533	528

Source data: Paul Bairoch, "Europe's Gross National Product, 1800–1975," and "International Industrialization Levels from 1750 to 1980," *Journal of European Economic History* 5:2 (1976), p. 297, and 11:2 (1982), pp. 302, 299.

Italy's forces nevertheless received in the interwar period a greater aggregate share of the national income than the armed forces of any other power except Nazi Germany, Imperial Japan, and in all probability Soviet Russia. Italian military expenditure – including the costs of the Fascist wars in Ethiopia and Spain in 1935–39 – was in absolute terms slightly greater than that of France and three-fourths that of Britain in the 1935/6–1938/9 period.[4] Yet once embarked on the Second World War, the armed forces' share of national income did not rise anywhere near as fast or as far as in the other contenders: the Italian war economy peaked in 1941 at the paltry level – by an authoritative recent estimate – of 23 percent of gross national product (Tables 2.4 and 2.5).

That the sums spent were so small relative to the economy and generated so little armed might was not accidental. Massive obstacles to military effectiveness in the realms of culture, politics, industrial expertise, raw materials, and energy supply, as well as in the concepts, organization, and technological skills of the armed forces themselves determined Italy's course throughout the Second World War.

4.   Knox, *Mussolini*, Table A.2.2, pp. 294–95.

Table 2.4. *Italian military expenditure and GDP, 1938–43*

	Army (percentage of total military expenditure)	Navy (percentage of total military expenditure)	Air Force (percentage of total military expenditure)	Colonies (percentage of total military expenditure)	Military expenditure as a percentage of state expenditure	State expenditure as a percentage of GDP (fiscal years)	Italian GDP as a percentage of 1938 GDP	Military expenditure as a percentage of GDP (current lire)
1938	33.0	14.8	19.1	33.1	31.1	20.8	100.0	**10.0**
1939	40.3	16.5	19.8	23.4	32.8	19.4	107.0	**8.0**
1940	52.2	11.6	17.3	19.0	45.4	22.8	104.5	**12.0**
1941	63.6	12.0	15.2	9.2	64.2	35.6	102.5	**23.0**
1942	61.7	14.2	10.7	2.0	56.4	37.8	103.0	**22.0**
1943	60.6	15.6	11.9	1.8	57.2	41.0	97.5	**21.0**

Table 2.5. *The contenders: military expenditure as a percentage of GDP* (at current prices)

	1939	1940	1941	1942	1943	1944
Italy	8	12	23	22	21	–
Germany	23	40	52	64	70	–
Japan	22	22	27	33	43	76
Britain	15	44	53	52	55	53
USSR*	–	17	28	61	61	53
USA	1	2	11	31	42	42

*at constant prices.

Sources: Italian GDP, state and military expenditure as a percentage of GDP, and base data for the armed forces percentages from Vera Zamagni, "Italy: How to Lose the War and Win the Peace"; all other powers from Mark Harrison, "The Economics of World War II: An Overview," both in Harrison, ed., *The Economics of World War II* (Cambridge, 1998), pp. 179 (Table 5.1), 199 (Table 5.13), 201-03 (Table 5.14), 21 (Table 1.8).

Three principal areas of cultural deficiency stand out. First and most important was the continuing imperviousness of much of Italian society to modernity. The chief features of that sovereign immunity were the prevalence of illiteracy, local and family allegiances that far outweighed loyalty to a distant and often only dimly perceived nation, a deep-rooted mistrust of authority, and often fierce resistance, conscious or unconscious, to precision and rational planning. All were qualities that extended far beyond the peasantry.

Illiteracy and semiliteracy did not merely mean a lack of command of the written word: they meant a lack of command of *Italian*, which in this period existed outside the schools and small educated elites only in Tuscany, Umbria, and the Rome area.[5] Mutually incomprehensible or barely comprehensible dialects were bound up with the "hundred cities" and tens of thousands of villages of Italy. *Campanilismo* – loyalty to the lands within sight of the local church steeple – and distrust of outsiders

5.   Marchesini, "Città e campagna," vol. 2, p. 34; for a detailed account, see Tullio De Mauro, *Storia linguistica dell'Italia unita* (Bari, 4th ed., 1991).

tended, especially in the South and islands, to outweigh the idea of nation and the Fascist appeals built upon that idea. The Church's as yet unbroken determination to retain its millennial hold on the village community further reinforced the peasantry's immunity to modernity. Finally, foreign rule and local misrule over many centuries had created the traditions that an American sociologist studying a southern Italian village in the 1950s famously described as "amoral familism."[6] The sociologist, Edward C. Banfield, subsequently earned much abuse for describing a phenomenon he did not create. Yet his concept was clearly applicable far beyond the South: this was a society short on mutual trust, cooperation, and spontaneous teamwork.

Altruism in the service of higher national purposes – precisely because it was perceived to be so rare – had a specific name: the "*senso dello Stato.*" That sense was strongest in the cities and in the North, where the Piedmontese state and its military traditions persisted, along with memories of the *Risorgimento* in both its Piedmontese-monarchical and radical-democratic incarnations. But "sense of the state" did not prevent the armament industry – located almost entirely in the Milan, Turin, and Genoa areas – from merrily defrauding that same state through illegal cartels and all manner of deceptive practices. Nor did it inhibit long-shoremen and servicemen from looting vital equipment and supplies from armored vehicles shipped to Libya in wartime. An Italian diplomat, with only slight exaggeration, noted in his diary after a brief visit to Rome and Milan in September 1940 that "he who supplies the troops with cardboard shoes is considered, in the end, a sort of hero."[7]

6.   Edward C. Banfield, *The moral basis of a backward society* (Glencoe, Illinois, 1958); the second Italian edition, *Le basi morali di una società arretrata* (Bologna, 1976), provides a sampler of the discussion that surrounded the book in Italy.

7.   See Ceva and Andrea Curami, *La meccanizzazione dell'esercito italiano dalle origini al 1943* (Rome, 1989), vol. 1, p. 451, on the "primordiali mancanze di struttura etica" of the longshoremen as well as massive damage to the machinery from careless handling; cardboard shoes: Michele Lanza (pseud. Leonardo Simoni), *Berlino, Ambasciata d'Italia 1939–1943* (Rome, 1946), p. 168.

A crippling parochialism of outlook was also hardly confined to the peasantry: it permeated Italian society, North and South, Left and Right, workers and industrialists and generals. Its symptoms were above all two: a profound lack of curiosity about developments outside Italy and a pervasive self-satisfaction that disaster rarely dented. The deficiencies of Italian weapons and of the armed forces' concepts for their employment, of which more later, offer a rich body of evidence substantiating the first point. And the second is perhaps best exemplified by the remarkable if hardly unique suggestion of an anonymous staff officer in the supreme command in January 1941 – as the armed forces were stalled in Albania, disintegrating in Cyrenaica, and pleading for German military help – that "the well-known excessive mental rigidity of the Germans can easily lead to errors of judgment that derive in great part from a cult of organization pushed to an extreme [*un assolutismo*] that blocks or distorts any vision of reality – a tendency that might be usefully tempered by greater contact with the mentality and intelligence of our race."[8]

Second among the most salient cultural impediments to military-industrial and military effectiveness was the absence of a well-developed military culture and traditions, except to some extent in Piedmont. "Italy," in the words of a leading army historian, "has never seemed well-inclined toward arms ... In reality one must admit that Italy has never been well-inclined *toward the state*, whatever its leadership."[9] What recent traditions existed were negative: battlefield defeat in the *Risorgimento*, by the Ethiopians at Adua in 1896, and at Caporetto, along with the army's inherited preference, much in evidence in its

8. Unsigned *Comando Supremo* memorandum on German intentions and future strategy, 24 February 1941, in Ceva, *Le forze armate* (Turin, 1981), pp. 572–73.

9. Quotation: Mario Montanari, *Politica e strategia in cento anni di guerre italiane*, vol. 1 (Rome, 1996), p. viii. For the origins of this condition, see especially Gregory Hanlon, *The Twilight of a Military Tradition: Italian Aristocrats and European Conflicts, 1560–1800* (London, 1998); for Piedmont, Walter Barberis, *Le armi del principe: La tradizione militare sabauda* (Turin, 1988).

distrust of Italy's greatest military leader, Giuseppe Garibaldi, and in the First World War, for passive obedience over spontaneity, enthusiasm, and initiative. Italian society consequently suffered from an almost universal lack of expertise and of interest in military affairs, "encouraged [as another authoritative Italian commentator has trenchantly put it] equally by left and right, anti-militarist circles and generals."[10]

Finally, society's peasant base, relatively small industrial sector, and narrowly selective educational system (85,535 university students, of whom only 13.6 percent were studying engineering, out of a total population of just under 44 million in 1939–40) meant a pervasive shortage of technical talent that placed severe limits on the extent to which the Italian armed forces could imagine, commission, operate, and maintain complex machinery. Italy's small stock of motor vehicles in 1939 – 469,000, against 1.99 million in Germany, 2.25 million in France, and 2.42 million in Britain – was itself suggestive of military-economic weakness. But even more revealing are the relative figures: 11 vehicles for each thousand people in Italy, 25 in Germany (two and a half times more numerous), 54 and 51 per thousand in Britain and France respectively (almost five times more numerous), and 227 per thousand in the United States (over twenty times more numerous). The Italian armed forces could not take even drivers, much less mechanics, for granted.[11]

It would however be both churlish and unfaithful to the evidence not to recognize that this society also possessed significant strengths – although often ones that Fascists did not appreciate. The Church preached, within limits, obedience to authority – as well as voicing the overtly un-Fascist thought that the enemy was also human. The mutual

10. Giorgio Rochat, *L'esercito italiano da Vittorio Veneto a Mussolini (1919–1925)* (Bari, 1967), p. 3.

11. Figures: table, DRZW 5/1:651; on the shortage of competent drivers, see for instance *Africa*, 1:117, and the AAR from November 1942 printed in Ceva, "4a armata e occupazione italiana della Francia. Problemi militari," in *8 settembre: lo sfacelo della quarta armata* (Turin, 1979), p. 98.

incomprehension of city and countryside, town-bred junior officers and peasant soldiers that had weakened the army's units in the First World War had been attenuated although not removed by the slow spread of primary education. The fragmentary military justice records of 1940–43 suggest a far lower incidence of desertion and other crimes – or of prosecutorial zeal – than in 1915–18.[12] Yet the peasantry retained the native endurance and fatalistic stubbornness that had rescued the *Regio Esercito*'s hierarchy from its own inadequacies on so many occasions in the Great War.

The relationships between regime, armed forces, and industry determined the extent to which the state was able to make good the cultural disadvantages and exploit the strengths already outlined. Despite the efforts of dictator and *Partito Nazionale Fascista* – of which the war of 1940–43 was the culmination – to shift the original balance between Fascism and the establishment, ultimate power remained in the hands of the king and the senior generals of the *Regio Esercito*, the only group in Italy powerful enough to throw Fascism out.[13] In foreign policy, Mussolini gradually emancipated himself from tutelage. In some areas of domestic policy the Party and its affiliates gained a virtual monopoly after the mid-1920s. But in military policy in particular Mussolini himself – conscious of his own lack of expertise and understandably reluctant to endanger his aura of dictatorial infallibility – habitually deferred to the professionals. He tended to intervene when their internecine quarrels became too heated, but avoided organizational or procurement measures, however necessary, that might provoke the hostility of significant numbers of senior generals and admirals, or of the monarch behind them.

---

12. See Rochat, "La giustizia militare nella guerra italiana 1940–43. Primi dati e spunti di analisi," *Rivista di storia contemporanea*, 1991:4, especially pp. 538–39.

13. For more on the regime's structure, Knox, *Common Destiny*, Chapter 2 and Conclusion; Emilio Gentile, *La via italiana al totalitarismo: Il partito e lo Stato nel regime fascista* (Rome, 1995); Alberto Aquarone, *L'organizzazione dello Stato totalitario* (Turin, 1965).

His strategic emphasis on Mediterranean primacy and a "march to the oceans" cut across the army's paramount position among the services, but the dictator largely failed to redistribute the armaments budget in support of his goals. He appointed as war minister a reforming junior general, Antonino Di Giorgio, then abandoned him hastily in 1925 in the face of the army establishment's wrath. He sometimes yielded, especially before 1936, to subordinates clever enough to maneuver him into positions, particularly over the fate of Austria or cooperation with National Socialist Germany, in which following his ideological priorities might seem unpatriotic. Yet monarchy and army, despite their latent power, were no more master in their own house than was the dictator. "Fascist merits," by the 1930s, might further a military career. King and armed forces glumly swallowed the forced removal of their Jewish comrades, including the designer of Italy's battleships, Umberto Pugliese.[14] The regime's demographic program made marriage mandatory after 1938 for officers aspiring to promotion, a much-hated regulation not suspended until 1941.

Mussolini sought to resolve the regime's duality, to settle the question of ultimate authority in Italy, through war.[15] But his very lack of authority constrained him to enter war by stealth in May–June 1940 in the wake of the German victories. A fear for his popularity greater even than the anxiety that tormented Hitler – who sought sporadically to spare German wartime living standards – dictated business as usual on the home front. Italy did not declare general mobilization, as Mussolini's Liberal predecessors had unhesitatingly done in 1915. Deference to civilian complaints apparently dictated the disastrous release of 600,000 troops from service in autumn 1940. Exemptions from call-up were

14. Ceva, "Fascismo e militari di professione," in *Ufficiali e società: Interpretazioni e modelli* (Milan, 1988), pp. 413, 419, 386, 424 note 24. After the Taranto disaster the regime found itself compelled to "aryanize" and reinstate Pugliese to supervise the repair of its damaged battleships.

15. See Knox, *Common Destiny*, Chapters 2 and 3.

lavish, and depended on connections as often as on the needs of war industry. The armed forces formally exempted roughly one million men at any given moment, but also declined to call large numbers of additional men of military age because they could neither feed, house, arm, nor train them, and because the scale of casualties was far smaller than that of the First World War.[16] University youth, who in general would have been most useful to the armed forces, were eligible for and in the majority accepted a scandalous deferment until age 26; university enrollment predictably doubled between 1940 and 1943.[17]

Mussolini, despite entreaties from the armed forces, resisted as late as January 1943 all attempts to impose on the industrial workforce the military discipline implemented as a matter of course in the First World War.[18] Well-placed observers such as Field Marshal Kesselring, who served as German theater commander from his arrival in late November 1941, lamented the "peacetime working methods" of Italian civilian dockyards, a complaint echoed in Italian sources. As late as 1942, civilian ministries still held partial jurisdiction over matters as decisive as the supply of longshoremen for service in Libya. Not until the end of May 1943, weeks after the loss of North Africa made the measure largely superfluous, did the high command secure the militarization of port

16. On exemptions, see the acid comment of Montanari, *L'esercito italiano alla vigilia della seconda guerra mondiale* (Rome, 1982), p. 227 and note 19; overall figures: Rochat, "Gli uomini alle armi 1940–1943," in his *L'esercito italiano in pace e in guerra* (Milan, 1991), pp. 267–68 and tables, and Dorello Ferrari, "La mobilitazione dell'esercito nella seconda guerra mondiale," *Storia contemporanea* 18:6 (1992), p. 1027 and note.

17. Rochat, "Qualche dato sugli ufficiali di complemento dell'esercito nel 1940," *Ricerche storiche* 18:3 (1993), pp. 630–31; also Ferrari, "Mobilitazione dell'esercito," p. 1025.

18. See VCSMG 1939–43 3:296–98, 302–03 and Curami, "L'industria bellica prima dell'otto settembre," in Romain H. Rainero, ed., *L'Italia in guerra: Il quarto anno – 1943* (Gaeta, 1994), pp. 326–28.

workers.[19] And rationing of some staple foods began only in December 1940 and remained incomplete even after the imposition of a more comprehensive system in September 1941. For many months the chief sacrifice demanded of the public was an irritating and militarily pointless ban on public dancing.

As early as the 1920s the regime had found itself unable to wield the terror which helped make sacrifice palatable in Soviet Russia and Nazi Germany. The outcry in 1924 after Mussolini's thugs had murdered a prominent Socialist adversary, Giacomo Matteotti, had revealed to the Duce, to his infinite disgust, a line that the Italian establishment would not let him cross. A series of attempts on his own life in 1925–26 had given pretext for creation of a "Special Tribunal for the Defense of the State." But that court put to death only nine men in peacetime, and twenty-two, mostly Slavs from the eastern borderlands, in war. Persistent political opponents risked mortal beatings or internal exile in the desolate South, but repression remained sporadic and selective, even after Mussolini's triumph in Ethiopia opened the road to a concerted attempt to make the regime more total. And despite Hitlerian exhortations in winter 1940–41 to use "barbaric methods such as shooting generals and colonels ... and decimating units," the armed forces apparently condemned to death fewer than 150 men between June 1940 and September 1943 – a record that contrasted sharply with the 4,000 or more death sentences, 750 executions, and numerous shootings without trial with which Italy's 1915–17 generalissimo, Luigi Cadorna, and his successor Armando Diaz had held Italy's peasant infantry in line in 1915–18. The well-meant advice that Ribbentrop ostensibly proffered in March 1943 – to shoot a hundred prominent Italians in order to bolster the regime's collapsing war effort – was not practical politics.[20]

Fear of offending constituted interests was characteristic of the war effort as a whole. No single authority other than Mussolini himself, whom neither temperament nor expertise had equipped for the task, coordinated weapons research, equipment procurement and production, and manpower mobilization. Although he was minister of each of the armed forces from 1925 to 1929 and 1933 to 1943, and supreme commander of the armed forces after June 1940, no functioning high command, much less one with powers over the war economy, emerged until summer 1941. Like Hitler, who similarly gave the professionals their head until 1938, and whose war economy and high command thereafter remained largely bereft of long-term planning, coordination, and rational management, Mussolini refused to tolerate centralization of power outside his own person. But unlike Hitler after the removal of Germany's war minister and army commander-in-chief in February 1938, Mussolini had to entrust to the fortunes of war the achievement of even a modest degree of direct control over the armed forces. And war prepared without such control – exercised with a rationality and expertise the Duce did not in any event possess – inevitably failed him.

The regime had nevertheless striven from its beginnings to prepare economy and society for Mussolini's long-foreseen conflict. A National Research Council under the nominal direction of the chief of general staff

20. Special tribunal: Aquarone, *L'organizzazione dello Stato totalitario*, p. 103 and note; Hitler (to Ciano, 8 December 1940), ADAP D/9/477, p. 685; ninety-two army death sentences in 1940–43 (partial data, estimated at 65 percent of the total, for the army alone; evidence of how many were actually carried out is lacking): Rochat, "La giustizia militare," pp. 536–37. For 1915–18, see Enzo Forcella and Alberto Monticone, *Plotone d'esecuzione: I processi della prima guerra mondiale* (Bari, 1968), especially pp. 433–512; Ribbentrop: Ernst von Weizsäcker, *Die Weizsäcker-Papiere 1933–1950*, ed. Leonidas E. Hill (Frankfurt a. M., 1974), p. 334 (perhaps reflecting ADAP E/5/184).

from 1925 to 1940, Marshal Pietro Badoglio, was responsible for directing military-industrial research. But it concentrated on autarchic nostrums such as the cultivation of guayule bushes, imported from the southwestern United States, as a rubber substitute. Potentially vital matters such as radar development, much less the implications of Enrico Fermi's nuclear work before his emigration to the United States in consequence of the racial laws, were not prominent on its agenda.[21]

An interministerial Supreme Defense Commission created in 1923–25 met annually for discussions held under Mussolini's supervision, but exercised no appreciable executive functions, which remained vested in the armed forces and in their rivals for influence and authority, the key civilian ministries. The Commission's chief organ, the Committee for Civil Mobilization, monitored many aspects of the war economy through branch offices throughout Italy, but lost much of its power in 1935 and was abolished in July 1940, leaving its dependent organizations homeless. The central strategic and economic concept upon which the entire structure rested was in any event faulty, with serious repercussions on armament production. As in Germany, the regime – in the face of raw material penury – gave investment priority to long-term infrastructure, heavy industry, and autarchic raw materials projects, with inevitable sacrifice in the medium term of deliverable combat power in the form of cannon, armored vehicles, aircraft, and warships.[22] As in Germany, although on a smaller scale and with far more crippling effect, a military-economic strategy predicated on a long war – which the Axis could not hope to

---

21. For the nationalist-autarchic character of much Italian interwar research, as well as the CNR's activities, see especially Roberto Maiocchi, "Scienzati italiani e scienza nationale (1919–1939)," in Soldani and Turi, eds., *Fare gli italiani*, vol. 2, pp. 41–86.

22. See especially Angela Raspin, *The Italian War Economy, 1940–1943* (New York, 1986), pp. 25–26, for investment priorities and levels, and Fortunato Minniti, "Le materie prime nella preparazione bellica dell'Italia 1935–1943," *Storia contemporanea* 17:1,2 (1986), pp. 4–40, 245–76, especially 2:275–76.

win – helped compromise the possibility of striking hard and swiftly enough at the outset to maximize the chances of a short war.[23]

Timing and Italy's geographic vulnerability compounded this fundamental strategic and military-economic error. The war effort proper – as opposed to the massive sums expended for munitions, vehicles, and supplies on Fascist wars in Ethiopia and Spain in 1935–39 – only began in 1940. The inability of industry to design adequate fighting machines and the long lead times between design and production then ensured that the armed forces did not receive modern equipment even in small quantities until 1942–43. But by that point Italy's oil stocks were largely exhausted and the Anglo-American conquest of North Africa had laid Italy's fragile rail network and the key industries of the Milan-Genoa-Turin triangle open to devastating air attack.[24]

Only one organization possessed executive powers over some aspects of the war economy. With Italy's war on Ethiopia, a General Commissariat for War Production emerged. But it failed to recreate anything resembling Liberal Italy's powerful Ministry of Arms and Munitions of 1915–18, which had successfully exercised direct control of industry and workforce, and had managed procurement contracts centrally on behalf of the services. The Commissariat merely allocated – or rationed – raw materials, but not labor or armaments contracts. It had little or no control even over medium-term armaments planning, and its wartime chief, General Carlo Favagrossa, spent 1941 and 1942 resisting – out of deference to the service staffs and ministries or from fear of responsibility – demands that he take command of procurement and

---

23. For the negative effects on German striking power in 1940–41 of the Four Year Plan's long-term autarchic priorities, see Richard Overy, *War and Economy in the Third Reich* (Oxford, 1994), p. 245.

24. See Achille Rastelli, "I bombardamenti aerei nella seconda guerra mondiale: Milano e la provincia," *Italia contemporanea* 195 (1995), pp. 309–42, and for the effects on aircraft production, Nino Arena, *La Regia Aeronautica 1940–1943* (Rome, 1982–94), vol. 3, pp. 69, 761; vol. 4, p. 792.

set priorities within the war economy. That task, along with even more pressing strategic and operational responsibilities, fell in summer 1941 to the reorganized *Comando Supremo* under General Ugo Cavallero, whose earlier career had included a four-year stint as chief of the Ansaldo armaments combine which had ended abruptly when the navy caught the firm fraudulently providing faulty armor and machinery.[25]

Until early 1943 the three services themselves controlled weapons development and production contracts with industry with virtually no coordination with one another and as little as possible with other economic and military-economic authorities, and without themselves possessing control of raw materials or labor allocation, or strong powers over industry.[26] Only after Cavallero's removal as a scapegoat for defeat in February 1943 did Mussolini and Cavallero's successor, General Vittorio Ambrosio, create a Ministry for War Production and devolve upon Favagrossa the powers he had earlier refused. Favagrossa immediately returned much of his new-found authority to the service procurement and testing departments, over which he deliberately assumed merely nominal control, or delegated it to coordination committees in which industry itself, following the example set in Albert Speer's reorganization of German war production, was the dominant partner. Favagrossa's new ministry was thus born dead, and made little difference to the war economy's performance in the brief period that remained before Italy's collapse in September 1943.[27]

25. For details see Ceva and Curami, *Industria bellica anni trenta* (Milan, 1992), Chapter 2.

26. Minniti, "Aspetti organizzativi del controllo sulla produzione bellica in Italia," *Clio* 4/1977, pp. 305–40, and the comments of Ceva and Curami, "Industria bellica e stato nell'imperialismo fascista degli anni '30," *Nuova Antologia* 2167 (1988), pp. 321–28.

27. See especially Minniti, "Aspetti organizzativi," pp. 337–340, and the incisive comments of Botti, "Strategia e logistica," pp. 237–40.

Nor did the regime possess the conviction or power to force upon Italian society the financial sacrifices demanded either in the democracies or in the other dictatorships. Although the disappearance or continued closure of most relevant archives make Italy's wartime financial decision making unusually opaque, the overall outcome is clear.[28] Gold and currency reserves threatened to run out as early as 1939–40, private capital was scarce, and Italy could tap neither the foreign loans that had furnished 13.2 percent of expenditure in 1915–18, nor the loot that helped fuel the war economies of Germany and Japan, nor the Lend-Lease that added 5 percent to Soviet gross domestic product in 1942 and 10 percent in 1943 and 1944.[29] Overall tax yields, despite a series of wartime increases and surcharges, *decreased* by 20 percent between 1939/40 and 1942/43.[30] Wealthy and powerful interests with friends in high places such as Galeazzo Ciano, whose own considerable fortune was a source of persistent gossip, regarded freedom from and evasion of taxation as an immemorial right. The regime, caught between the wrath of the possessing classes and the legions of small savers upon whose continued credulity the government's credit rested, ultimately opted for

28. For what little is known about the process of decision, see Giuseppe Maione, *L'imperialismo straccione: classi sociali e finanza di guerra dall'impresa etiopica al conflitto mondiale (1935–1943)* (Bologna, 1979), which rests largely on the rich personal papers of the finance minister, Paolo Thaon di Revel.

29. For some of Germany's "external inputs," see Werner Abelshauser, "Germany: Guns, Butter, and Economic Miracles," in Harrison, ed., *Economics of World War II*, pp. 143 (table 4.7: occupation charges and clearing debt) and 161 (table 4.17B: forced and foreign labor); Lend-Lease: Harrison, "The Soviet Union: The Defeated Victor," ibid., p. 287.

30. Massimo Legnani, "Sul finanziamento della guerra fascista," in Gaetano Grassi and Legnani, eds., *L'Italia nella seconda guerra mondiale e nella Resistanza* (Milan, 1988), pp. 302–06; through 1939, Felice Guarneri, *Battaglie economiche fra le due guerre* (Bologna, 1988) is also useful.

inflation.[31] The inability to tax effectively played a role, alongside a host of other factors, in Fascist Italy's failure to expend much more than 20 percent of gross domestic product per year on its last war.

In its dealings with Italian industry the regime confronted many of the same interests that it feared to tax, and it was in those dealings that it showed its lack of organizational ability and determination most conspicuously. The Duce might on occasion fulminate that FIAT must cease to think of itself as "a sacred and untouchable institution of the state" because "it had large numbers of workers."[32] In foreign policy he steered Italy to war and ruin without tolerating interference from the industrial elite. But in economic and military-economic matters both he and the generals showed a seemingly limitless deference to the large industrial combines: domestic political stability, as Mussolini had interpreted it since the 1920s, appeared to demand it.

The state's massive bail-out of Depression-stricken banks and industry in 1933 had placed under public ownership more of heavy industry than in any other Western society: 90 percent of merchant shipping, 80 percent of shipbuilding, 75 percent of pig-iron production, 45 percent of steel, and a wide variety of other holdings – a fifth to a quarter, measured in terms of capital, of Italian industry.[33] In practice – which long survived Fascism – state-owned or part-owned industries acted as independent fiefdoms whose only connection to the state resided in the immunity from bankruptcy that it offered. The regime's ownership did however give it an apparent economic interest even in the informal collusion, covert or overt cartels, and tariff barriers that maintained Italy's high domestic price levels – until it came to pay those same prices for military

31. For Ciano's role, see especially Bottai, 6 June 1942; Ciano, 5, 6 June 1942; Giuseppe Gorla, *L'Italia nella seconda guerra mondiale: Diario di un milanese, ministro del re nel governo di Mussolini* (Milan, 1959), pp. 243–44.

32. Quotation: Valerio Castronovo, *Giovanni Agnelli* (Turin, 1971), p. 436.

33. Figures: Raspin, *War Economy*, pp. 41–42; Ernesto Cianci, *Nascita dello Stato imprenditore in Italia* (Milan, 1977), pp. 278–79.

equipment. It also offered, through the Committee for Civil Mobilization, yet another powerful tool for preventing competition. New plants needed bureaucratic approval, and existing firms invariably blocked – with bogus counter-applications designed to trigger a state veto of the interlopers on grounds of duplication of effort – all attempts to enter their markets.[34]

The dictator harbored a deep ideological distrust of foreign investment, and consequently favored FIAT by obstructing Ford's attempts to enter the Italian market from the 1920s through 1932. Mussolini and the generals then reinforced the perverse economic effects of this policy by allowing FIAT and its joint-venture partner, Ansaldo, to achieve a monopoly over the production of armored fighting vehicles. Cavallero had presided over the creation of the monopoly in the early 1930s as chief of Ansaldo; as Badoglio's successor at the *Comando Supremo* he then helped to cement it in place throughout Italy's war.[35] The industrialists rarely hesitated to play their trump card: the threat of worker unrest if production shut down. Industry's very long lead times from prototype to production and inability or unwillingness to produce better machines than the "anachronistic and pathetic" FIAT CR42 biplane, the inadequate Breda Ba65 and unserviceable Ba88 ground attack aircraft, the deadly (to its crews) SM85 dive-bomber, the useless 3.5-ton L3 FIAT-Ansaldo tankette, and the same firm's underpowered, undergunned, and mechanically unreliable M13/1940, M14/1941, and M15/1942 medium tanks also paradoxically strengthened its position. Both army and air force accepted long runs of vehicles and aircraft that had performed poorly

---

34. See the description of Ceva, "Grande industria e guerra," in Rainero and Biagini, eds., *L'Italia in guerra: il primo anno – 1940* (Rome, 1991), p. 44.

35. Castronovo, *Agnelli*, pp. 453–63; Ceva and Curami, *Industria bellica anni trenta*, pp. 99–105; *Meccanizzazione*, vol. 1, pp. 157–75 and Chapter 15; Ceva, "Rapporti fra industria bellica ed esercito," Rainero and Biagini, eds., *L'Italia in guerra: Il secondo anno – 1941* (Gaeta, 1992), pp. 228–29; on Mussolini and foreign investment, see Claudia Damiani, *Mussolini e gli Stati Uniti 1922–1935* (Bologna, 1980), pp. 251–54, 308.

or been proven useless in battle for fear of ending up with no weapons at all, and out of consideration for "the need for work of the FIAT production line," as the air force leadership slavishly described it in internal discussion. FIAT produced almost 2,000 CR42s – more than any other Italian combat aircraft – between 1938 and 1944; the air force was still ordering them as late as March 1943.[36]

The inadequacies of industry itself indeed meshed so perfectly with the regime's deficiencies as coordinator and contractor that the attempt to distinguish cause from effect is often futile. What is beyond dispute is that Italy's weapons and weapons systems were the least effective, least numerous, and most overpriced produced by a major combatant in the Second World War. Italian steel cost four times the world market price. The new *Littorio*-class battleships which reached the navy in 1940 and after cost by one estimate twice what they would have if built in French shipyards which were themselves scarcely low-cost producers.[37] And in fighting machine design, metallurgy, assembly-line technique, machine tool production, precision instrumentation, communications electronics, and radar and sonar, Italian industry entered – and largely left – the war in a condition of stubborn and parochial backwardness. Research and quality control in vital areas such as armor was primitive or nonexistent; the riveted plates of FIAT-Ansaldo's first medium tank to see extensive combat, the M13/1940, shattered like glass.[38] Aircraft and tank design were virtuoso trial-and-error performances by individual *progettisti* rather

36. Quotations: Arena, *Aeronautica*, vol. 1, p. 28 (Ba65/88: pp. 79, 80, 89–90, 639–40; SM85: 80, 641–42; CR42 biplane: 87–88); Curami, "Piani e progetti dell'aeronautica italiana, 1939–1943. Stato maggiore e industrie," *Italia contemporanea* 187 (1992), p. 254; tanks: Ceva and Curami, *Meccanizzazione.*

37. Ceva, "Grande industria," pp. 41, 48–49.

38. See the photographs of knocked-out M13 tanks in the March 1942 report for the *Comando Supremo* on vehicles and tactics in North Africa by Col. M. Bizzi, NARA T-821/250/000100ff., and excerpts of its text along with other documentation in Ceva and Curami, *Meccanizzazione*, vol. 2, pp. 270–301, 328–52.

than team efforts; a single individual at Ansaldo designed *all* Italian tanks and armored cars between 1933 and 1943.[39] Unsurprisingly, no satisfactory tank ever emerged. Despite the early capture and transport to Italy for study of a Soviet T-34, the war's best medium tank, FIAT-Ansaldo's best effort was a moderately sturdy 75mm assault gun equipped with a low-velocity weapon. Nor did the combine tolerate competition from superior foreign machines such as the medium tank that Skoda offered in 1941. FIAT-Ansaldo also successfully if covertly resisted production in Italy of the Panzer III or IV, for which Germany – and Hitler in person – intermittently offered designs, patents, and even machine tools.[40]

Although air production was oligopolistic rather than monopolistic, FIAT's aircraft division distinguished itself by designing and selling to the air force "perhaps the worst monoplane fighter of the Second World War," the open-cockpit G50.[41] The aerodynamic sophistication apparent, for instance, in the Japanese "Zero" – an aircraft that despite similar engine power to the G50 and the contemporary Macchi MC200, carried 20mm cannon instead of the Italians' ineffectual machine guns – was almost wholly absent. Industry likewise failed until 1942–43 to produce a serviceable ground-attack aircraft: those with which the air force began the war were more deadly to their crews than to the enemy. Aero engine design revolved around copies and descendants of foreign engines licensed in the 1920s and early 1930s. The inability of the state-controlled

39. Ibid., vol. 1, p. 273; six individuals (Marchetti, Rosatelli, Gabrielli, Zappata, Castoldi, and Longhi) were responsible for the ten aircraft that gave an effective contribution to Italy's Second World War air effort (CR42, G50, MC200, MC202, Re2001, SM79, SM84, BR20, Cant Z506, Cant Z1007): Minniti, "La politica industriale del Ministero dell'Aeronautica. Mercato, Pianificazione, Sviluppo (1935–1943)," *Storia contemporanea*, 12:1–2, (1981), 1:25.

40. Ceva and Curami, *Meccanizzazione*, vol. 1, pp. 363–67, 380–87.

41. FIAT G50: Ceva, "Grande industria," p. 39 (the essay is also the best summary of recent research; for a carefully documented history of the armor monopoly, see Ceva and Curami, *Meccanizzazione*, vol. 1, Chapters 9, 11–16).

petroleum industry to produce high-octane fuels or lubricants that did not wreck engines also limited innovation. All attempts to design the reliable 1,500-horsepower-class engine needed to propel cannon-armed monoplane fighters at 400 mph failed miserably. The Piaggio firm gleefully falsified test results after falling under suspicion because its engines routinely failed in flight. The air force took the matter to Mussolini, but Piaggio continued to produce engines so sloppily manufactured that they were dangerous. The air force's own representative on Piaggio's board, when challenged, nonchalantly insisted that air force quality control technicians were excessively severe: "But haven't you figured it out? It's the *Germans* who are fighting the war."[42]

The ultimate solution to the aero engine bottleneck appeared to be licensed production by Alfa-Romeo and FIAT of the Daimler-Benz DB601 and DB605 engines that powered Germany's first-line fighters. But unfortunately for the war effort, the air ministry neglected to buy simultaneously the rights to the Messerschmitt Bf109, a step that might have speeded quantity production of effective fighters in place of FIAT's biplanes. In the event, an adequate DB601-powered fighter, the Macchi MC202, did appear in small numbers in summer 1941, but the Alfa-Romeo plant set up to produce the DB601 drastically limited aircraft production by shipping a mere seventy-four engines in 1941.[43] Italy's first truly competitive fighters, the MC205, Re2005, and FIAT G55 (one of the few bright spots in FIAT's wartime record) became available in small numbers immediately before final collapse in summer 1943.

Only the navy designed its ships and some weapons in-house, and had somewhat better luck. But the Ansaldo combine under Cavallero nevertheless sold it armor-plate with falsified proof test results, and installed vital ship parts – such as propeller shafts – that had been covertly welded

---

42. "Ma non avete ancora capito che tanto la guerra la fanno i tedeschi": Curami, "I riflessi delle operazioni nello sviluppo della Regia Aeronautica," in Rainero and Biagini, eds., *1941*, p. 508.

43. Curami, "Piani e progetti," p. 256.

to disguise cracks resulting from poor casting technique. Industry also furnished the navy throughout the war with carelessly manufactured and thoroughly inaccurate main gun ammunition.[44]

Production methods and coordination remained backward. Except in part for the small-arms industry, Italian firms were resolutely artisanal: too few skilled workers slowly hand-crafting obsolete weapons.[45] In a world increasingly dominated by industrial-scientific research organizations, large design teams, and the standardized models and mass production by semiskilled labor adopted in the United States, Soviet Russia, and Germany after 1942, the failure of Italy's armaments effort was foreordained — although the available industrial capacity, if employed with a minimum of rationality and an eye to developments abroad, might have produced far more serviceable equipment in far greater quantities. Japan, with less than twice Italy's total industrial potential, produced aircraft and ships in sufficient quality and quantity to prolong for forty-four months the unequal contest it had naively begun at Pearl Harbor. Its navy's air striking force — a complex of seven fleet carriers and 474 aircraft — held world primacy between spring 1941 and spring 1942.[46] And Soviet Russia, with 1938 per capita levels of industrialization and

44. Curami, "Commesse belliche e approvvigionamenti di materie prime," in Rainero and Biagini, eds., *1940*, pp. 62–64, offers a thoughtful introduction to the issues surrounding Italian aero engines, fuels, and lubricants; DB601 delays: Curami, "I riflessi delle operazioni," p. 506; Ansaldo scandal: Ceva and Curami, *Industria bellica anni trenta.*

45. "L'industria aeronautica ha mantenuto il suo carattere originale: cioé artigiano!" (air ministry report of 1942, printed extensively in Arena, *Aeronautica*, vol. 3, pp. 726–32); likewise Fougier to Ambrosio, 15 April 1943, *Direttive Superaereo*, 2/2:698.

46. On the qualitative edge achieved in many areas until American electronics and systems engineering came into play, see David C. Evans and Mark R. Peattie, *Kaigun: Strategy, Tactics, and Technology in the Imperial Japanese Navy 1887–1941* (Annapolis, MD, 1997), especially Chapters 8, 9 and pp. 507–08; for the creation of 1st Air Fleet (the carrier striking force), pp. 349–52.

GNP lower than Italy's, a society still two-thirds peasant, and less than half Italy's motor vehicles in relation to population, had created by 1941 an immense mass army equipped with 24,000-odd tanks whose quality far surpassed anything Fascist Italy ever produced, and in part anything available to – or even projected by – the attacking *Wehrmacht*.[47]

Japan – until the U.S. submarine campaign throttled its economy in 1943–45 – and Soviet Russia nevertheless had priceless advantages that Italy lacked: raw materials and energy supplies. Yet Italy's destitution was far from total: the Germans discovered mounds of secretly hoarded raw materials when they occupied north Italy in autumn 1943. And even an abundance of steel, copper, aluminum, coal, oil, and rubber could not have remedied the defects of industry itself, nor the conceptual, organizational, and technological failings of the armed forces.[48] But Italy's overall resource dependence was nevertheless both impressive and crippling. To function normally the economy theoretically required twenty-one to twenty-two million tons of imports annually, of which half was coal and a third oil. Approximately three-fifths of that twenty-one million tons passed in peacetime through Gibraltar and Suez, as the Italian navy and the dictator had long lamented. In war, the planners projected that greater use of land transport would reduce that proportion to two-fifths of all imports.

In the event, about 60 percent of Italy's overall energy consumption in 1940–42 came from foreign sources.[49] Only Germany's assurance of

---

47. DRZW 4:75. The Soviet border armies deployed 14,000 to 15,000 tanks; the Germans attacked with 3,648 tanks and assault guns (DRZW 4:977).

48. This is the thesis of Andrea Curami and others, in contrast to the numerous postwar accounts that stress raw material shortages as the source of Italy's military-industrial failure; see especially Curami, "Commesse belliche."

49. Peacetime annual imports: Air staff memorandum, 1 April 1940, *Direttive Superaereo*, 1/1:94; wartime projections: Umberto Spigo, *Premesse tecniche della disfatta* (Rome, 1945), p. 84 (estimates from the Commissione Suprema di Difesa, of which Spigo had been secretary). External energy supplies: Vera Zamagni, "Un'analisi macroeconomica degli effetti della guerra," in Zamagni,

March 1940 that it would provide Italy's entire coal import requirement by rail made Fascist Italy's last war possible; despite seasonal shortages due to weather conditions along the vital rail lines through the Alps, the Germans delivered the twelve million tons of coal that they had promised in 1940/41, eleven million in 1941/42, and twelve million once again in 1942/43. Hydroelectric power, which produced 40 percent of Italy's steel in 1942, increased from fifteen million kilowatt-hours in 1938 to around twenty million in 1941–42. Overall energy consumption remained steady from 1939 to 1942, then dropped by roughly a quarter in 1943.[50]

These were static or declining inputs which did not permit the massive wartime expansion that occurred in the United States, Britain, and Soviet Russia. Italian GDP peaked in 1939 and declined thereafter, whereas that of all other major combatants except France did not peak until 1942–44.[51] Even Germany, which of the major contenders suffered most from resource constraints, was able through conquest of the raw materials, plants, and labor of its neighbors to increase its production of coal – its chief energy source – by roughly 30 percent between 1938/39 and 1943/44.[52] Italy's meager steel production (which amounted in 1938 to about a tenth of Germany's and 38 percent of Japan's) slowly dropped from 2.32 million tons in 1938 to 1.73 million tons in 1942, due in part to a shortfall in imports of foreign scrap iron and steel.[53]

ed., *Come perdere la guerra e vincere la pace: L'economia italiana tra guerra e dopoguerra 1938–1947* (Bologna, 1997), p. 52 (table).

50. Zamagni, "Un'analisi macroeconomica," pp. 16–17, 45 (table 1A4), 52 (table); German coal exports to Italy: DRZW 5/1:576.

51. Harrison, "The Economics of World War II," Table 1.3, p. 10 (peak GDP achieved in 1942: Japan; in 1943: Britain; in 1944: Germany, USA, Soviet Russia.)

52. DRZW 5/1:576.

53. Figures: Akira Hara, "Japan: Guns before Rice," and Zamagni, "Italy: How to Lose the War and Win the Peace," in Harrison, ed., *Economics of World War II*, pp. 230 (Table 6.3), 184 (Table 5.3).

And for the armed forces, petroleum was an even more critical bottle-neck than steel: less than 1 percent of the petroleum products that the armed forces and civilian economy consumed in 1938 had come from inside Italy. By 1942 overall petroleum consumption, including imports, had fallen (in terms of energy content) to 35 percent of the level of 1938. That crippled the navy, the armed forces' largest consumer of crude oil; it also throttled domestic motor transport for industrial raw materials and products, food distribution, and passengers, adding to the already massive frictions within the war economy. Italy's resource dependence meshed with the weaknesses already described to make the errors and inadequacies of Italy's war preparations before 1940 irredeemable.[54]

Production of armaments and munitions either stagnated or declined after 1941. The navy took delivery between June 1940 and September 1943 of only 240,000 tons of warships, about a third of Italy's tonnage at the outset; capital ship construction largely ended, stalling key projects that included two belated aircraft carriers. Aircraft production peaked in 1941 and fell thereafter. When the plants the army had belatedly commissioned in 1938 for its new generation of artillery were ready in 1941–42, energy shortages kept production well below planned output. Capacity for one key although characteristically obsolescent item, the 47mm light anti-tank gun, was 290 units per month in February 1942, but coal and electricity shortages and industrial disorganization held production to 170, barely enough to replace combat losses.[55]

Italy's overall production of equipment and munitions was enough to supply meagerly fewer than twenty divisions actually in contact with the enemy.[56] And total 1940–43 production was diminutive by international

---

54. Steel production, petroleum: Zamagni, "Un'analisi macroeconomica," pp. 44 (table 1A3), 52 (table).

55. *Comando Supremo* memorandum, 6 February 1942, Ceva, *La condotta italiana*, pp. 201–02.

56. Cavallero, in minutes of meeting, 6 March 1942, ibid., p. 208.

standards: roughly 60,000 transport vehicles, 7,000 artillery pieces (of which over half were the 47mm anti-tank gun), 4,152 armored fighting vehicles (of which only 535 had guns of 75mm or larger), and somewhere in the neighborhood of 10,000 artillery pieces; German and United States tank production to the end of 1943 was 18,600 and 57,585 respectively. The Italian air force took delivery in 1940–43 of 10,389 aircraft of which three quarters were bombers, fighters, reconnaissance, or transport; Germany's aircraft production over the same period was 62,239 and that of the United States was 157,000.[57] Those numbers were the single most decisive influence on Italy's fate.

57. Figures: Ceva and Curami, *Meccanizzazione*, vol. 1, pp. 474–75 for armor; remaining figures from Ceva, "Italy," in I. C. B. Dear and M. R. D. Foot, eds., *The Oxford Companion to the Second World War* (Oxford, 1995), p. 585 (pp. 459 and 1183 respectively for the German and U.S. figures).

3

MEN AND MACHINES: THE ARMED
FORCES AND MODERN WARFARE

From the beginning the question of whether Italy would retain a measure
of dignity in defeat rested first of all with the armed forces. And of the
armed forces, the army was by far the most important, for it absorbed
almost two-thirds of the military budget, dominated the high command,
and alone held the power to destroy the regime. "Men, our indisputable
resource," not machines, and mind over matter were the *Regio Esercito*'s
twin credos – a cultural limitation that long antedated Fascism and
proved almost impervious to experience in 1940–43.[1] Numerical superiority in infantry was in the army view the decisive factor in war, a view
supposedly confirmed by the experience of 1915–18. The *Regio Esercito*
had acquired numerous machines by that war's end, but its leaders had
never accepted what the German high command had recognized as early
as mid-1916: warfare had become "machine warfare."[2] Belief in the

---

1. For the quotation (General Armando Diaz, 1923) and an excellent introduction
    to interwar army thought, see Antonio Sema, "La cultura dell'esercito," in
    Cultura e società negli anni del fascismo (Milan, 1987), pp. 91–116. For the very slow
    assimilation after 1940, especially at the highest levels, of the principles of
    machine warfare, see Ceva and Curami, *Meccanizzazione*, vol. 1, pp. 310–14.
2. See Michael Geyer, "German Strategy in the Age of Machine Warfare, 1914–
    1945," in Peter Paret, ed., *Makers of Modern Strategy* (Princeton, 1988), pp. 537–54.

*U.S. troops examine a disabled FIAT-Ansaldo M14 tank, Tunisia, 1943 (U.S. National
Archives 208-AA-260-EE).*

human will paralleled faith in numbers; both together perhaps contributed to the army's tolerance until 1939 of FIAT-Ansaldo's 3.5-ton L3
tankettes, which were easily perforated by machine-gun fire and had on
occasion succumbed to Ethiopians wielding stones. Reverence for the
human spirit and a culturally determined faith in genial improvisation
may also have helped to cause the army's universally attested disdain for
cadre and unit training.

Like its German counterpart after 1933, the army made its doctrinal
and force structure decisions under the Fascist regime with considerable
freedom, subject only to the dictator's demands for fighting power. But
the structure the *Regio Esercito* chose for itself, unlike that erected by its
German counterpart and eventual ally, perpetuated the "atavistic intellectual narrowness" later detected and analyzed in detail, after several
false starts, by the army's postwar official historians.[3]

Reverence for numbers dictated as many divisions as the army budget
permitted. Corporate self-interest powerfully reinforced doctrinal
choice: the higher officer corps had grown disproportionately during
the First World War and had subsequently exploited its bargain with
Fascism to reestablish its numbers after forced personnel cuts in 1918–22.
The more divisions, the more command positions for its members – a
logic that culminated in 1937–38 with the decision of the chief of staff and
undersecretary of the army, General Alberto Pariani, to increase the
peacetime army from forty-odd to seventy-odd divisions by decreeing
that each would have two infantry regiments – the "*divisione binaria*" –
instead of the usual three.

Regardless of the structure of its divisions, the army leadership's insistence on maintaining as large a force as budgetarily feasible condemned
the   service   to   intellectual   torpor   and   physical   immobility.
Nondiscretionary expenses consumed all available funds: regular officer

---

3.   For this courageous phrase, accompanied by much astute analysis, see
      Montanari, *Alla vigilia*, especially p. 251; likewise his *La campagna di Grecia*
      (Rome, 1980) and *Africa*, works in the best traditions of Clausewitzian *Kritik*.

pay; enormous static bureaucracies dictated by the need to employ as many regular officers as possible; and the numerous installations and immense stocks of basic equipment – rifles, mess kits, canteens, rucksacks, uniforms, and blankets – that the inflated force structure required. Combat units consequently remained at less than half strength throughout most of the year during peacetime, suffered massive shortages of crew-served weapons, vehicles, horses, and mules, and were rarely able to train companies or even platoons as units. The army leadership also economized on its junior cadres, with disastrous consequences for tactical expertise and unit cohesion to be described later.

Machines were low on the army's scale of priorities, and the machines it commissioned were correspondingly inadequate. The war ministry's bureaucratic "labyrinths" alone – even discounting industry's manifest shortcomings – made failure almost inevitable. Each new equipment item or weapon required the approval of the artillery (or engineer, or motorization) technical office, the appropriate department of the ministry itself, the inspectorate of the branch concerned, the training section of the army staff, and finally the ministry secretariat. If even one of these organizations proposed a minor modification, the entire process had to begin once more. It took six months to approve a Molotov cocktail anti-tank weapon that the technical staff had put together and successfully tested in less than a week in July 1940. This system, and the ministry's return in July 1940 to its traditional daily closing hour of 2 P.M., so compounded the dysfunctions of industry that it is surprising that the army received any new equipment at all before 1943.[4]

The army's highest priority was artillery, the weapon most congenial to its 1915–18 conceptual framework. But strangely – in view of its straightened circumstances – the service demanded as early as 1929 a

---

4. Labyrinths: Cavallero, *Diario 1940–1943*, p. 582; Mario Caracciolo, *E poi? La tragedia dell'esercito italiano* (Rome, 1946), pp. 58–60; closing time: Soddu to subordinates, 61920, 27 August 1940, ACS, Primo Aiutante di Campo, Sezione Speciale, bundle 67, folder "Circolari Varie 1940."

total renewal of all artillery, a course upon which Germany only embarked because forced disarmament after 1918 had left it no alternative. As a senior artillery officer pointed out in 1933, Italy could simply refurbish, with immediate effect and at considerable savings, many of the excellent weapons produced before 1915 on German and French licenses or captured thereafter from Austria-Hungary. New shells and propellant charges were feasible, and modern gun carriages, off-road tractors, and half-track carriers would have worked wonders. But the half-track only came to Italy in wartime as a belated means of saving rubber, and the sometimes excellent new cannon the army finally ordered in 1938 reached the troops in small numbers only in 1941–42. In the event, the immense bulk of the army's artillery in 1940–43 remained that of 1915–18; the British counterparts of two key Italian weapons, the 100/17 howitzer and the 105/28 gun, outranged them by 3,000 and up to 8,700 meters respectively, and were considerably more mobile.[5]

Conceptual blinkers narrowed further by penury also slowed the army's fitful attempts to acquire an effective medium tank. FIAT-Ansaldo, great though its faults, enjoyed the army's tolerance throughout. And although the last prewar chief of staff, Pariani, correctly foresaw as early as 1936–37 that a drive on Suez would be the strategic center of gravity of Italy's coming war, he planned to fight that war primarily with truck-borne infantry. Italy's first medium tank, the failed M11/39, had its main gun rendered almost useless by its placement in the hull rather than in a turret, a solution apparently dictated either by inability to design turret mechanisms, or the alleged need to reduce vehicle width to fit

---

5. Refurbishment of artillery: Ceva and Curami, "Industria bellica e stato," pp. 326–29 and note 24; Ceva, "Rapporti fra industria bellica ed esercito," pp. 220–21; half tracks: Ceva and Curami, *Meccanizzazione*, vol. 1, p. 411; artillery ranges (25-pounder, 4.5″ gun): Brian R. Sullivan, "The Italian Soldier in Combat, June 1940–September 1943: Myths, Realities and Explanations," in Paul Addison and Angus Calder, eds., *Time to Kill: The Soldier's Experience of War in the West, 1939–1945* (London, 1997), p. 186, and *Africa*, 3:708.

Italian roads. One of Italy's few generals with experience of commanding armored units in combat, General Ettore Bastico, was apparently so intimidated by his colleagues' opposition to the new weapon that at a meeting of senior generals called to discuss the future of armor in November 1937 he conceded that "the tank is a powerful tool [*mezzo*] but let us not idolize it [*non gridiamogli osanna*]; let us reserve our reverence for the infantryman and the mule."[6] Innovation was and remained suspect, because it meant scrapping a force structure that derived from the army's deeply felt conception of war and directly served the interests of the officer corps.[7]

What was truly remarkable was how little, and how slowly, the shock of war changed the army's reverence for infantry and mules. After the *Wehrmacht*'s destruction of Poland in September 1939 and the penury and confusion revealed by the Italian army's own partial mobilization that autumn, the army staff began to have second thoughts about its 120- to 126-division target figure for the war army. Despite an attempt by Pariani's successor as army chief of staff, Marshal Rodolfo Graziani, to hold the line at 100 divisions, the final figure selected for activation in spring 1940 was 73.[8]

The 73 divisions of June 1940 grew to a nominal 91 by mid-1943, despite the catastrophic defeats in North Africa (December 1940–February 1941), Russia (November 1942–February 1943), and Tunisia (January–May 1943) that eliminated 34 divisions. Cavallero – who had

---

6. "Il carro é un mezzo potente che non dobbiamo disconoscere; ma non gridiamogli osanna. L'osanna riserviamolo per il fante e per il mulo": Botti, "I generali italiani e il problema dei corazzati: la riunione tenuta dal Generale Pariani il 23 e 24 novembre 1937 sul carro armato e i suoi riflessi," *Studi storico-militari 1993* (Rome, 1996), pp. 211–14, 241.

7. Italy is noteworthy by its absence from the best recent analysis of the origins of the major weapons systems of the Second World War: Williamson Murray and Allan R. Millett, eds., *Military Innovation in the Interwar Period* (Cambridge, 1996).

8. Figures: Montanari, *Alla vigilia*, pp. 280–81, 305–06 note 35; Carlo Favagrossa, *Perché perdemmo la guerra: Mussolini e la produzione bellica* (Milan, 1946), p. 115.

won his spurs in 1915–18 in the operations section of the supreme command – claimed to perceive as early as 1941 that "the general experience of the war. . . has emphasized the importance of quality rather than numbers." A few officers at the *Comando Supremo* recognized by July 1941 that "a single motorized division, EVEN FOR DEFENSE AND OCCUPATION MISSIONS, has the capability of four infantry divisions, while it eats only a fourth as much and requires only a fourth as much transport from Italy."[9] Yet Cavallero failed to motorize fully a few picked divisions while eliminating the many useless mouths that were in part responsible for the armed forces' North African logistical nightmare. Mussolini's own rage for numbers and the political imperative of outnumbering the Germans in that vital theater were doubtless partly responsible.[10] But the root cause was the army hierarchy's own continuing belief in numbers. Cavallero sought to bring Italian forces in North Africa up to sixteen divisions, of which all except two or three would of necessity be foot infantry.[11] In the event, he maintained the equivalent of at least eight foot infantry divisions in North Africa until El Alamein. As late as July 1942 the *Comando Supremo* proposed to add a further 67,000 troops to the mostly immobile 150,000 already overseas.[12]

At the army's high point in April 1943 it thus numbered almost 3.7 million officers and men. Its combat units were as underequipped,

9.   Cavallero to Roatta, 8 June 1941; *Comando Supremo* office note, July 1941 (emphasis in original), both in Ceva, *La condotta italiana*, pp. 151, 110. The author of the note was probably Colonel Giuseppe Cordero Lanza di Montezemolo, chief of the operations section for Africa, and the *Comando Supremo*'s sharpest brain.

10. The latter is the thesis of Ceva, *La condotta italiana*, pp. 76, 109–110.

11. Cavallero diary, 20 July 1941, ibid., p. 77; similarly, army staff memorandum on reinforcement of North Africa, 23 May 1941 (110,000 additional men, but only 14,000 vehicles and tanks), in Ceva, *Le forze armate*, pp. 582–87.

12. *Comando Supremo* memorandum, "Ripartizione tonnellaggio negli avviamenti in A.S.," 22 July 1942, NARA T-821/144/000486–91.

undermanned, inadequately officered, and poorly supported as they had been at the outset. Its overall "mobility ratio" – thirty-eight men under arms to each truck in its inventory – had scarcely budged from 1940 to 1943. Its bloated and static rear area commands had absorbed 500,000 men, a full third of the personnel stationed in Italy and the islands. The gigantic Roman bureaucracies possessed one officer for every thirteen enlisted men, and a largely superfluous entity such as the horse cavalry school at Pinerolo employed 3,650 officers and men.[13]

As in the interwar period, the technological poverty that accompanied the army's numerical hypertrophy was self-inflicted. Badoglio was so uninterested in mechanized warfare that his only recorded comment on a perceptive army intelligence analysis of German methods in July 1940 was "we'll study it when the war is over." It apparently required Mussolini's intervention that same month to compel the war ministry bureaucracy to begin work on specifications for a 75mm-gun tank – which in the event FIAT-Ansaldo failed to produce before collapse in 1943 rendered it useless.[14]

The army's wartime record on motor transport was only slightly less disastrous. The war ministry had failed to anticipate before June 1940, or to recognize thereafter, the sheer numbers of vehicles required and the fact that fighting might not be confined to hard-surfaced roads; for off-road mobility Italian units in North Africa had to rely largely on captured British trucks and Bren carriers. And in areas such as communications, where relatively small investments could have produced dramatic results, the army failed dismally. Italian tank crews suffered without

13. Rochat, "Gli uomini alle armi," pp. 271, 278–80, 290 (Table H); for the army's size over the course of the war, Tables A, B, C, pp. 284–86 and Ceva, "Italy," p. 592 (graph); "mobility ratio" (men to truck or artillery tractor): 1:38, 1 June 1943; 1:40, 1 June 1940 (calculated from Ceva, *Le forze armate*, pp. 263, 349, and Rochat, "Gli uomini alle armi," Table C).

14. Knox, *Mussolini*, p. 26; Ceva and Curami, *Meccanizzazione*, vol. 1, pp. 297–301, 360, 393–95, 481, 484; vol. 2, pp. 532–33.

voice radios until 1941. Even after that, the army lacked a long distance radio that could operate on the move. Nor did anyone in Rome think to provide inexpensive items such as the compensated vehicle compasses essential in the desert – this despite thirty years of Italian military experience in Libya. When the reconnaissance units of the Italian mobile divisions fighting alongside the *Afrika Korps* belatedly received their first armored cars in 1941–42, commanders had to stop their vehicles and walk away from them to take bearings with hand compasses. Even basic infantry weapons such as the excellent and inexpensive 81 mm mortar were in short supply and scantily provided with ammunition until 1941. The bureaucracy had also ensured that the army's basic weapon, the bolt-action rifle, came in two entirely different calibers, and the sampler of machine guns issued at various times to the units fired at least seven distinct and incompatible types of ammunition.[15]

The navy made rather more effective use than either army or air force of the relatively small resources that it commanded. By 1940 it had created a balanced fleet built around an intended total of eight new or modernized battleships. That was an achievement accompanied by considerable sacrifice: the navy's priorities were the reverse of the army's – it bought ships first and funded manpower with what little money remained. The result was overwork and personnel turbulence among its cadres: naval officers in 1940 amounted to 5.4 percent of enlisted manpower whereas in France and Britain the proportions were 7.5 percent and 9.2 percent respectively.[16] Nevertheless, even the conscripts among the navy's crews were an elite, and the navy's prestige attracted a high proportion of volunteers.

Yet the *Regia Marina* also suffered from unduly narrow technological, operational, and tactical horizons. Its conception of war was that of Tirpitz and Jellicoe; the long-range clash of battle fleets remained the

---

15.   See Sullivan, "The Italian Soldier in Combat," pp. 184–85.
16.   USMM, *L'organizzazione della marina durante il conflitto* (Rome, 1972–75), vol. 1, pp. 261, 272–73, graph 14.

decisive act of war, despite the example of feverish innovation elsewhere, most notably in the greatest of the Axis navies, that of Imperial Japan. The Italian navy staff failed to appreciate the potentially crippling mismatch between Italy's lack of oil and a battle fleet that consumed immense quantities of that commodity. It also failed to develop adequately or rejected outright more fuel-efficient and deadlier technologies and techniques that would have served Italy best in 1940–43 if prepared in advance: aircraft carriers, torpedo aircraft, mines, submarines, frogman-guided torpedoes, and radar. When offered the opportunity to construct at least one of the three or four aircraft carriers feasible within the 60,000 tons allotted to Italy under the 1922 Washington Naval Treaty, a committee of admirals had in Mussolini's presence and with almost perfect unanimity scornfully rejected the idea in 1925, although by that point all other major navies, including that of France, already possessed carriers. The navy staff flirted indecisively with the concept once more in 1935–36; possible solutions included conversion of the transatlantic liner *Roma*. The autocratic chief of staff, Admiral Domenico Cavagnari, ended all deliberation with an emphatic and peremptory marginal "NO!!!" in August 1936. He and key subordinates publicly, repeatedly, and vehemently denied thereafter that the navy needed aircraft carriers.[17] Only after the Taranto disaster and Cavagnari's dismissal did Mussolini himself intervene to press for the conversion of the *Roma*. The navy staff still resisted, alleging insuperable practical obstacles, and Mussolini gave in. Not until July 1941, after defeat – in part due to British carrier-based torpedo-bombers – at Matapan, did the navy consent to take up the project once more, perhaps at Cavallero's insistence. Neither the *Roma* nor a second converted liner were ready by September 1943, and no solutions were as yet in sight for critical issues that had taken the

17. See especially Cavagnari's famous March 1938 parliamentary speech, noteworthy for its "peremptory and arrogant tone," in Giorgio Giorgerini, *Da Matapan al Golfo Persico: La Marina militare italiana dal fascismo alla Repubblica* (Milan, 1989), pp. 444–45.

British, U.S., and Japanese carrier forces the best part of a decade to
resolve – from specialized pilot training to the provision of launching
catapults, "navalized" fighters, and the dive-bombers and light torpedo-
bombers that the aircraft industry had so far been unable to produce.[18]

The navy did see the usefulness of land-based torpedo-bombers to
support the fleet and strike at enemy shipping. But neither navy nor
Badoglio were able to move the air force to form the necessary units
until late 1939, although the navy had developed an aerial torpedo so
excellent that the Luftwaffe bought 300 of them. The navy staff likewise
recognized the vital role of mines, to which it assigned the task of block-
ing the Sicily channel to east-west British traffic. But Cavagnari refused
to adjust spending priorities to reflect the importance of that mission.
Battleships came first, and in 1940 the navy entered the war with mines
that were almost all First World War surplus.

Submarines had a higher priority, and by June 1940 Italy had one of the
largest submarine forces in the world. But the navy failed to create a force
that rivaled those of Italy's ally and adversaries either doctrinally or
technologically. Misplaced faith in the daytime submerged attack,
failure – as in the British navy – to follow German doctrinal progress,
and consequent technical-tactical defects that ranged from a submersion
time three times that of German boats, to a surface speed of only
11–12 knots, to inadequate torpedo capacity and too-short periscopes,

---

18.   The best brief analysis of navy resistance to the aircraft carrier is Alberto Santoni,
      "La mancata risposta della Regia Marina alle teorie del Douhet. Analisi storica del
      problema della portaerei in Italia" in *La figura e l'opera di Giulio Douhet* (Caserta,
      1988), pp. 257–69 (Cavagnari's veto, p. 262); also the scathing account of
      Giorgerini, *Da Matapan al Golfo Persico*, pp. 420–445, and VCSMG 1939–43
      2:74–75; carrier aircraft problems in Curami, "I riflessi delle operazioni," pp. 495–
      504; ship details in USMM, *Le navi di linea italiane* (Rome, 1973), pp. 339–54.
      Santoni, "La battaglia di Matapan," in Biagini and Rainero, eds., *1941*, pp. 419–33,
      offers an informed summary of the battle and of the debates surrounding it, but see
      also Mattesini, *Il giallo di Matapan* (Rome, 1985).

rendered Italy's submarine force relatively ineffectual. Like its Japanese ally, the navy failed equally in anti-submarine warfare: sonar, effective depth charges, and use of aircraft against submarines arrived only belatedly.[19]

The one major naval weapon of the Second World War that Italy developed first – the "*maiale*" ("hog"), the frogman-guided "slow torpedo" that sank the battleships *Valiant* and *Queen Elizabeth* at Alexandria in December 1941 – was born an orphan. The weapon built on a tradition inaugurated in the First World War, when Italian swimmers and torpedo boats had accounted for two Austro-Hungarian battleships. But the *maiali* were anything but a navy staff product: they did not fit *Supermarina*'s Jutland-style operational concept. Only the emergencies of 1935–36 and 1940 gave the devoted band of diving enthusiasts at the La Spezia submarine flotilla a chance to develop their weapons: the *maiali*, the explosive speedboats that accounted for the cruiser *York* in March 1941, and the frogman-borne limpet mines that destroyed shipping at Gibraltar, Algiers, and elsewhere. Navy staff indifference starved the program between 1936 and the Munich crisis of 1938.[20] Only after the navy's first abortive encounter with the British fleet, off Calabria on 9 July 1940, did Cavagnari suddenly discover that he had a weapon that cost little, risked little except the skins of those skilled and brave enough to employ it, and offered much. Had the maiali been operationally ready in June 1940, Italy could have launched the devastating initial blow that the Germans, British, and French expected or feared, but never came.

Radar was a marked exception to Italy's generally poor record in developing new technologies, but not to the navy staff's rule of rejecting

---

19. Mussolini, in meeting minutes, 29 January 1943, VCSMG 1939–43 4:287; Cavallero, *Comando Supremo*, pp. 189–90, 195; USMM, *L'organizzazione*, vol. 1, pp. 135–49.

20. For the development history of the *maiali*, see Archivio dell'Ufficio Storico della Marina Militare, Rome, "Mezzi d'assalto," bundle 1, and USMM, *I mezzi d'assalto* (Rome, 1972), Chapter 1.

innovation. An isolated team of researchers at the naval communications school in Livorno, with minimal funding and almost no encouragement from Rome, developed from 1935–36 onward a series of increasingly effective prototype search radars. Industrial firms in Florence and Milan, FIVRE and SAFAR, developed and produced (respectively) the necessary ultra-high-frequency final amplifier tubes and cathode-ray display tubes derived from pioneering television research. But the navy staff suffered throughout from what a historian of the research effort has described as "inertia and intellectual backwardness."[21] Cavagnari and his chief subordinates saw no purpose in deploying even experimentally the strange devices emerging from the Livorno workshop. Until mid-1941 the navy consigned each successive prototype to storage after successful static trials against ships and aircraft at ever-increasing ranges.

The Taranto disaster, which resulted in part from British achievement of surprise in the absence of Italian land-based radar defenses, was insufficiently persuasive. As late as February 1941 the navy's ordnance chief rejected any practical application of Italy's radar technology as "futuristic," and the battle fleet commander, Admiral Angelo Iachino, refused an offer of three prototype radars to mount on his ships. Then came the night action off Matapan in which the battleships *Warspite, Valiant,* and *Barham* annihilated two Italian heavy cruisers; in its wake, intercepted British tactical communications persuaded the Italian navy staff that the British had somehow located the doomed Italian squadron from beyond visual range. Even then, the ordnance bureaucracy managed to so slow production and deployment that the Germans had to provide Italy's first operational naval radars. SAFAR ultimately produced roughly a hundred sets, and both the Germans and the Western powers – in 1943–44 – found Italy's radar technology more advanced in some respects than their own, at least until the advent of operational microwave radar in early

---

21. Luigi Carillo Castioni, "I radar industriali italiani. Ricerche, ricordi, considerazioni per una loro storia," *Storia contemporanea,* 18:6 (1987), p. 1260.

1943. The navy had squandered the opportunity to profit from the one key technology of the war in which Italy had initially been competitive.[22]

Even the conventional surface fleet on which the navy staff had lavished most of the naval budget had avoidable defects. The main fleet striking forces of *Littorio*-class battleships and *Zara* and *Bolzano*-class heavy cruisers were up to world standards except for the single detail most vital in the daylight long-range combat for which the navy had designed them: the accuracy and reliability of their main guns. Cavagnari and associates accepted from industry an amazing 1 percent tolerance in shell weight and a similar lack of uniformity in propellant charges; they also failed to correct serious rangefinder, loading system, firing circuit, and shell fuse defects revealed in exercises. The navy staff was fully aware before 1939 that Italian battleship and cruiser salvos grouped so loosely that hitting the enemy was problematic. In the preliminary daytime action off Matapan, the battleship *Vittorio Veneto* and its accompanying heavy cruisers had overwhelming superiority of force, achieved surprise, and fired 636 rounds from their main batteries at a British light cruiser squadron without a single hit. The *Bismarck*, two months later, sank the *Hood* and put to flight Britain's most modern battleship, the *Prince of Wales*, by firing roughly the same number of rounds as had the *Vittorio Veneto*.[23] Most of Italy's light cruisers were foreseeable disasters; they achieved trial speeds in the vicinity of 40 knots in calm seas, but sometimes disintegrated when hit and lacked

22. See in general Carillo Castioni, "I radar industriali italiani," pp. 1221-65; quotation: pp. 1238–39; also Enrico Cernuschi, *Marinelettro e il radiotelemetro italiano: Lo sviluppo e l'evoluzione del radar navale (1933–1943)* (Rome, 1995), pp. 61–62.

23. See, among much other literature, the illuminating discussion of the navy's gunnery in Ceva, "Notizie e riflessioni sugli ultimi anni della Ansaldo S.A. 'privata' (1929–1933)," *Nuova antologia* 2122 (1999), pp. 91–131; USMM, *L'organizzazione*, vol. 1, pp. 97, 104–05; and Santoni, "La battaglia di Matapan," p. 428.

protection against heavy weather. Destroyers tended to swamp; the battle fleet lost two escorts and most of their crews in this manner while returning from the second battle of the Sirte in March 1942. Other navies had similar difficulties, but tended to discover and correct them in peacetime; the Japanese navy inaugurated a radical rebuilding of defective cruisers and destroyers after storm disasters in 1934–35.[24] But in the Italian case, most defects of this kind emerged only in combat, and too late for remedy.

The air force, unlike the army and navy, was largely bereft of a conception of war that might have given direction to its armament efforts. In theory the air staff revered the "absolute air warfare" that Giulio Douhet had prophesied in the 1920s, despite some competition from the ground-attack doctrine for which General Amedeo Mecozzi doggedly campaigned throughout the interwar period. In practical terms the air force devoted the bulk of its funding before June 1940 to three-engine and two-engine medium and light bombers wholly incapable, in their speed, bomb load, range, navigation aids, radio communications, and bombsights, of implementing Douhet's concept. The air staff recognized the need for a long-range four-engined bomber, and had seriously considered the idea of purchasing production rights to the Boeing B-17 Flying Fortress. But it ultimately opted – on grounds of the prospective superiority of the Italian machine – for the Piaggio P108 "flying feebleness" (as the former deputy chief of the air staff described it after the war). A few P108s entered combat belatedly in 1942, but were so unreliable mechanically that they frequently disappeared without trace over the Mediterranean.[25] The Savoia-Marchetti SM79 trimotor, which had made its debut in Spain, remained by default the *Regia Aeronautica*'s most effective bomber; its planned successor, the SM84, proved so slow, unstable, and unreliable that the air force withdrew it from service in 1941–42.

---

24. See Evans and Peattie, *Kaigun*, pp. 240–45.
25. Pricolo on his rationale for rejecting the B-17: Curami, "Piani e progetti," p. 252; "Vere debolezze volanti": Giuseppe Santoro, *L'aeronautica italiana nella seconda guerra mondiale* (Rome, 1957), vol. 2, p. 473; Arena, *Aeronautica*, vol. 2, p. 586.

Open-cockpit biplane fighters made up the next largest group of aircraft; the air force leadership's persistent attachment to the biplane throughout the late 1930s contributed to freezing the *Regia Aeronautica* in backwardness as much as the inadequacy of the monoplane prototypes that industry offered in 1938–39, after all other major air forces had made the transition to monoplanes.[26] The air force leadership also failed to demand high-octane fuels and high-performance petroleum-based lubricants from industry in the late 1930s, while development time yet remained; Italy largely fought the war with castor oil in its aircraft engines. General Francesco Pricolo, air force chief from 1939 to 1941, sought to make a virtue of these deficiencies by standardizing them. In early 1940 he scornfully rejected quantity production of a promising monoplane fighter prototype, the Reggiane Re2000, because its manufacturers had markedly improved its test-flight performance with high-octane fuel. The aircraft and its variants finally entered service in small numbers in 1941–42.[27] Air Ministry departments and air staff in any event could not always agree on which aircraft to produce, and rarely proved able to stick to a specification once arrived at. The continual requests for design changes and variants that bedeviled the development of aircraft such as the Cant Z1018 medium bomber were only the most conspicuous examples of a type of mismanagement also found abundantly in the German aircraft industry. As Mussolini – not the first or last political leader to utter such a complaint – lamented in January 1943, "we arrive at perfection [only] when it is useless."[28]

26. See Ceva, "L'evoluzione dei materiali bellici in Italia," in Ennio Di Nolfo, Romain H. Rainero, and Brunello Vigezzi, eds., *L'Italia e la politica di potenza in Europa (1938–1940)* (Milan, 1985), pp. 365–69; Arena, *Aeronautica*, vol. 1, pp. 87–88.

27. On air ministry and staff fondness for the CR42, see especially Arena, *Aeronautica*, vol. 1, pp. 87–88; for the Re2000 and 2001, Curami, "Piani e progetti," pp. 248, 250, 254.

28. On the Cant Z1018, see NARA T-821/479/001049ff. and 480/000127ff.; Mussolini: VCSMG 1939–43, 3:286.

A wide variety of other crippling deficiencies testified to the air force leadership's lack of insight into the three-dimensional nature of modern warfare. Refusal or inability to cooperate with the navy was not confined to the torpedo-bomber issue. The air staff organized timely experiments in the mid-1930s to determine the best technique for bombing shipping. The absence of suitable aircraft and ordnance ruled out the use of dive-bombers carrying heavy armor-piercing bombs, a system found highly effective elsewhere but not inaugurated in Italy until the Luftwaffe provided 100-odd Junkers Ju87 Stukas from autumn 1940 onward. Unlike any other major air force, the *Regia Aeronautica* instead inexplicably concluded that 50-kilogram bombs dropped by level bombers could inflict "unquestionably mortal" damage on warships of up to 10,000 tons.[29] Italy therefore entered the Second World War with a shortage, not remedied even in part until 1941, of the heavy armor-piercing bombs needed to make an impression on the British Mediterranean Fleet. Italian fuses, in common with those of many of the combatants at the outset of the war, proved unreliable, and bomb casings often split open on impact. Incendiaries used briefly over Malta had the disconcerting habit of bursting immediately upon release, destroying the aircraft. Despite research throughout the conflict, the air force failed to procure an illumination rocket that worked.[30] Bombsights and bombing procedure remained rudimentary: the SM79, for instance, lacked stabilizing gyroscopes and an intercom between pilot and bombardier. To confer with the pilot or request a second pass over the target, the bombardier had to crawl up to the cockpit. The consequent lack of communication led an entire

29. See the excerpts from a detailed report of 1938 or 1939 by General Pietro Pinna, vice-chief of staff, in Arena, *Aeronautica*, vol. 1, pp. 82–83.

30. Francesco Pricolo, *La Regia Aeronautica nella seconda guerra mondiale* (Milan, 1971), pp. 140–42; Romeo Bernotti, *Cinquant'anni nella marina militare* (Milan, 1971), p. 230; Donald G. Payne (pseud. Ian Cameron), *Red Duster, White Ensign* (New York, 1960), pp. 78, 229; Hugh Lloyd, *Briefed to Attack* (London, 1949), p. 45.

formation to loose its bombs on the Italian fleet rather than on the British during the battle off Calabria.[31]

Air defense was likewise an orphan. The radar and flak systems that the Luftwaffe brought south in its deployment in December-January 1940–41 to shore Italy up and cover Rommel's passage to Tripoli were a revelation. But no integrated Italian air defense system of radars, fighters, and anti-aircraft artillery (which in any event belonged not to the air force but to army, navy, and Fascist Militia) appeared until 1942. A major deficiency of both aircraft and crews was their limited capacity for instrument flying, night flying, and blind navigation – but in mid-1940 Pricolo sought to increase the experience level of the first-line units by closing down the air force's very effective Instrument Flying School and dispersing its personnel and accumulated experience. In September 1940, an Italian air corps dispatched abortively to foggy Belgium at Mussolini's insistence to aid the Germans against Britain lost five aircraft during the flight north from Italy, and a further thirty-three from fog, rain, icing, navigational error, and enemy action.[32] In North Africa, where Italian aircraft had been flying since 1911, air units in 1940 still lacked sand filters for their engines. The result was an epidemic of engine and machine-gun failure from sand thrown up by the propellers: one light bomber, in the words of the official historian, tended to "self-deactivate" in all respects during takeoff.[33] Experience did ultimately teach a degree of wisdom; Pricolo held back the first precious squadrons of MC202s, the first operational Italian aircraft mounting a DB601 engine, until they could be fitted with sand filters, despite the wrath of Cavallero at the *Comando Supremo.*

31. Pricolo, *La Regia Aeronautica*, p. 261.

32. Unsigned memorandum for Mussolini, 29 September 1940, ACS, Ministero dell'Aeronautica, Gabinetto, 1940 bundle 63; Arena, *Aeronautica*, vol. 1, pp. 114–16, 226–27, 232.

33. Knox, *Mussolini*, p. 23, the Pricolo-Porro correspondence cited there, and Arena, *Aeronautica*, vol. 1, pp. 90–91 (Ca310).

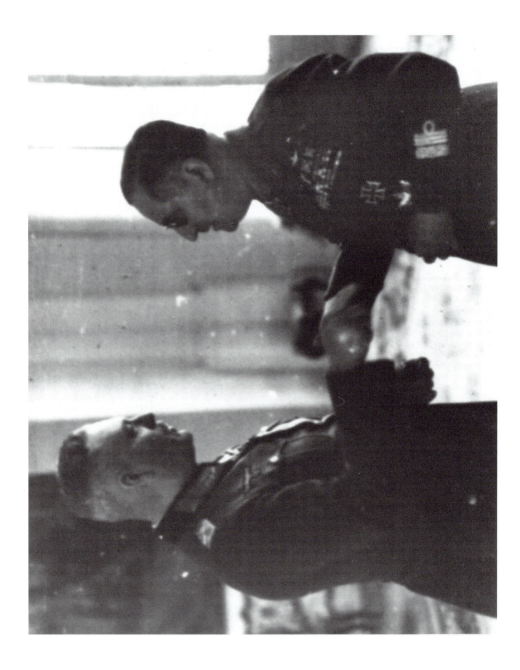

4

STRATEGY

Fascist Italy's approach to the art of matching ends and means in war, and its machinery for strategic decision making, were predictably eccentric – although less so than that of its German ally, where the dictator's power, by autumn 1942, had melted and consumed such vestiges of professional autonomy as remained to the Prusso-German army after its decapitation in 1938. At the outset Mussolini induced Victor Emmanuel III to delegate at least in part the royal prerogative of the supreme command: as of 11 June 1940 the Duce was officially commander of "the troops operating on all fronts." He took that precarious appointment – sanctioned by a mere proclamation rather than a royal decree with legal force – as a license to commit strategic folly despite his limited control over the internal mechanisms of the armed forces. That ambiguity, which reflected the dualism at the heart of the Italian state, was characteristic of the regime.

Immediately under Mussolini, a chief of general staff (from 1925 to December 1940, Marshal Pietro Badoglio) advised the Duce on strategic issues and war preparation, and was at least theoretically answerable for interservice coordination. After 4 June 1940, under a characteristically vague charter that Mussolini had drawn up, Badoglio was also responsible for translating the Duce's strategic directives into orders for each of the

Wehrmacht High Command meets Comando Supremo: Keitel (left) and Cavallero at Salzburg, April 1942 (U.S. National Archives 242 -HLB-FH4-5204-8).

armed forces, and for ensuring the services' timely and coordinated employment. In that capacity, Badoglio called and chaired a series of meetings of the service chiefs of staff at which some limited discussion of strategic issues occurred – but always with an eye to the Duce, who often read the minutes. And Mussolini, as minister of each of the armed forces, also maintained a parallel chain of command in which the service undersecretaries – who were, not coincidentally, also the service chiefs of staff in the case of the navy and air force – reported directly to him without necessarily consulting Badoglio. To complete the disarray, the chief of general staff until 1941 had virtually no staff; his *Comando Supremo* could neither plan operations nor even monitor adequately the performance and actions of the services, upon whom he was almost totally dependent for information. Even without the Duce's frequent strategic inspirations, this was a system designed to maximize dictatorial power rather than decision-making coherence. Badoglio's rival since the 1920s and successor in 1940–43, Cavallero, markedly reinforced the *Comando Supremo's* position and increased its staff upon his return from theater command in Albania in May–June 1941. But the improved efficiency of the high command merely allowed Mussolini to squander Italy's limited resources with greater speed and thoroughness.

Italian strategy in 1940–43 was an unstable amalgam of Mussolini's sudden and often flamboyant inspirations and the more prosaic calculations of the chief of general staff and service chiefs. Its chief characteristics were causally interrelated: myopia, dissipation of effort, passivity, logistical ineffectiveness, and great and ever-growing dependence on the German Reich. Together they ensured that Mussolini's concessions to the need for the utmost speed and concentration of force before Italy's economic weakness laid it low ("better to lose a war in three months than win it in three years") remained purely verbal.[1]

---

1.   Quotation: Botti, "La logistica dei poveri: organizzazione dei rifornimenti e amministrazione dell'Esercito nel 1940," *Memorie storiche militari 1992* (Rome, 1994), p. 441; likewise 411.

Strategic myopia derived both from the cultural limitations already described and from the institutional inadequacy of the Italian intelligence effort, and was even more decisive in shaping Italian strategy than the "short-war illusion," the assumption of swift German victory often described as the chief source of Italian insouciance in 1940. Few members of the Italian leadership had much understanding of the limited role the Mediterranean area played in the world balance of power.[2] Fewer still understood the military implications of the massive economic power wielded by the enemies or potential enemies of the Axis. Even those who had some grasp of Italy's vulnerability sometimes lacked the imagination to see that Britain, although itself under siege, might be capable of mounting a theater-wide counterattack by late 1940. Churchill's August 1940 decision to send many of Britain's tanks to Egypt for early use against Italy, despite the German cross-Channel threat, was an act wholly beyond Rome's imagination. And fewer still in the Italian leadership understood that the United States, although practically disarmed in 1939, might deploy huge naval, air, and ground forces to the Mediterranean with astonishing speed. As late as June 1943, Cavagnari's successor as naval chief still quaintly regarded his British antagonists as "the most powerful navy in the world."[3]

The separate intelligence organizations of the three services did little to remedy this myopia. Those of the army and air force made spectacular – and in the army case, perhaps deliberate – overestimates of French forces in May–June 1940, doubling French ground strength in Tunisia and striking terror into the hearts of Graziani and Badoglio. In September 1943 the army intelligence apparatus also apparently multiplied German

---

2. See the skeptical and documented view (following Hillgruber, *Hitlers Strategie*) of Klaus Schmider, "The Mediterranean in 1940–1941: Crossroads of Lost Opportunities?," *War and Society* (Australia) 15:2 (1997).

3. Riccardi to Ambrosio, 23 June 1943, in Renato Sicurezza, "Le operazioni in Tunisia e nell'Italia meridionale: l'aspetto navale," in Rainero, ed., *1943*, p. 50.

armored strength around Rome.[4] Cavallero attempted to rationalize the
system in 1941 by creating a centralized coordination and assessment
organ at the *Comando Supremo*, while increasingly confining the three
service intelligence branches to operational matters. The army branch
made a major contribution to Axis strategy and operations in June 1942,
after securing the U.S. Army BLACK cypher through a brilliant embassy
burglary: a decrypted message from the U.S. military attaché in Cairo
analyzing British disarray after the fall of Tobruk helped trigger
Rommel's final dash on Egypt.[5] But ability to understand Italy's overall
strategic situation in relation to that of its allies and enemies remained
weak, nor did dictator or *Comando Supremo* welcome strategic knowledge
that impinged on their prerogatives. The naval academy disciplined a

4. Carlo De Risio, *Generali, servizi segreti, e fascismo* (Milan, 1978), pp. 28–34, 227;
    Knox, "Fascist Italy Assesses its Enemies, 1935–1940," in Ernest R. May, ed.,
    Knowing One's Enemies (Princeton, 1984), p. 351. USE, *Le operazioni delle unità
    italiane nel settembre–ottobre 1943*, pp. 99–104, defends army intelligence against
    the charge of overstating German strength, but mistakes table of organization
    strength ("Soll") for actual strength in the 3rd *Panzergrenadier* Division status
    report of 1 September 1943 (facsimile in Giuseppe Castellano, *Roma Kaputt*
    [Rome, 1967], pp. 225–27; original in BA-MA RH 26–3/12, Teil 2), and
    endorses the army staff's implausible total of 150 tanks assigned or attached to
    the division by 9 September. The 1 September status report shows only three
    Mk. III command vehicles actually present.
5. Compare *Africa*, 3:363–64 with S.I.E. decrypt Bl 174 of 23 June 1942: Fellers to
    War Department, 791, 20 June 1942, Appendix 8 to (undated) internal Italian
    intelligence narrative (translation), "The Contribution of the Information [sic]
    Service to the May–June 1942 Offensive in North Africa," NARA RG 457/
    1035 (Records of the National Security Agency; my warmest thanks to Brian R.
    Sullivan for copies of this and other documents from this source); also De
    Risio, *Servizi segreti*, pp. 111–12, and David Alvarez, "Axis Sigint Collaboration:
    A Limited Partnership," in Alvarez, ed., *Allied and Axis Signals Intelligence in
    World War II* (London, 1999), p. 7.

civilian economist on its teaching staff for publishing in spring 1942 statistical projections (later proven accurate to within 5 percent) suggesting that in 1943 the Western powers would build slightly more tonnage than they would lose to the Axis submarine offensive. Naval intelligence did not arrive at a similar conclusion – which bore heavily on the timing of the Anglo-American counteroffensive in the Mediterranean theater and on the outcome of the war – until spring–summer 1943, long after the Western powers' strategic reach had become all too obvious.[6]

Badoglio, with his habitual pithiness, summed up at a chiefs of staff meeting in 25 September 1940 both the prevailing military-geographic outlook and the widespread obliviousness to the future: "If we succeed in moving [the British Fleet] out of the Mediterranean, we will dominate the Mediterranean and nothing will be able to stop us." The far more sophisticated Cavallero harbored similar delusions throughout. He confided to his diary three weeks after Pearl Harbor that "the possession of Tunisia" [by Italy] would mean that "the war in the Mediterranean is won." The Anglo-American landings in Morocco and Algeria in November 1942, despite their unparalleled scale, inspired in him the bizarre notion that the Axis would have "won the war" if the remnants of the French fleet were to join Italy and Germany.[7] As for Mussolini, the spectacle the Western powers had made of themselves at Munich and his occasional contacts with Neville Chamberlain had long since persuaded him that the British "were no longer . . . of the stuff of Sir Francis Drake and of the other magnificent adventurers who created the Empire," a view he apparently revised only in late 1940. The United States, "land of

---

6.   For organizational details, see especially "Attribuzioni della centrale S.I.M.," 21 February 1943, NARA T-821/127/000722–23, and "Ordinamento del Servizio Informazioni," 23 April 1943, 127/001050–52; Epicarmio Corbino's shipping estimates: Ezio Ferrante, "La marina mercantile italiana e la lotta per le comunicazioni marittime nel secondo conflitto mondiale," in Rainero and Biagini, eds., *1940*, pp. 137–38.

7.   VCSMG 1939–43, 1:84; Cavallero, *Diario 1940–1943*, pp. 300, 550.

Negroes and Jews" led by a paralytic, was likewise both too feeble and too distant to threaten Italian ambitions. Its main strategic role, Mussolini suggested on one occasion in autumn 1941, was to make Italy more essential to the Germans.[8]

Few in the ruling group and military leadership thus saw the underlying meaning of Pearl Harbor. The king, whose own strategic horizons were defined by the traditional territorial aims of the House of Savoy such as Corsica and Nice, was pleased at news of Japanese victories. Mussolini was delighted to declare war on the United States in parallel with Hitler on 11 December 1941; the Duce, Cavallero, and the service chiefs do not seem to have ever discussed the consequences. The crushing American naval victory over Japan at Midway in early June 1942, which made U. S. intervention in the Mediterranean certain that autumn and winter, does not even appear in diary sources from within the ruling group.[9] Ambrosio (at that point army chief of staff) and the king naively thought as late as mid-1942 that Russian collapse would compel Britain and the United States to make peace.[10] They were obviously unaware that the armament and force plans that the United States had approved in July 1941 for the coming war were predicated on reducing Germany to rubble and conquering it without Soviet help.

8. Mussolini, in Ciano, 11 January 1939; on the USA: 6 September 1937, 15 April 1939, 28 May, 5 July, 13 October, 30 October 1941; Mussolini apparently intended his fleeting and isolated prophecy that the United States would send an expeditionary corps to Egypt (6 November 1941, ADAP D/13/454, p. 614) as an attempt to persuade a Hitler triumphant in the East that the Reich still needed its Italian ally.

9. Ciano, 3 and 8 December 1941; for the king's view that Italy "was not complete" without Nice and Savoy, Paolo Puntoni, *Parla Vittorio Emanuele III* (Milan, 1958), p. 88 (April 1942). The minutes in VCSMG 1939–43, 2–3 covering the crucial months of late 1941 and early 1942 do not mention the United States at all.

10. Ciano, 4 August, 1 June, 23 February 1942.

Of the key figures, only Ciano – as a result of early diplomatic service in Latin America and China – appreciated the military-economic power and global reach of the United States; except for a brief period in November 1941, he remained convinced that U.S. intervention was coming and would lead to Axis defeat. Yet neither his complaints and misgivings throughout 1941–42 nor the doubts of his Foreign Ministry subordinates had much bearing on Italian policy or strategy, despite their wide circulation within Roman high society.[11] Not until October 1942, as news thickened of Anglo-American convoys of unprecedented size gathering at Gibraltar, did Italian intelligence and key figures in Rome begin to appreciate what was in store. Only days before the Anglo-American landings in Morocco and Algeria, Mussolini was still manfully promoting the view that the Western powers aimed only at punishing Italy from the air, a position he maintained well into the following spring. The "mongrel character [*grosse Rassenmischung*]" of the U.S. Army was in any event an ostensible impediment to battlefield effectiveness.[12]

Even the destruction of the Tunisian bridgehead and the ensuing almost bloodless surrender of the fortress island of Pantelleria, Italy's counterpart to Malta, on 11 June 1943 generated little urgency. Three weeks before the Anglo-American landings in Sicily that triggered the regime's collapse, Ambrosio claimed grandiloquently to Mussolini that

11. For Ciano's views, see especially Ciano, 20 July, 8 December 1941; Bottai, 25 July, 7 August, 9 October, 23 October, 21 November 1941, 30 January, 10 September 1942; Alberto Pirelli, *Taccuini 1922/1943* (Bologna, 1984), pp. 327, 347, 348, 349, 375 (and for their leakage, see especially ADAP D/13/354, Puntoni, *Parla Vittorio Emanuele*, p. 64 [22 July 1941], and Ciano, 2 August 1942).

12. Ciano, 9 October, 1, 4, 7 November 1942; Bottai, 10 September, 10 October, 4 November 1942; ADAP E/4/68; ADAP E/4/98, pp. 170–72; E/5/158, p. 300; E/5/192, p. 379; VCSMG 1939–43, 4:370. *Africa*, 4:91–95 is detailed and eloquent on Italian and Axis failure in November 1942 to understand what impended.

"the enemy knows the value of our soldiers" and predicted that an attack on the islands or the peninsula, "apart from doubts about its success, would have a purely local effect" without major strategic consequences.[13]

Yet the greatest strategic blind spot of the political leadership and high command was incomprehension of its ally. Even those, including the dictator himself, who appear to have leafed through *Mein Kampf* were oblivious to the approach of BARBAROSSA until Italian military intelligence began to harden in mid-May 1941. But both then and later, Italian assessments of German aims rested in part on a primitive version of the "rational actor model" beloved by economists and political scientists, the superstition that decision makers seek results "optimized" in terms of the observer's *own* code of values. German decisions as seen from Rome thus almost invariably confirmed the widespread Italian view that the Germans were above all else stunningly stupid. Ciano's puzzlement at the first news of the coming attack on Russia ("it's a dangerous game, and one that I think lacks a precise purpose") suggests the extent to which even the most astute failed to understand Hitler's racist logic – which Hitler admittedly disguised by justifying his actions to his allies in often implausible strategic terms.[14]

The Italian leadership almost invariably diagnosed Hitler's refusal to compromise with Stalin in winter–spring 1942–43, which left Italy facing the Western powers' Mediterranean offensive with only limited German help, as a mere case of "mistaken conduct of the war." Only the ambassador in Berlin, the otherwise lightweight Dino Alfieri (or his astute staff) appears to have understood the reality: "Hitler is in fact still dominated and pervaded . . . by the fanatical will – to use the adjective that recent

---

13. Ambrosio to Mussolini, 18 June 1943, printed in De Felice, *Mussolini l'alleato* (Turin, 1990), vol. 1/2, p. 1134; see also the pitiless analysis of Elena Aga Rossi, *A Nation Collapses: The Italian Surrender of September 1943* (Cambridge, 2000), pp. 42–44.

14. Ciano, 14 May 1941.

[German] propaganda has brought into fashion – to continue the war against Russia . . .". Cavallero's successor Ambrosio and others instead wasted much effort pressing Mussolini to steer Hitler toward a "realistic vision" of the situation.[15] That an ideological ferocity wholly beyond anything seen in Fascism determined Hitler's course in Russia as in the "Jewish Question," and that Italy must therefore seek its own salvation sooner rather than later, was an insight to which Italy's rulers came only slowly and hesitantly.

Dissipation of effort was an even more powerful element of Italian strategy than myopia: it finished the job, begun by the army's force structure, of so diluting the armed forces' striking power that they became incapable of securing even local victories. Mussolini himself was the chief villain. His inability to postpone gratification in 1940 and his obsession with demonstrating Italy's usefulness as an ally thereafter generated an ever-longer list of actual and potential commitments that precluded concentration on the strategic center of gravity of Italy's Mediterranean war, which could only be the swift conquest of Egypt and of the oil of the Persian Gulf beyond.

The Duce's omnidirectional aggressiveness found its first expression within days of entering the war, when he badgered his generals into attacking France across the Alps. Fortunately for Italy the Germans had rendered the French incapable of counterattack, although outlying French fortifications held the Italian columns with much slaughter while the French navy bombarded Genoa and surroundings at will.[16]

These demonstrations that the armed forces were incapable of over-coming an already defeated enemy should have counseled thenceforth

---

15. DDI 9/10/141, p. 175 (21 March 1943); Ambrosio memoranda for Mussolini, 17 February and 24 March 1943, in *Africa*, 4:428, 695.

16. See USE, *La battaglia delle Alpi Occidentali* (Rome, 1981), especially pp. 201–07, and USMM, *Le azioni navali in Mediterraneo dal 10 giugno 1940 al 31 marzo 1941* (Rome, 1970), pp. 85–91.

the strictest concentration on a single objective. Italy's definitive war aims program of 26 June 1940 nevertheless outlined claims fully in line with Mussolini's longstanding ideological goals: from Nice, Corsica, Tunis, Malta, and southern Switzerland to Cyprus, Egypt, Iraq, Djibouti, the Gulf coast of Arabia, and Aden. And Mussolini was determined to secure these objectives before Hitler could arrive at a bilateral deal with Britain that left Italy empty-handed.[17] Within days of France's exit from the war on 22–24 June, Mussolini therefore launched or approved four new enterprises in addition to the attack on Egypt, which he and Badoglio had initially scheduled for 15 July.

Mussolini granted his East African theater commander, Amedeo of Savoia-Aosta, authorization to seize British Somaliland – a dusty and strategically useless corner of Africa that nevertheless proved the only territorial prize that Fascist Italy conquered with its own unaided forces in the entire course of the war. The dictator also pressed ground and air participation in the prospective invasion of Britain on a far from enthusiastic Hitler, and moved the army staff to prepare an attack on southern Switzerland in concomitance with an expected German drive from the north. In fulfillment of the ambitions held since 1927 he also ordered – with the enthusiastic approval of the army staff's de facto chief, Mario Roatta, reputed to be Italy's most astute senior general – preparations for a massive invasion of Yugoslavia that would require up to forty-five divisions, more than half the army. Partly on Ciano's advice, the Duce added in July–August 1940 a fifth potential theater: an attack on neutral Greece from Albania and a landing on Corfù. In the next months the navy also sent almost thirty submarines to Bordeaux to join the German U-boat campaign in the Atlantic.[18]

---

17. DDI 9/5/114, and Mussolini (12 July) in Pirelli, *Taccuini*, p. 272. On war aims and the "specter of peace" in summer 1940, Knox, *Mussolini*, pp. 137–38, 142–45.

18. See Knox, *Mussolini*, Chapter 4 (pp. 165–67, 171–72, 174–76, 193 for Roatta's role); 45 divisions: Badoglio to Mussolini, 8 August 1940, NARA

The vivisection of Switzerland soon fell into abeyance; Hitler preferred to settle that account after final victory. He also flatly vetoed the Yugoslav operation, which could only proceed if Germany provided 5,000 trucks (with drivers) for an action that contravened the Reich's own pressing strategic interest of keeping war as far as possible from Romania's all-important oil. The Germans also limited Italy's contribution to the war against the British Isles to some 200 aircraft operating from Belgium until December 1940 – when pressing German hints, the rigors of the northern winter, and Italy's Mediterranean disasters compelled their withdrawal. Yet by September 1940 the generals and Mussolini had discovered yet another enemy, the defeated but ever-recalcitrant French, and had begun assembling ground forces for three further, and possibly concurrent, major operations: landings in Tunisia and Corsica, and an invasion of southern France.[19]

Two Mussolini decisions in October 1940 partially clarified this confused situation, while further compounding the dissipation of Italy's meager resources. The first was the demobilization of 600,000 of the 1.2 million men under arms within Italy, which Mussolini decided on 1 October, apparently as a consequence of the pressing needs of agriculture. Badoglio accepted the measure with complacency, since it would rule out the Yugoslav operation, which he had guardedly opposed. Roatta nevertheless warned that much of the army would become unserviceable for many months as a result.

But demobilization went forward even after Mussolini demanded on 14–15 October the implementation of his second and even more fatal inspiration, Italy's attack on Greece. Badoglio and the service chiefs appear to have had mild misgivings about this course, but the army staff's

---

T-821/126/000777–79; Santoni, "The Italian Submarine Campaign," in Stephen Howarth and Derek Law, eds., *The Battle of the Atlantic 1939–1945* (London, 1994), pp. 323–26.

19. On all this, see Knox, *Mussolini*, Chapter 4; for Hitler's suggestion that Italy withdraw the air corps from Belgium: ADAP D/11/369, p. 538.

position was particularly flaccid, perhaps reflecting Roatta's enthusiasm for the attack on Yugoslavia; strategic megalomania was not confined to the Duce.[20] From 1 November 1940, two days after his troops crossed the Greek border, Mussolini and Badoglio gave their new Balkan theater priority over North Africa, diverting to Albania the trucks laboriously assembled for shipment to Libya to support the drive into Egypt. And although Albania had revealed itself by mid-November as a bottomless pit that implacably consumed men, munitions, and the few machines Italy could muster, Mussolini insisted, in response to real or imagined French slights, that the armed forces continue preparations to occupy Corsica, Tunisia, and southern France. That requirement and the ever-increasing demands of the Albanian front taxed the *Regio Esercito* beyond its limits. Once Britain took the offensive at Taranto on 11–12 November and in the Egyptian desert on 9 December, the armed forces and regime faced – simultaneously – defeat in the Balkans at the hands of a third-rate power, the loss of North Africa to Britain, total defeat at sea, organizational chaos caused by the army's precipitate remobilization, and the increasing possibility of domestic upheaval.[21]

Yet neither German aid – the Luftwaffe, Rommel, and fresh consignments of raw materials and equipment – nor the German strategic guidance that inaugurated the *guerra subalterna* in January–February 1941 prevented further dissipation of Italy's assets. Mussolini reacted badly to German help. His outward show of comradely gratitude concealed a complex of emotions, of which historians have emphasized fear of German domination to the point, on occasion, of ascribing the Duce's excesses to terror of the Germans rather than ideological ambition. Yet far more important than the fear and resentment constantly rekindled by German slights – Hitler's repeated messages in the middle of the night to

20. For Roatta's views, and the narrow limits of military opposition to the Greek operation, see Knox, *Mussolini*, pp. 193, 209–221.

21. Knox, *Mussolini*, pp. 260–72; De Felice, *Mussolini l'alleato*, vol. 1/1, pp. 728–48, 976–81.

announce faits accomplis, the savage and persistent mistreatment of Italian workers in Germany, the drunken ramblings by Nazi potentates about Italy's approaching future as a German colony – was a burning envy of his former junior partner.

The reversal of Mussolini's fortunes as German power grew after 1937, and especially in and after the great German victories of 1940, was double-edged in its consequences. German power liberated the Duce to be himself, but also filled him with envy and fury. Hitler's successes opened the appalling prospect that to Hitler rather than to Mussolini himself would go the historic honor of consummating the Fascist revolution. The stark contrast – visible by winter 1940–41 to both Italian and foreign opinion – between stunning German victories and catastrophic Italian defeats was a supreme humiliation that unless swiftly reversed would deprive the regime of its legitimacy and its future. The secretary of the Party, Adelchi Serena, put it too mildly by far in reporting Mussolini's pervasive and enduring ill-temper to a fellow minister in late June 1941: "He's jealous of Hitler."[22]

Jealousy and ideology were at the root of the dictator's desire, frequently invoked to his ministers, to prove Italy in the "comparative examination" of war. The "problem of proportionality between what the Germans have done in this war and what we have done and will do" had "inevitable political repercussions" and had to be resolved. Italy could "not be less present [on the eastern front] than Slovakia." "We must pay off our debt to our ally"; the regime's future and Italy's independence demanded it. To his ministers he stressed the urgency of the matter in the language of fear, a language the Duce's ministers understood far better

---

22. Gorla, *L'Italia*, p. 211; Gerhard Schreiber, "La partecipazione italiana nella guerra contro l'Urss: Motivi fatti conseguenze," *Italia contemporanea*, 191 (1993), pp. 250–52, provides a catalog of the Duce's anti-German diatribes in 1941–43, as recorded by Ciano and others; see also the interpretation of De Felice, *Mussolini l'alleato*, vol. 1/1, pp. 387–89.

than ideological imperatives: a victorious Germany would "dictate its law to us as well as to the vanquished" unless Italy demonstrated its worth. And as in summer 1940, although with less reason, Mussolini may have continued to fear a bilateral Anglo-German deal – this time after Soviet defeat – that would sell out Italy's Mediterranean aspirations.[23] To reclaim its lost ideological honor, to assert its position as the first of Hitler's satellites, to prove however belatedly its worth as an ally, and to earn Hitler's continuing support for its Mediterranean ambitions, Fascist Italy incurred great and increasing burdens for which its armed forces were little more prepared than for the "parallel war" in which they had failed in 1940.

The first major new task was policing the Balkans after Germany dismembered Yugoslavia and crushed Greece in April–May 1941. Mussolini's longstanding aim of Balkan hegemony entailed the gleeful absorption of as much territory as Hitler was willing to concede, whatever misgivings army staff and *Comando Supremo* might voice.[24] Italian forces were inevitably unprepared for the partisan insurrection that broke out in earnest after June–July 1941 throughout the former Yugoslav territories, from Italy's occupation zones and annexed lands in Slovenia and Dalmatia to its protectorates in Montenegro and Croatia. Guerrilla uprisings followed in Greece and eventually even in Albania. By early 1942 Italy had committed almost 30 divisions and a quarter of the army's manpower to a counterinsurgency campaign that

---

23. Mussolini to the Council of Ministers: Bottai, 5 July 1941; also Gorla, *L'Italia*, pp. 217–18; similarly, Bottai, 25 September, 14 October 1941, 7 February 1942; Ciano, 22, 24, 30 June, 10 October, 24–25–26 November 1941; Mussolini to Cavallero, 24 July 1941, in Ceva, *La condotta italiana*, p. 169. For Mussolini (also in the Council of Ministers, 5 July 1941) on the prospects of an Anglo-German peace after BARBAROSSA: Gorla, *L'Italia*, p. 219; for possible implications, Schreiber, "La partecipazione italiana," p. 250.

24. Roatta, in Ciano, 29 April 1941.

was beyond even the Germans so long as their war with Soviet Russia lasted.[25]

New obligations in the Balkans were not the only consequence that summer of Mussolini's determination to prove Italian arms in any theater in which his ally was at war. News of Hitler's aim of invading Russia prompted him, in the first weeks of June 1941, to press Italian forces on his ally, as he had the previous year for the attack on Britain. Despite Hitler's friendly advice that the Duce could best help the Axis cause by concentrating on the Mediterranean theater, Mussolini insisted on sending three divisions to Russia in July 1941, and followed up with repeated vain requests that he be permitted to send further troops. He pressed Cavallero to ready 20 divisions for spring 1942 – a figure that gives the measure of his delusions about the capabilities of his military-economic instrument. Even the king's disapproval did not chasten the dictator. Cavallero, who was well aware of the potentially catastrophic consequences of diverting materiel and cadres from North Africa, feebly attempted to reduce the commitment to six divisions. Hitler finally took pity on Mussolini at the end of November 1941, as the advance on Moscow stalled, and accepted for the future drive on the Caucasus the Alpine divisions that Ciano eagerly offered on Mussolini's behalf.[26]

By August–September 1942 Italy thus had 229,000 men deployed in static positions along the Don, guarding the northern flank of the German drive on Stalingrad. Italian 8th Army's stock of almost 18,000 trucks and artillery tractors, 946 artillery pieces, almost 300 47mm anti-tank guns, 52 modern anti-aircraft guns, and 50-odd MC200 and MC202

25. Divisions in the Balkans: Cavallero memorandum for Mussolini, 6 January 1942, in Ceva, *La condotta italiana*, p. 196; strength (1 December 1941): 596,127 officers and men in the Balkans out of 2.48 million total strength (Rochat, "Gli uomini alle armi," Table B.1, p. 284).

26. For the king's efforts, see Puntoni, *Parla Vittorio Emanuele*, p. 65; Ciano and Hitler: ADAP D/13/522, pp. 734–35.

fighters – spread thinly through nine divisions and supporting units – proved wholly inadequate against the Red Army version of machine warfare. But even a fraction of the materiel and skilled manpower deployed in Russia would have massively increased the mobility, fire-power, and tactical skill of the experienced but attenuated Italian divisions and air units that accompanied Rommel in the final Axis drive on Egypt.[27] The equipment sent to Russia was forfeit in any case: it vanished, along with over 80,000 dead and missing officers and men, in the Stalingrad catastrophe. By the time of Italy's final withdrawal from the eastern front in spring 1943, almost 60 percent of Mussolini's expeditionary force were dead, wounded, incapacitated by frostbite, or missing in action.[28]

By mid-November 1942, even before defeat in Russia, Montgomery's victory at El Alamein and the Anglo-American landings in Morocco and Algeria placed Italy before desperate choices. Yet in this final defensive phase of the *guerra subalterna,* Duce and *Comando Supremo* tolerated no violation of the principle of dissipation of effort. They immediately committed seven divisions to the occupation of southern France alongside the Germans. In mid-November Ambrosio and Cavallero debated the withdrawal of three divisions from Russia to help defend Italy, but reached no conclusion.[29] In backing Germany's intervention in Tunisia with their own troops, Mussolini and Cavallero also evaded the fundamental question that Ambrosio had posed – and had characteristically failed to press home – at a chiefs of staff meeting on 17 November 1942:

27. See the masterly account of these events, and of their strategic and military-economic implications, in Ceva, *La condotta italiana,* Chapter 5, "La dispersione delle forze," as well as his "La campagna di Russia nel quadro strategico della guerra fascista," *Il politico,* 1979/3; also Schreiber, "La partecipazione italiana."
28. Figures: Schreiber, "La partecipazione italiana," p. 269.
29. See Ceva, "4a armata,"; VCSMG 1939–43, 3:893 and Cavallero, *Diario 1940–1943,* p. 576 (17 November 1942); Ambrosio sought at this point to withdraw only the three divisions of the expeditionary corps sent in 1941, not the entire

could the Axis successfully fight for long in Tunisia, on the far side of a sea, however narrow, that Anglo-American air and naval power would soon dominate totally? The Italian leadership preferred instead to under-estimate the speed with which the maritime powers could build up their forces, toyed with chimerical notions of a decisive offensive westward toward Morocco, and in the end set its sights on "delaying as long as possible the loss of Africa."[30]

Even before Ciano and Cavallero, as Mussolini's emissaries, met with Hitler at his eastern headquarters in mid-December 1942, the decision to fight to the end in Tunisia had been set in stone, and largely by default. Cavallero waffled repeatedly over the extent to which, and where, Rommel should fight during his long retreat from El Alamein. Of the key figures, only Rommel and – more mutedly – Ambrosio recognized that what remained of Libya was indefensible because it could not be supplied, and that fighting on in Tunisia made sense only to hold a bridgehead through which to evacuate the shattered remnants of the Axis army. But Hitler, with the encouragement of his navy and of the *Wehrmacht* High Command, was no more willing to retreat from Africa than from Stalingrad. He trumped Rommel's plea for an "African Dunkirk" with his own peremptory demand for a "Mediterranean Verdun."[31] The operational and tactical clumsiness of the Anglo-American drive on Tunis did the rest; in an involuntary act of strategic genius,

Italian army in Russia, as suggested in Schreiber, "La partecipazione italiana," p. 265.

30. VCSMG 1939–43, 3:885, 3:890–93; see also Mussolini's bizarre and belated suggestion that the Axis strike at the Western powers through Spain (ADAP E/5/252, p. 483 [26 March 1943] and Ceva, "Momenti della crisi del Comando Supremo," in Rainero, ed., *1943*, pp. 101–33).

31. Rommel, Hitler: *Africa*, 4:9, 44, 186–87, 442–43; Walter Warlimont, *Inside Hitler's Headquarters* (New York, 1964), pp. 307–12; Basil H. Liddell Hart, ed., *The Rommel Papers* (New York, 1953), pp. 365–66; *Kriegstagebuch des Oberkommandos der Wehrmacht (Wehrmachtführungsstab)* (Munich, 2nd. ed.,

the Anglo-American leadership lured fresh German and Italian forces onto a killing ground dominated by Western airpower, beyond a sea the Axis could not command. Timely withdrawal and the staking of Italy's remaining forces on pushing the Americans and British off the Sicilian beaches would have mightily improved Axis chances of disrupting the Western powers' strategy by delaying the invasion of France in 1944. Conversely, the surrender in early May 1943 of almost a quarter of a million irreplaceable veterans and the destruction of much of their air and naval support determined the fate of Sicily and of the Italian war effort.

After myopia and dissipation of effort, strategic passivity: the inertia and fatalism of Mussolini's chief advisers sounded throughout a powerful counterpoint to the dictator's frenetic activism. At no time either before or during the war of 1940–43 did the service staffs or chief of general staff produce an agreed and coherent overall strategic concept, a war plan designed to translate into reality either the dictator's immoderate goals or some more modest subset thereof. The army, perhaps enlightened by Mussolini's geopolitical musings about Mediterranean domination, identified Egypt as Britain's most vital position and as Italy's key to hegemony as early as 1935. Thereafter both its chief of staff after autumn 1936, Pariani, and the theater commander in Libya, the Fascist leader and air marshal Italo Balbo, entertained notions of a drive on Suez. But neither created forces capable of fighting their way across the 500-odd kilometers of desert between the Libyan frontier and Alexandria. And despite Pariani's delightful suggestion to Mussolini that Italy must wage a *guerra brigantesca*, a brigands' raid upon the fat and unwarlike democracies, the Italian leadership failed to prepare the forces needed to carry out the general's grandiose but not entirely fanciful vision of a coordinated Axis

1982), 1942, vol. 2, pp. 1040–41, 1943, vol. 1, pp. 130–31, 1943, vol. 2, p. 1603; Michael Salewski, *Die deutsche Seekriegsleitung 1935–1945*, vol. 2 (Munich, 1975), p. 251. Ambrosio: see his critical remarks in VCSMG 1939–43, 3:885, 890, but also his agreement to fighting on, 3:886, 892.

war: "attack on Egypt, attack on the [British and French] fleets, [German] invasion of France."[32]

Badoglio was the unchallengeable master of strategic passivity. That posture accorded with his phlegmatic temperament – but the marshal almost certainly also intended to prepare thereby the means to disassociate himself from defeat.[33] In December 1937 he made a show of considering Pariani's notion that Italy's major effort in any war with the Western powers must be the conquest of Egypt. But as war approached the marshal repeatedly and decisively vetoed all offensive planning: "to study operations that do not correspond to reality means to dull the brain and waste time." Italy must first "close the house doors" in Libya with fortifications as outmoded in concept as they were tedious and expensive to build; a fraction of the resources squandered on the fortified belt around Tripoli might have relieved in part the port bottlenecks at Tripoli, Benghazi, Tobruk, and Sollum that so constrained the Axis forces in 1940–42.[34]

Balbo, who fought hard to keep the Egyptian offensive plan alive throughout autumn and winter 1939–40, finally surrendered to the defensive because his forces lacked the medium tanks needed to take on the British, and because it was amply clear that the army staff had no intention of providing them.[35] In spring 1940, Badoglio helped to scotch any prospect of coordination with the Germans by damning

32. Pariani, quoted by Mussolini, in Bottai, 31 October 1936; in Ciano, 14 February 1938.

33. See the remarks of Ceva, in *Africa settentrionale 1940–1943* (Rome, 1982), pp. 166–67, and *La condotta italiana*, pp. 121–22 on the "resigned but farsighted passivity" of the high command.

34. Badoglio quotations: VCSMG 1925–37, pp. 421–23, VCSMG 1939–43 1:19; also Badoglio to Graziani, 15 November 1939, ACS, Carte Graziani, bundle 41.

35. Dorello Ferrari, "Il piano segreto di Balbo," *Studi storico-militari 1984* (Rome, 1985), pp. 80–86; ACS, Carte Graziani, bundle 41 for the correspondence on which Ferrari's unfootnoted work rests.

joint operations as unpatriotic; the marshal was ever skillful in playing upon the dictator's fear of appearing weak.[36] The three services, although apparently without mutual consultation, likewise failed to prepare the surprise attacks on the enemy fleets and bases – on the model of Japan's opening assault on Port Arthur in 1904 – that might have opened the road to Suez and to Mediterranean domination. Such blows required instruments – *maiali* and landing craft for the navy, torpedo-bombers, dive-bombers, paratroops, and amphibious forces for air force and army – that had no place in their respective concepts of war and for the coordinated use of which no joint intelligence or planning mechanisms existed. The naval leadership was in any case highly averse to risking its capital ships for any purpose whatsoever. In April 1940 Cavagnari had prophesied to Mussolini – for the record – that Italy risked arriving at the peace table "not only without territorial bargaining counters, but also without a fleet and possibly without an air force." His subsequent conduct, in the words of the German naval liaison chief, showed a single-minded determination to "strive for the greatest possible security."[37] The naval leadership's ultimate unspoken purpose was to preserve the fleet as an end in itself by disguising it as a diplomatic bargaining counter.

The armed forces thus entered the war under directives dictated by Badoglio's insistence on the defensive, despite a Mussolini demand in March–April 1940 for an aero-naval offensive "all along the line." Passivity endured even after the marshal's minimum condition for Italian intervention – "that a *puissant* German action . . . should have so genuinely prostrated the enemy forces that every audacity would be justified" – had been met. The decision to declare war on the Western

---

36. The intimidatory intent of Badoglio to Mussolini, 4 April 1940 (Biagini and Ferdinando Frattolillo, eds., *Diario Storico del Comando Supremo* [Rome, 1986–], 1/2:174–75) is unmistakable.

37. Cavagnari to Mussolini, 14 April 1940, printed in USMM, *L'organizzazione*, vol. 1, pp. 351–52; Weichold to German navy high command, 1 September 1940, German Naval Records (NARA T-1022), file PG 45951.

powers was a tacit trade-off: Badoglio and the service chiefs acquiesced to war in return for the dictator's toleration of their total inaction.[38]

German victories then gave the Duce the opening he needed to implement his inchoate intention of somehow forcing generals and admirals to fight. As Pariani had pointed out dryly the preceding year, Italy could not expect to realize its wide-ranging objectives "from a defensive posture."[39] Yet even the stunningly favorable situation created by French collapse and Britain's ejection from the Continent did not inspire Badoglio to audacity. In his first chiefs of staff meeting of the war, on 25 June, he gave perfunctory instructions for air attacks on Gibraltar and Malta, and tacit absolution to the navy's refusal, recorded in a staff study dated 18 June, to prepare a landing on Malta despite the fact that the island's defenses at that point consisted of five understrength British battalions, the local regiment, and three biplane fighters. The chiefs of staff, perhaps out of deference to the navy's well-known reluctance, also passed over in silence the prospects of a fleet action now that French collapse had evened the odds between Royal Navy and *Regia Marina*. And at this point Badoglio saw the attack on Egypt not as a war-winning blow but as a mere large-scale raid ("*una puntata decisa*") designed "to give the Duce that [necessary] element of substantiation for our claims toward Egypt." At no time during the meeting did Badoglio or anyone else give any sign of seeing the need for an overall strategic concept: all were waiting passively for the Germans to lay Britain low.[40]

The closest Italy came to a coherent war plan during its unique period of strategic opportunity in summer 1940 was a Badoglio inspiration in mid-August, never implemented, for a drive northward from Italian East

38. Knox, *Mussolini*, especially pp. 121–23; Badoglio's conditions for war: Badoglio to Mussolini, 5298, 11 April 1940 and 5306, 13 April 1940, Biagini and Frattolillo, eds., *Diario storico del Comando Supremo*, vol. 1/2, pp. 190–93.

39. VCSMG 1939–43 1:6.

40. VCSMG 1939–43, 1:64; navy staff memorandum, 18 June 1940, USMM, *L'organizzazione*, vol. 1, pp. 356–60.

Africa in concurrence with Graziani's thrust into Egypt. But even that effort lacked coordination with the navy, which fiercely resisted suggestions that it assist the drive on Suez by sweeping the British from the seas, even though its basic operational directive of 29 May 1940 enjoined an offensive stance in the central Mediterranean. After retiring in confusion from a slower British force off Sicily on 9 July, the Italian battle fleet conducted a search-and-evade sortie on 31 August. By mid-September the naval leadership had converted Badoglio to its cause: "to conceive of a naval battle as an end in itself is absurd," the marshal conceded in a directive approving the navy's stance. *Supermarina* replied with the suggestion that its primary mission should be to keep the army in North Africa supplied – a task to which it largely held henceforth while lamenting the ostensibly "scarce and limited strategic objectives" available to its main force, and insisting that convoy duties must take absolute precedence over offensive operations against the British fleet.[41]

The absence of a war plan of any kind, much less one that coordinated Italy's entire effort in support of the conquest of Egypt, made it easier for Mussolini to open new theaters in the name of doing *something*. It was no accident that the decision to attack Greece, although triggered by Mussolini's fury at Germany's occupation of Romania in October 1940 without consultation with Italy, immediately followed the navy's renunciation of the offensive and Graziani's confession that a further advance in Africa would be possible only after long delay.[42]

In the *guerra subalterna* that followed Italy's disasters, the Italian high command's role was even less active than in the "parallel war." Like

---

41. Navy staff memorandum, Di.N.A. n.0, 29 May 1940, USMM, *L'organizzazione*, vol. 1, pp. 353–54; Badoglio to Cavagnari, 16 and 28 September 1940; navy staff memorandum, 22 September 1940, all in *Direttive Superaereo*, 1/1:249–57; navy staff memorandum n. 31, 10 February 1941, in *Africa* 1:686; see also the scathing analysis of navy passivity in 1940–42 in Mattesini, *La battaglia aeronavale di mezzo agosto* (Rome, 1986), pp. 15–18, 20–23.

42. Knox, *Mussolini*, pp. 205–06, 207–08.

the *Wehrmacht* high command and the German army staff, which inevitably regarded the Mediterranean as a secondary theater even before BARBAROSSA, the *Comando Supremo* and the Italian command in North Africa stood by aghast as Rommel repeatedly hijacked Axis strategy. After renewed staff studies of a Malta landing by the three services began belatedly at the *Comando Supremo's* request in spring 1941, the proposed operation took shape from autumn onward as a joint Italo-German enterprise. The navy's almost total failure to get shipping through to North Africa in November 1941 gave the matter urgency, even after Kesselring's forces, fresh from the Russian winter, had descended to Sicily to punish the island fortress. Yet although Cavallero had made Malta his highest priority, Italian preparations so dragged that the Axis was unable to cap with an air and sea landing the Luftwaffe's devastating bombardment of March–April 1942. Readiness was still far from assured by the time of Rommel's conquest of Tobruk in June 1942. Cavallero and Kesselring consequently had no answer to Rommel's furious demands for a drive on Alexandria, or to the decrypted U.S. Army report from Cairo suggesting that the allegedly incompetent British army was on the verge of collapse.[43]

After Rommel's final failure to break the El Alamein position in early September 1942, the *Comando Supremo* watched the approach of disaster as if hypnotized. In late March 1943, Ambrosio, now chief of general staff, belatedly asked Mussolini – as he had asked Cavallero in November 1942 – the right question: "Does it make more sense to play the enemy's game by continuing to throw men and equipment into the Tunisian furnace, or rather to save them for the heavy tasks to come?" But Ambrosio almost immediately, if perhaps unconsciously, destroyed his own case by conceding that unless persuaded otherwise, "[o]ur ally does not feel

---

43. See the balanced account in *Africa*, 3:354–64; partial (and not entirely congruent) texts of Fellers to War Department, 791, 20 June 1942, in ibid., pp. 363–64 and in Appendix 8 to "The Contribution of the Information [sic] Service to the May–June 1942 Offensive," NARA RG 457/1035.

himself directly and immediately threatened by an attack on the Italian peninsula and will care little if it is put to fire and sword: thus once Tunisia is evacuated, he won't send us a thing."[44]

Ambrosio's prediction reflected fears widespread in the high command, but was nevertheless wrongheaded.[45] Hitler's sense of mission and attachment to his own power had long since committed him to maintaining the Duce, and the Führer was acutely aware that the capacious airfields of the Po Valley were a mere hour by Lancaster or B-17 from Munich. But fear of abandonment – and of German revenge if Italy sought to leave the war – nailed the Italian leadership to the spot until the Anglo-American assault on Sicily in July 1943. Hitler brushed aside Mussolini's timid advocacy of a peace with Stalin that would free German forces for the Mediterranean. Even after Sicily was virtually lost, and despite increasing pressure from Ambrosio, behind whom stood the king, Mussolini himself failed to summon the courage to tell Hitler face to face at their conference at Feltre, near Venice, on 19 July that Italy must leave the war.

That failure triggered a last, almost despairing attempt to escape paralysis: the king's belated decision to remove Mussolini on 24–25 July. The regime's overthrow proved easy. Fascism had failed that spring to repress convincingly strikes in Turin and Milan in which the clandestine Communist movement had played a role.[46] The Fascist regime thus no longer fulfilled its original political and social function in the eyes of the monarchy and the Italian establishment. Its inability to use terror inspired contempt, and not only among the Germans. Its endemic corruption had reached new depths under the pressure of

---

44. Ambrosio "Appunto per il Duce," 24 March 1943, in *Africa*, 4:694–97.

45. See for instance Fougier to Ambrosio, 15 April 1943, *Direttive Superaereo*, 2/2:705.

46. See especially De Felice, *Mussolini l'alleato*, vol. 1/2, pp. 921–37, and Tim Mason, "The Turin Strikes of March 1943," in his *Nazism, Fascism, and the Working Class* (Cambridge, 1995), pp. 274–94.

wartime scarcity and the mission of supervising food supplies and rationing that Mussolini had unwisely devolved upon the Party. Above all else,
the regime's long career of defeat from the Albanian mountains in 1940 to
the Sicilian beaches in 1943 had generated a genuine revulsion, shared by
a significant portion of the Fascist elite itself, against the Duce and all his
works. But as one astute foreign ministry official claimed to have predicted to the king's chief adviser in June 1943, the problem was not how to
remove Fascism, surrounded as it was by universal if belated execration.
The problem was this: "The day Mussolini is thrown out, the Germans
will be on top of us."[47]

Ambrosio and Roatta, to whom it fell to face that event, vacillated
helplessly, caught between their inescapable need for German troops
to save southern Italy from the Western powers and their fear of the
vengeance those same troops would exact when Italy changed sides.
They asked for another two German divisions three days before
Mussolini's removal, and were still requesting additional forces on 15
August, after thirteen picked German divisions had already deployed. By
early September the Germans dominated northern and central Italy with
sixteen divisions in the peninsula and islands.[48] Meanwhile Badoglio,
recalled to power as Mussolini's successor after a long clandestine candi-
dacy following his resignation as chief of general staff in December 1940,
sought quaintly to placate Adolf Hitler with his word of honor as an

---

47. DDI 9/10/406: quotation, p. 530. This very detailed and pithy account by
    Leonardo Vitetti – from his own papers – of a conversation on 9 June 1943
    with Prince Acquarone, minister of the king's household, shows almost
    superhuman insight on Vitetti's part. Perhaps he wrote it down in August–
    September.

48. Ambrosio remarks to chiefs of staff, 22 and 26 July 1943, NARA T-821/125/
    000369–70, 000364, 000357, 000353–54 (oddly, these meetings do not appear in
    VCSMG 1939–43, vol. 4); Roatta to the Germans, 15 August, in Aga Rossi,
    A Nation Collapses, pp. 61–62; German forces: 12 August, DDI 9/10/681, p. 855;

officer while secretly approaching the British and Americans.[49] The marshal's overriding strategic objective was self-preservation and perhaps even the preservation of the monarchy, to be achieved by manipulating the Western powers while evading combat with the Germans.

Until the Sicily landings the Italian leaders had radically underestimated British and American power. Now they wildly overestimated both the Allies' strategic interest in the Mediterranean and their operational reach, which was circumscribed by the range of the British and American fighters newly based on Sicily. Although any "officer with a pair of dividers could figure out that the Gulf of Salerno was the northernmost practicable landing place," as an American admiral remarked before the fact, Badoglio and Ambrosio secretly arranged Italy's armistice with General Dwight D. Eisenhower on 31 August 1943 in the hope that the Western powers would land at the mouth of the Tiber with fifteen divisions and save both government and capital without the need for Italian action.[50] To prevent "an immediate German reaction provoked by indiscretions," Badoglio expressly forbade forewarning the huge Italian force in the Balkans, and reportedly told Ambrosio he was willing to sacrifice half a million men to preserve secrecy. Ambrosio's directives to the armed forces were in consequence deliberately fragmentary, purely defensive, and mentioned the approaching armistice only

8 September: Kesselring, *Memoirs*, p. 182. For the view from the German side, *Kriegstagebuch des Oberkommandos der Wehrmacht*, 1943, vol. 2, pp. 814–15, 820, 825, 847, 850, 855, 865, 868, 871, 881–82, 1447–48.

49. ADAP E/6/204; 217, p. 373; 275; DDI 9/10, Appendix, documents 1, 2, 3. On 31 July an Italian crown council took in Badoglio's presence the decision "to enter immediately into contact with the Allies for the purpose of concluding an armistice" (in the words of the new foreign minister, Raffaele Guariglia: *Ricordi* [Naples, 1949], pp. 585–86).

50. Quotation: Samuel Eliot Morison, *Sicily–Salerno–Anzio: January 1943–June 1944* (Boston, 1954), p. 249.

belatedly and in bizarre Aesopian language.[51] When the Americans
stressed that action was imminent, Badoglio confessed sheepishly that
he was unready to fight the Germans around Rome or anywhere else,
thus forcing the cancellation of an audacious improvised operation by the
82nd Airborne Division aimed at securing the city with Italian help.[52]
Badoglio had eliminated all danger of "a romantic and bloody adventure"
in which the Italian armed forces fought the Germans in an organized
fashion.[53]

Paralysis turned to panic the following day, 8 September, when
Eisenhower duly announced the armistice and U.S. 5th Army landed at
Salerno. Badoglio, Ambrosio, and the king escaped Hitler's vengeance by
instantaneous disorderly flight to the Anglo-American camp. As a means
of ensuring the Italian leaders' fundamental objective – the safety of their
own persons and the "continuity of the state" – this measure was a short-
term success. In the longer term it helped destroy the monarchy;
Badoglio saved himself and the king by deliberately leaving the armed
forces leaderless and without clear orders in the face of swift and savage
German counteraction.[54] Only ships and aircraft escaped; a chastened

---

51. See the pointed and carefully documented analysis of Aga Rossi, *A Nation
Collapses*, pp. 60–63, and the *Comando Supremo* orders in her *L'inganno reciproco:
l'armistizio tra l'Italia e gli angloamericani del settembre 1943* (Rome, 1993),
pp. 337–49.

52. For Badoglio's decision to cancel the operation, see Maxwell Taylor to AC of
S, G-3, Allied Forces Headquarters, 9 September 1943, and log of Taylor
mission, September 1943, by Col. W. T. Gardiner, USAAF, Maxwell D. Taylor
Papers, National Defense University Library, Washington DC (my thanks to
Brian R. Sullivan for copies of these documents); also Albert N. Garland and
Howard McGaw Smyth, *Sicily and the Surrender of Italy* (Washington, DC,
1965), pp. 485–505, and Aga Rossi, *L'inganno reciproco*, pp. 395–413.

53. For the phrase, used pejoratively and naively by Vitetti to Acquarone, see DDI
9/10/406, p. 536.

54. On the intentions of Badoglio and Ambrosio, see the considered judgment of
Aga Rossi, *A Nation Collapses*, pp. 62–63, 82–89, 91–103.

Mussolini became part of the *Wehrmacht's* immense booty.[55] Strategic paralysis had produced the worst conceivable outcome: the dissolution of the Italian armed forces, the demoralization of Italian society, and the division and devastation of the country at both German and Anglo-American hands.[56]

The fourth major distinguishing characteristic of Italian strategy in 1940–43 was that its logistical base was wholly inadequate to the demands of war. Overseas campaigning in Ethiopia and Spain did not move Badoglio or the navy staff or Pariani – despite the general's vision of a drive on Suez – to acquire an analytical understanding of the projection of Italian power overseas, or to create the necessary organizational framework; force structure megalomania evidently imposed blinkers in this area as well. And despite the years of tension with Britain from summer 1935 onward, it was not until 1938 that army and navy began to consider, although inevitably without coordination with one another, the specific case of North Africa.[57]

The logistical fiasco that attended Mussolini's almost bloodless seizure of Albania in April 1939 showed that existing arrangements failed even in the absence of an enemy. Yet neither service developed a sense of urgency. The navy based its planning on the assumption that the British and French navies would largely interdict Italian traffic with Libya from the outset of war. The navy therefore could not be held responsible for

55. A vast polemical literature exists; see especially Carlo Pinzani, "L'8 settembre 1943: elementi ed ipotesi per un giudizio storico," *Studi Storici*, 13:2 (1972), pp. 282-337, and Aga Rossi, *A Nation Collapses* and *L'inganno reciproco*.

56. For a pioneering (and much-contested) attempt to assess the long-term impact of September 1943 on Italian national consciousness, see Ernesto Galli della Loggia, *La morte della patria* (Rome, 1996).

57. This and succeeding paragraphs owe much to the pioneering explorations of Ferruccio Botti, *La logistica dell'esercito italiano, 1831–1981*, vols. 3 and 4 (Rome, 1994–95); "La logistica dei poveri"; "Problemi logistici del secondo anno di guerra – aspetti interforze," in Rainero and Biagini, eds., *1941*, pp. 291–327; and "Strategia e logistica."

providing continuous overseas supply; it was up to the army to stock the colony in advance with the supplies and equipment required for any land campaigns it might choose to undertake. The army, in its disorganization and penury of 1939–40, was unable to meet even Libya's defensive requirements. The navy had also failed to arrange the construction of the specialized ships needed for the overseas transport of tactically loaded units, vehicles, and even fuel; the landing craft that the Western powers found so useful for bypassing port bottlenecks as well as for amphibious operations; and the escort vessels needed to defend convoys against submarine and air attack. *Supermarina* also presided over the loss at the very outset of 36 percent of Italy's merchant shipping, stranded outside the Mediterranean when Italy declared war. A prewar staff study had assumed, with apparent resignation, a loss of 50 percent of Italian tonnage through enemy action or internment in neutral ports. Cavagnari had received notice of Mussolini's warlike intentions, if not the date of Italy's intervention, at the beginning of April. But no one attempted to notify the ships until 7 June.[58] As for the air force, it made almost no preparation to provide the other services with air transport, an ostensibly subordinate mission that it disdained.

Italy thus joined Hitler's war without the logistical doctrine, organization, or preparations required to fight effectively either a short Mediterranean war or a long one. Each service maintained its own distinct logistical system, and no standardized or even commensurate units of measure for munitions, fuel, food, equipment, and clothing existed. Pricolo had plaintively noted this deficiency at a chief of staffs meeting in November 1939, and Badoglio had sagely concurred; but no one apparently followed up.[59] The absence of an interservice doctrine and organizational framework meant that by 1941 supplies to North Africa,

---

58. For what little is known about this extraordinary oversight, see Ferrante, "La marina mercantile italiana," pp. 133–34. On the navy's prewar shipping loss projections, see the cryptic remark in USMM, *L'organizzazione*, vol. 1, p. 253.
59. VCSMG 1939–43 1:23.

to take only the most striking example, flowed through five separate and often conflicting channels: army, navy, air force, Ministry for Italian Africa, and *Wehrmacht*. At the center, a multiplicity of organizations fought over one aspect or another of overseas supply. The army staff's transport office (*Direzione Superiore Trasporti*) might have provided centralized direction for overseas shipments, but resistance from the Ministry of Communications, the other services, and other parts of the army bureaucracy rendered it ineffectual.

At the periphery, at the ports in Italy, Albania, and North Africa, even greater confusion reigned. At each port, army and navy respectively maintained separate "embarkation and disembarkation offices" and "shipping and embarkation commissions"; delicate interservice negotiations attended the loading of each ship. The resulting confusion as well as the absence of ships capable of carrying army units complete with their equipment meant that during the panicked Albanian build-up of November 1940–January 1941, units often arrived and proceeded into combat against the Greeks without vehicles, artillery, or even crew-served weapons. Attempts to streamline overseas logistics during the first year of war by placing both Albanian and Libyan ports under centralized authorities, and subsequent extensive personal intervention by Cavallero, did not make the system notably more effective. Authority over shipping at Naples, the key port for North Africa, remained divided between multiple and conflicting authorities until December 1942 – by which time reform was superfluous. The ports also lacked the skilled and disciplined labor force that the British had secured by organizing stevedore battalions at the outset of the war.

Logistical pathologies so constrained Italian military performance that after mid-1941 Cavallero found himself compelled to supervise personally the movement of supplies to North Africa. The chief of general staff devoted the immense majority of the 300 service chiefs' meetings held in 1942 to detailed discussion of the movements of individual ships.[60] Italy

---

60. VCSGM 1939–43, 3:vi–xxi.

had a dictator to decide its strategy (a subject rarely central to the chiefs' deliberations), and the North African convoy war indeed lurched from sinking to sinking, but Italy's supreme military and naval authorities could surely have employed their time more profitably. That they did not was evidence of the extent to which the armed forces were not merely incapable of creating an effective logistical system, but also unwilling or unable to cooperate at all except through ad hoc negotiations at the highest level.

Given these circumstances, the lament of many military and naval memoirists that failure to seize Malta on the one hand and Mussolini's sheepish renunciation in 1940 of the purported chance to occupy the ports of Tunis and Bizerte at the French armistice on the other doomed the Axis campaign in North Africa is unpersuasive.[61] Malta was vulnerable in 1940, and its early elimination would certainly have eased Axis logistics in winter 1941–42. But once Rommel drove on Egypt in summer 1942, Malta was largely out of the picture: submarines and aircraft based in Egypt and other eastern Mediterranean bases and supported through the Red Sea–Cape of Good Hope route decimated Italian shipping bound for Benghazi and Tobruk. Tunis and Bizerte, like Malta, would have been useful in supplying Tripolitania. But at the time of the 1940 armistice it was far from clear that the French colonial authorities and fleet would surrender tamely: continued French belligerency in North Africa and the Mediterranean provoked by Italian territorial demands was an outcome from which the Duce rightly shrank.[62] In any case, the Tunisian ports were even further west than Malta: the road from Tunis to Alexandria was 2,000-odd arid kilometers. The decisive logistical constraints on Axis strategy were neither Malta nor Tunis, but port capacity, organization, anti-aircraft protection, and air cover in eastern

---

61. See for instance Roatta (who lobbied for seizing Tunis in June 1940), in his *Otto milioni di baionette* (Verona, 1946), p. 104.

62. See the analysis in Knox, *Mussolini*, pp. 127–28, 131–33.

Libya, the absence of effective Italian navy arrangements for across-the-beach landing of vehicles, fuel, and supplies, and the long roads between ports and front that consumed much of the fuel the navy actually delivered.[63]

The consequence of myopia, dissipation of effort, strategic passivity, and logistical incoherence was the loss of Italy's independence – in four stages. Mussolini and the Italian military leadership had confessed Italy's dependence in August 1939 by making their intervention in Hitler's war contingent on Berlin providing 18,153,000 tons of coal and strategic raw materials, 150 heavy anti-aircraft batteries, and numerous other items.[64] Hitler's ultimate answer had come the following spring: the promise of 12 million tons of coal per year by rail and the conquest of western Europe. Italian dependence in 1940 thus remained latent and concealed until the armed forces failed to establish their domination of the Mediterranean and Middle East in July–September 1940, Britain's hour of greatest peril.

By August 1940 General Franz Halder, the German army's chief of staff and organizer of Hitler's victories, saw clearly that German forces alone could "help the Italians erect their Mediterranean empire."[65] In the four months that followed, the Italian armed forces proved that without immediate massive German help, Italy's war effort and the Fascist regime were as incapable of defense as they had been of offense. The army barely avoided total defeat in Albania, but was unable to drive Greece from the war; Cavallero and Mussolini launched a renewed offensive in March

---

63. For the relationship between Luftwaffe sorties against Malta and Axis supply flow to North Africa, see DRZW 6:752 (a vivid graph); on the impact of motor transport within Africa, see Martin van Creveld, *Supplying War: Logistics from Wallenstein to Patton* (Cambridge, 1977), Chapter 6, "Sirte to Alamein," and DRZW 6:756–57; useful reflections on Malta's role in Giorgerini, *Matapan*, pp. 504–13.

64. DDI 8/13/293; see Knox, *Mussolini*, p. 43 and Ciano, 26 August 1939.

65. Halder, *Kriegstagebuch*, vol. 2, p. 46.

1941 which collapsed miserably amid heavy Italian casualties. Between December 1940 and February 1941, the army lost up to 150,000 of the 244,500 men it had deployed to North Africa as well as well over half their vehicles.[66] The navy temporarily lost half of its battleship force at Taranto, failed (along with the air force) to catch the British battleships that shelled the vital Genoa area in February 1941, and suffered a stinging setback off Matapan at the end of March. Italy in essence had no air defense except that brought south by the Luftwaffe after December 1940, and at no time an effective air defense; the first modest RAF bombardments of the northern cities produced disquiet, and the final crescendo of air bombardment from autumn 1942 onward generated increasing panic.[67] Neither Italian actions nor even Rommel's arrival with the handful of German reconnaissance and anti-tank units that later grew into the *Afrika Korps* averted the final and definitive loss of Libya in spring 1941. Only Churchill's second greatest strategic error after his underestimation of the Japanese, the decision in February 1941 to divert ground and air forces to aid Greece rather than pressing on in Libya, saved Italy's 129,000 largely noncombat troops and 209 tankettes huddled near Tripoli.[68] With Germany – without Italian knowledge – turning eastward, Italy and the Fascist regime lay at Britain's mercy.

66. Figures: *Africa*, 1:167 note 149, 168 note 161 (manpower and trucks as of September–October 1940); losses, according to fragmentary Italian data: 1:385, 1:443 note 5.

67. USMM, *Azioni navali*, 1, Chapter 12; Pricolo reprimand to subordinate units, 19 February 1941, *Direttive Superaereo*, 1/2:526–27; Fougier to Ambrosio, 15 April 1943 (confessing that "the country is in practice without effective [air] defense"), ibid., 2/2:705; Simona Colarizi, *L'opinione degli italiani sotto il regime, 1929–1943* (Bari, 1991), pp. 397–98.

68. Italian strength and prospects: *Africa*, 1:396–98, 2:18, 73 note 22 (the vast majority of the 129,000 were garrison and service troops; available combat units only contained 25,000 men); on the British decision, see especially the severe judgment of Schmider, "The Mediterranean in 1940–1941," pp. 24–27.

Italy's open dependence on Berlin in the ensuing *guerra subalterna* expressed itself most graphically in the astonishing wish list that the army staff presented to the Germans at the end of 1940. To continue the war, the army urgently required equipment for thirty divisional and twenty corps artillery battalions with vehicles and copious munitions, almost 8,000 trucks, 750 ambulances and specialized vehicles, 1,600 light anti-aircraft guns, 900 88 mm anti-aircraft guns (with tractors, search-lights, rangefinders, sights, and munitions), 800 medium tanks, 300 armored cars, 675 anti-tank guns, 9,000 mules, 300 medium- and long-range radio sets, 20,000 rolls of concertina wire, half a million engineer stakes, 10 million sandbags, and numerous lesser desiderata.[69] The Italian high command also pleaded with increasing urgency for the deployment to Libya of German armored divisions; Badoglio and Mussolini had spurned such forces the previous summer and autumn, but high command and regime now swiftly swallowed their pride.

Given the Italian record to date, Hitler saw little point in diverting to the *Regio Esercito* German equipment needed to mount BARBAROSSA. Rome received some French and Czech booty, small additional consignments of raw materials, and little else except the temporary commitment of German forces. That limited intervention was from the beginning an economy-of-force effort to prevent Italian collapse until Soviet defeat freed the *Wehrmacht* to drive Britain from the Mediterranean and Middle East.[70] Yet Germany's exiguous forces thenceforth carried the weight of the Mediterranean war.

Italy's inability to supply North Africa smoothly without German air support demonstrated the extent of dependence. Only the Romanian oil

---

69. Roatta to Cavallero, Guzzoni, 40900, "Materiali e mezzi da richiedere al Reich," 17 December 1940, NARA T-821/127/000651–54 and Rintelen to Oberkommando der Wehrmacht, g.Kdos Nr. 317/40, 20 December 1940, NARA T-77/590/1771374–76.

70. Führer directive 32, "Vorbereitungen für die Zeit nach Barbarossa," 11 June 1941, ADAP D/12/617.

that the Germans controlled permitted the movement of Italy's convoys and battle fleet. And offensive warfare was largely German: Rommel's armor by land, and by sea the Luftwaffe, U-boats, and German light surface forces that sank 72 percent (by tonnage) of the British warships and 80 percent of the British merchant shipping lost in the Mediterranean between June 1940 and September 1943.[71] The Malta operation, the securing of French permission to use Tunisian ports, and the seizure of Tunisia itself in November 1942 likewise required German forces or German support.

Within this framework, the Italian high command was largely powerless to control the pace of the offensive war against Britain, as Cavallero's inability to mount the Malta operation without German units and assent demonstrated. Yet until the *guerra subalterna* entered its final defensive phase in autumn 1942, Cavallero and Mussolini nevertheless had some degree of negative power over German strategy: they could try to control Rommel through their management of his supply lines, and they succeeded in preserving a separate and nominally supreme Italian command structure both in North Africa and in Rome. Hitler cooperated. He had never been tender toward his allies as a people, and had concluded by 1940 – with special reference to Ciano – that "every second Italian [was] either a traitor or a spy." He gave Mussolini a sharp private "ruler across the knuckles," in the Duce's words, after the attack on Greece had failed. But he also demanded of his subordinates that they cloak German domination with enough tact to spare the Duce's prestige in front of his own

---

71. Figures: Mattesini and Santoni, *La partecipazione tedesca alla guerra aeronavale nel Mediterraneo (1940–1945)* (Rome, 1980), pp. 595ff., Tables A, B; also summarized by Giorgerini, *Matapan*, pp. 498–500, and endorsed by De Felice, *Mussolini l'alleato*, vol. 2, p. 1109 and note; also the record of Luftwaffe X Fliegerkorps (73 percent of all British Mediterranean tonnage sunk in January–May 1941), in Mattesini, *L'attività aerea italo-tedesca nel Mediterraneo: Il contributo del 'X Fliegerkorps' gennaio–maggio 1941* (Rome, 1995), pp. 270–71.

ministers and the Italian public.[72] That concession, fear of British air attacks on the Romanian oil fields or on Germany itself staged from the Mediterranean theater, and the Fascist regime's implicit ultimate threat – to collapse – gave Mussolini and Cavallero enough leverage to preserve Italy's nominal theater command and continuing German assistance even after the crises of winter 1940–41 had passed.

In the final defensive phase of the *guerra subalterna*, the Germans gradually dropped even the pretence of courtesy and consultation, as Italy's dependence became ever more total. Hitler alone took the decision to occupy Tunisia, merely summoning Ciano to hear it on Mussolini's behalf. The rout of the Italian army in Russia, which resulted from the conjunction of its own inadequate force structure with the unrealistic demands the German high command had placed upon it, offered the Germans a welcome scapegoat for their own grievous strategic and operational blunders. Hitler harangued the Duce by letter about the heroism that German units had displayed. Ribbentrop, with characteristic tact, lectured the Italian ambassador in Berlin about Italy's purported responsibility for the loss of German 6th Army at Stalingrad and the imperative need to remedy through "extraordinarily drastic measures . . . executed with lightning speed" the "frightful *déroute* and panic" that had overtaken Italian forces on the Don. The Führer, after all, customarily had officers who abandoned their positions court-martialed and shot.[73]

A long-running Italo-German disagreement over Balkan occupation policy simultaneously came to a head as Anglo-American preponderance in the Mediterranean theater grew. The German leadership hammered away at the Italian economy-of-force policy of supporting Mihailovic's

---

72. Hitler, in Gerhard Engel, *Heeresadjutant bei Hitler* (Stuttgart, 1974), p. 88; ADAP D/11/369 and Ciano, 22 November 1940; Fricke minute, 8–9 January 1941, in Gerhard Wagner, ed., *Lagevorträge des Oberbefehlshabers der Kriegsmarine vor Hitler 1939–1945* (Munich, 1972), pp. 181–82.

73. ADAP E/5/135, pp. 233–34; E/5/148, p. 266; E/5/184, pp. 353–57.

Chetniks against Tito's Communist partisans. Both groups, Hitler insisted, were a mortal threat to Axis communications to Greece in the event of the Anglo-American landing there that British deception operations had led him to expect. The Führer personally stressed his "genuine angelic patience" over the issue, and openly accused the Italian army and high command of having created the partisan and Chetnik problem by past tolerance and perpetuated it by present sabotage.[74] Finally, Hitler and Ribbentrop, invoking the examples of Clemenceau, Stalin, and the Führer's own "brutality" (a word with highly positive connotations in the Nazi lexicon) in the occupied territories, demanded openly that Mussolini show greater ruthlessness in Italian internal politics and in his dealings with his own *Comando Supremo* and officer corps.[75]

Unlike the emollient Cavallero, Ambrosio sought with a certain naiveté to "stand up to the Germans." He and the navy staff and Mussolini largely evaded the March 1943 demand of Hitler, conveyed through the new chief of the German navy, Admiral Karl Dönitz, that the *Regia Marina* be placed under German tutelage, with advisers, trainers, and small German detachments at all levels, in order to ensure the passage of supplies to Tunisia. They also resisted German insistence that the fleet sacrifice its last destroyers on doomed supply runs to Tunis and Bizerte.

But Italy's situation soon made even small displays of independence a luxury. Mussolini and Ambrosio repeatedly demanded German air reinforcements throughout winter and spring 1942–43. In February Ambrosio felt compelled to ask the German high command for yet another huge list: 750 tanks, 7,400 trucks, 750,000 anti-tank mines, 500 aircraft, 326 radar sets, forty sonar sets, eight frigates, twelve motor torpedo boats, and thirty fast minesweepers. Few of these items were

---

74. DDI 9/10/339, pp. 449, 451; for the unfolding of the issue, see above all ADAP E/5/135, pp. 229–32; E/5/158, pp. 294–96; DDI 9/10/61.

75. ADAP E/5/184, p. 357; DDI 9/10/203, p. 263.

available, "given the current enormous requirements of the German army." Ambrosio therefore forwarded in April an even more immense list of requirements: 1,250 tanks, 372 artillery pieces, 1,350 anti-tank guns, 7,400 trucks, naval and aviation fuel, 500 aircraft, aircraft engines, and numerous other items.[76] Further desperate pleas for more Luftwaffe support on the eve of the fall of Tunisia followed. Italian enthusiasm for German troops in Sicily and Italy was more qualified, but by May–June 1943 the *Regio Esercito* possessed a single more or less motorized infantry division and one partially equipped armored division outfitted with the lamentable FIAT-Ansaldo M15/42. Mussolini and Ambrosio therefore accepted first three and then four German armored and motorized divisions for Sicily and the peninsula. On 19 June, after the fall of Pantelleria, they also requested 2,100 artillery pieces, 800-odd tanks, and the astonishing total of 2,000 aircraft.[77]

As the Italian-held sectors of the Axis front in Sicily collapsed, Mussolini ordered the assembly of a final gigantic list for Hitler that reiterated the request for 2,000 combat aircraft, a figure that was almost two-thirds of the Luftwaffe's front-line fighter and bomber strength at a time when the eastern front was in crisis and the Reich under heavy bombardment; between 24 and 30 July Bomber Command erased much of central Hamburg. And even in the absence of constant Anglo-American air attack, southern Italy's airfields, railroads, and ports were incapable of supporting many more aircraft than already deployed. That point Hitler, in an unprecedented diatribe on Italian logistical,

76. Salewski, *Seekriegsleitung*, vol. 2, pp. 258–65; destroyers: VCSMG 1939–43, 4:367, 369, 372, 87; DDI 9/10/220, p. 290; De Felice, *Mussolini l'alleato*, vol. 2, pp. 1114–16; *Comando Supremo* wish list file: NARA T-821/30/000169–71, 000182–91, 000333–45; also 000251–91; VCSMG 1939–43, pp. 63–81 (Kesselring's bemused reaction: p. 66); DDI 9/10/242.

77. VCSMG 1939–43 4:376, 379, 152, 165; DDI 9/10/517, p. 669.

organizational, and leadership failings, drove home to Mussolini in person in the final conference of the Axis alliance at Feltre on 19 July.[78]

By then both parties to the Axis had come to regard Italian requests for aid as largely instrumental. Field Marshal Wilhelm Keitel, chief of the *Wehrmacht* high command, dismissed the demand for 2,000 aircraft as an "alibi." Italian dependence was now so total that the implicit threat to collapse unless miraculously rescued left Hitler's associates unmoved. Hitler himself was already preparing countermeasures, codenamed *Alarich* after the King of the Goths who had imposed a puppet emperor upon Rome before sacking it in 410 AD. The Reich would hold north-central Italy whatever the Italians did.[79] In Rome, Ambrosio compiled a master list of broken German promises for Ciano's successor at the foreign ministry, Giuseppe Bastianini, who presented it to Mussolini with the pressing suggestion that – as in September 1939 – the Duce demand the immediate and full satisfaction of Italy's needs.[80]

But Mussolini's fear of crossing Hitler had now indeed become paramount, given Italy's total dependence. That fear prevented any confrontation at Feltre over ending Italy's war. Subsequently, Badoglio's ever-increasing terror of *both* Hitler and the Western powers precluded any attempt to refuse the divisions the Germans were pouring southward

78. Luftwaffe actual first-line strength, 30 June 1943: 3512; 31 July 1943: 2947: Williamson Murray, *Strategy for Defeat: The Luftwaffe 1933–1945* (Washington, 1983), p. 188. Hitler on Italian organization, infrastructure, and command: DDI 9/10/505, 531, pp. 688–89; ADAP E/6/159, pp. 267–70; some unexploited airfield capacity in *central* Italy apparently did exist (Arena, *Aeronautica*, vol. 4, p. 52).

79. See especially Josef Schröder, *Italiens Kriegsaustritt 1943: Die deutschen Gegenmassnahmen im italienischen Raum: Fall 'Alarich' und 'Achse'* (Göttingen, 1969), Chapter 3.

80. Enno von Rintelen, *Mussolini als Bundesgenosse* (Tübingen, 1951), p. 204; DDI 9/10/517 and note 4; 516 and appended draft message to Hitler.

across the Brenner and along the Riviera. In the end Anglo-American terror won: the coldly delivered threat of Eisenhower's chief of staff that "if necessary, [Rome] would be destroyed" was persuasive in view of the ever-intensifying Anglo-American air campaign that had severely damaged Milan, Turin, La Spezia, Naples, and the capital.[81] The collapse of the armed forces in September 1943 set the definitive seal on Italian dependence: the embarrassed passivity of Badoglio and the king in the face of the American offer of airborne forces for Rome and their refusal to fight the Germans – anywhere – at the armistice ensured lengthy Anglo-American tutelage.

81. DDI 9/10/737, p. 903; Arena, *Aeronautica*, vol. 4, pp. 510–70 offers a summary of the air campaign and its effects, but see also Rastelli, "I bombardamenti aerei."

5

OPERATIONS

"Operation is movement" was the principle on which General Hans von Seeckt refounded the post-1919 German armed forces. They in turn imposed that principle on the forces of Germany's main adversaries. The purpose of movement was the surprise concentration in time and/ or space of strength against enemy weakness within a theater of war, in execution of a campaign plan designed to achieve the strategic objectives of the state. The conduct of operations required a doctrine that fostered the combined employment of the three services and the combination of arms – their coordinated use – within the ground forces. Operations, the Germans discerned, also required a particular command structure and style. Unity of command was highly desirable; creative freedom for subordinates within the framework of their superiors' intent was vital; and commanders capable of exploiting that freedom were indispensable. Operational success also required a force structure that combined foresight, coordination, movement, and striking power: intelligence and reconnaissance, supremely effective communications, mechanization to the greatest extent possible, massive firepower, and lavish logistical support to sustain both fire and movement. A further prerequisite was constant training exercises to test and refine the ability of both leaders and large ground, air, and naval units to frame and execute campaign plans.

Total war, 19 July 1943: while Mussolini meets Hitler at Feltre to seek a way out, USAAF heavy bombers devastate Rome's rail yards and the surrounding housing areas (U.S. National Archives 208-MO-103).

The Italian armed forces in 1940 recognized virtually none of these principles except in a purely verbal sense. The inability to plan campaigns had been the root cause of the great defeats of 1848–49 and 1866. The Great War had taught little; tactical stalemate had so crippled movement that only the Germans and the British in Palestine and in the West after July 1918 learned much about the conduct of operations. The *Regio Esercito* simply threw away the experience gained in its one major operational success, the Vittorio Veneto offensive of October 1918, despite the vital role of Cavallero himself in its planning and execution.

Ethiopia was the unique exception. On the eve of war, Mussolini and Baistrocchi, his army chief of staff, promulgated new *Directives for the Employment of Major Units* premised upon the notion that Italy's resource dependence ruled out wars of attrition: "Ours must be a war of movement."[1] To that end, Mussolini insisted in pressing upon the army leadership unprecedented numbers of men and machines. Ultimately a coherent and moderately effective campaign plan, based on successive bounds forward and lavish logistical support, took shape.[2] Technological superiority, from caterpillar tractors imported from the United States to mustard gas dropped from aircraft to truck columns partly supplied by air, assured the swift victory needed to end the campaign before Italy succumbed to economic and diplomatic pressure. Yet the armed forces, and especially the army, came to regard many of these innovations – and particularly their coordinated use – as somehow inapplicable to other theaters. In 1940–43 neither the service staffs nor the *Comando Supremo* ever *planned* a campaign, in the sense of defining a set of coherent operational steps designed to lead to the achievement of a strategic objective.

The authors of the Directives and of subsequent army doctrine implementing Pariani's vision of a "war of rapid decision" (*guerra di rapido corso*) also paid lip service to the concept known in German doctrine and

1.　Quoted in Montanari, *Alla vigilia*, p. 256.
2.　For the planning, Rochat, *Militari e politici*.

practice as the creation of a *Schwerpunkt,* of "massing where one wishes to create superiority of forces."[3] Yet in 1940–43, the armed forces normally despaired of achieving surprise through concentration at unexpected times or places and made virtually no use of deception, the systematic control of enemy expectations. Dissipation of effort – the uniform distribution of weakness and failure – not concentration was as characteristic of Italian operations as of strategy. In the French Alps and Greece, in pursuit of Mussolini's megalomaniacal objectives, the army advanced on broad fronts and suffered defeat in detail. In the defense, the desire to be strong everywhere usually precluded the accumulation of mobile reserves; Graziani's December 1940 débâcle and the rapid collapse in East Africa the following spring bore witness to this vice. Thereafter, at least in Africa, the Germans selected the *Schwerpunkt.* But they also imposed on the Italian army in Russia an overstretched cordon deployment that Russian armor ripped to shreds after the Stalingrad fighting had consumed the German mobile reserves that might have plugged gaps in the Italian front.

Cooperation and integration between the services were likewise no more present operationally than strategically. No doctrinal framework for integrated ground-air or naval-air campaign planning existed at the outset, nor did one develop. Not until mid-1941 did Italian aeronaval defeat at Matapan and German air-land victory on Crete suggest to the Comando Supremo that cooperation between navy and air force required a doctrinal and procedural framework. The resulting agreement – a sort of treaty between warring states – that Cavallero brokered in summer–autumn 1941 improved coordination but was no substitute for a joint navy-air force command to conduct the Mediterranean war at the

---

3. See the lengthy analysis of the *Directives* in Filippo Stefani, *La storia della dottrina e degli ordinamenti dell'esercito italiano* (Rome, 1984–86), vol. 2/1, pp. 345–65. For the German concept as employed in the Second World War, Oberkommando des Heeres, H.Dv. 300/1, *Truppenführung,* I. Teil (Berlin, 1936), paragraphs 28, 44, 323, 389.

operational level.[4] Army-air force cooperation likewise lacked a doctrinal framework; fear of subordination to the other services prevented the air force from acknowledging and exploiting the full versatility of air power. Until 1941 and in part thereafter, the air staff devoted as little thought as possible to the conduct and coordination of ground support, air transport, supply drops, and paratroop operations.

The services' command structure and style was if anything even less well-adapted to the conduct of operations than Italian doctrine. Even before the Germans arrived, the high command that revolved chaotically around Mussolini was unable to coordinate the divergent operational impulses of the service staffs. Nor did Cavallero's strengthening of *Comando Supremo* prerogatives in 1941 end the tendency of army and navy to plan and conduct operations in isolation from one another while relegating the air force to a supporting role. When the *Comando Supremo* proposed a joint ground, sea, and air attack on Tobruk in June 1941, the navy flatly refused to cooperate.[5] Even after the great convoy crisis of November–December 1941 that brought the descent of Kesselring as *Oberbefehlshaber Süd* under the theoretical authority of Mussolini, no joint air-naval operations center and staff emerged. The chiefs and deputy chiefs of staff, meeting under Cavallero's chairmanship with Kesselring and the German service representatives, did however help shape the plans for the grandly conceived Malta operation of winter–spring 1942.[6] Other such meetings helped direct the relatively successful concentration of Italian air and naval forces against the Malta convoys of June and August 1942 – although in the end the Italian and German navies quarreled with their air forces over providing fighter escort for a cruiser sortie.[7]

---

4. "Norme generali per la cooperazione aeronavale nel Mediterraneo," 1 October 1941, *Direttive Superaereo*, 1/2:748–63; in addition see especially Mattesini, *Mezzo agosto*, pp. 32–33.

5. Mattesini, *Mezzo agosto*, pp. 20–22.

6. VCSMG 1939–43 3:467–70, 476–77, 481–83, 491–92, 498–504, 515–18.

7. See especially *Africa*, 3:545–54; also Santoro, *L'aeronautica*, vol. 2, Chapter 21.

In theory the overseas theater commands in North Africa, the Dodecanese, East Africa, and Russia had authority over more than one service. But in the most vital Italian theater, North Africa, the command structure became ever more complex and less effective as the war continued. The arrival of the Germans meant duplication in all things. Not even Cavallero, for all his reputation within the armed forces for "servility to the foreigner," was willing to create a theater command structure that included all three services and both allies – for Italian dependence meant that Germany would almost certainly provide the commander-in-chief. Indeed for obscure reasons of his own Cavallero, in August 1942, actually deprived Marshal Ettore Bastico, the North African theater commander, of control both of the Italian air force and of logistics. Only in Tunisia, and then largely thanks to the availability of a skillful and forceful high-level Italian commander, General Giovanni Messe, did a structure that partially integrated the two allies briefly arise.[8]

At theater level and below, the army repeatedly demonstrated its structural and intellectual incapacity in the conduct of mobile warfare. Staffs such as that of the Italian expeditionary force in the Ukraine were immobile, weighed down with as many as 150 officers, compared to 66 in a German corps staff.[9] In the judgment of a general staff officer with long experience with the Italian army,

> The command apparatus is . . . pedantic and slow. The absence of sufficient communications equipment renders the links to the subordinate units precarious. The consequence is that the leadership is poorly informed about the friendly situation and has no capacity to redeploy swiftly. The working style of the staff is schematic, static [*unbeweglich*], and in some cases lacking in precision.[10]

8.   *Africa*, 3:871–73; 4:339–43.

9.   Italian corps: Deutsches Verbindungskommando b. ital. Expeditionskorps in Russland to DVst.b.it.AOK 8., 7.8.1942, NARA T-501/326/000149–50; German corps: Martin van Creveld, *Fighting Power* (Westport, CT, 1982), p. 50.

10. Gyldenfeldt report, 8 August 1942, NARA T-501/320/000289–95; for corroboration see Becker, "Erfahrungsbericht als Verb. Offz. bei der Ital. mot.

The army's performance on all fronts and much Italian testimony confirms this picture. The only exceptions were the few Italian mobile units, such as the *Ariete* and *Trieste*, that operated with the *Afrika Korps*. These units also suffered from inadequate communications and vehicles. But by dint of practice alongside the Germans, their staffs acquired the experience and some of the habits of mind needed to cope with rapidly changing situations in a war without fixed fronts, under the leadership of the most volcanically unpredictable of Germany's generals. The commander of the *Ariete* armored division at El Alamein, General Francesco Arena, found Rommel's tendency to give operation orders over the radio rather than in writing a shade eccentric, but nevertheless sought to educate the *Comando Supremo* about "the advantages of a morale and operational nature" of the German practice of commanding from well forward.[11] Not everyone learned. Rommel's titular superior throughout most of the campaign, Bastico, continued to regard German scurrying about the battlefield as undignified, bizarre, and productive of "excesses the consequences of which I believe [Rommel] himself does not understand."[12]

The army's command structures fit poorly with operations. Its command style was flatly incompatible with their effective conduct. Mutual mistrust, clique rivalries, and personal feuds divided the higher officer

Div. 'Pasubio,'" 15 August 1941, NARA T-312/360/7934956–57; Giuseppe Mancinelli, *Dal fronte dell'Africa settentrionale (1942–43)* (Milan, 1970), pp. 15, 175, points out that poor communications helped engender the schematism the Germans lamented; see also (among much evidence in army files) Caracciolo to Corpo d'Armata Celere, 22 February 1942, NARA T-821/86/001024. For more on the German view of the Italians in Russia, see Jürgen Förster, "Il ruolo della 8a armata italiana dal punto di vista tedesco," in *Gli italiani sul fronte russo* (Bari, 1982).

11.   Arena AAR, 13 December 1942, NARA T-821/31/000018–20.

12.   Bastico on Rommel: *Africa*, 3:117; Rommel on Bastico: "a fundamentally decent man with a sober military understanding and considerable moral stamina": Liddell Hart, ed., *The Rommel Papers*, p. 382.

corps. In Rome, General Ubaldo Soddu, undersecretary for war and deputy chief of Badoglio's *Comando Supremo*, feuded with the equally unprincipled and inept Giacomo Carboni of military intelligence (SIM), while intriguing to supplant first Badoglio and then the commander of Italian forces in Albania, Sebastiano Visconti Prasca. Badoglio sought to undermine Graziani and was the sworn enemy of Cavallero from the mid-1920s. Cavallero removed Alfredo Guzzoni, who had attempted to loosen FIAT-Ansaldo's grip on armored vehicle production while minding the *Comando Supremo* during Cavallero's winter 1940–41 absence in Albania. He replaced Gastone Gàmbara of the mobile corps in North Africa for communicating with Ciano behind Cavallero's back, and for "intellectual indiscipline" in a dispute between Rommel and Cavallero. He prevailed on Mussolini to retire Pricolo of the air force for failing to jump at Cavallero's word of command. And he sent Roatta – who had supported Guzzoni on the tank issue – off to command the Italian army in Yugoslavia in early 1942.[13] At a less exalted level, the East African command had unwisely attempted to turn rivalries to operational advantage in the attack on British Somaliland: "We ... placed at the head of the [attacking] echelons officers whom we knew to be hostile to one another, hoping that this would put wings on their feet." The unexpected result was that "both of them concentrated essentially on preventing the other from getting there."[14]

Commanders habitually oversupervised their subordinates in obsessive detail. Graziani found it necessary to emphasize in 1940 to his chief subordinate, Mario Berti, the need for "*absolute precision*" and "a complete and absolutely true outline" of the motor transport requirements of one of Berti's divisions. Graziani's apparent assumption that Berti would otherwise get it wrong – or lie – was an astonishing commentary on the abilities

13. Guzzoni and Roatta: Ceva, "Rapporti fra industria bellica ed esercito," pp. 227–29; Gàmbara: *Africa*, 3:74, 104–05; Cavallero, ironically in view of his own past at Ansaldo, also had Gàmbara investigated for corruption.

14. Trezzani to Badoglio, 25 August 1940, quoted in Knox, *Mussolini*, p. 154.

and ethos of the higher officer corps.[15] The marshal also invaded Berti's field of responsibility by dictating in detail the operational plan (which in any event miscarried chaotically) for the advance into Egypt.[16]

A concomitant of mistrust and oversupervision was the sport of "*palleggiamento delle responsabilità*," or the passing of decisions to subordinates or superiors, while storing up evidence with which to damn them in case of disaster.[17] Graziani bitterly resented his transfer to North Africa in June 1940, and sought to minimize his own responsibility for immobility by sending Rome the minutes of councils of war with his subordinates. Cavallero's frequent envoy to North Africa and the *Comando Supremo*'s sharpest brain, Colonel Giuseppe Cordero di Montezemolo, reported in December 1941 the persistence of a

> command style [*modo di comandare*] ... not suited to this kind of war: commanders show little initiative, [and] ask for orders on matters within their own sphere, as if to place the responsibility [for decision] on their superiors. These in turn contribute to this situation by tying their subordinates down and checking over in advance the orders [the subordinates] issue.

The unloading of responsibility upon ever-lower levels of command likewise accompanied the high command's precipitate flight in September 1943. In no aspect of war were the differences between Italian and German military culture greater, for in Germany a century's traditions and the *Reichswehr*'s meditations on the First World War dictated parsimonious orders, creative freedom, and thirst for responsibility at all levels.[18]

---

15. Graziani to Berti, 26 August 1940, ACS, Carte Graziani, bundle 42 (emphasis in original).

16. See Montanari's critical analysis in *Africa*, 1:103, 119.

17. This is the origin of Graziani's wonderful collection of papers at the ACS.

18. Cavallero, *Diario 1940–1943*, p. 279. On Prusso-German leadership traditions and their consequences in the Second World War, see Knox, *Common Destiny*, Chapter 5. An outstanding example of similar Royal Navy methods is Admiral

The vicious circle of mistrust and oversupervision stemmed in part from the very nature of the *Regio Esercito*'s higher officer corps. The senior service had always had difficulty recruiting from the nation's limited pool of educated talent. During the First World War, Italy's greatest prime minister after Cavour, Giovanni Giolitti, had cruelly remarked that the generals he had dealt with were the products of a society that consigned to army careers the "stupidest sons of the family," the "black sheep and half-wits."[19] Their successors in the second round of the thirty years' war of 1914–45 suffered from an epidemic lack of energy and self-confidence. The commander of one of Italy's two armies in Albania described in his after-action report the abilities of his division and corps commanders with language more bureaucratic than Giolitti's, but no more merciful:

> Some did not show sufficient strength of character, physical robustness, professional competence and initiative together with love of responsibility. Too many have presumably arrived at high rank by virtue of administrative drudgery, and without having well understood the meaning of the leadership of men and the active employment of units on the battlefield.

Corporate self-defense and barracks army routine had also produced a sedentary and overage higher officer corps: colonels of fifty, divisional commanders in their late fifties, and corps and army commanders of sixty or more.[20] Symptomatically, some of the paratroops who trained in 1941–42 for the Malta landing appear to have believed that their divisional

Sir Andrew Cunningham's masterful restraint – despite excellent communications between his operations room in Alexandria and the forces in contact – during Admiral Philip Vian's brilliant convoy defense against *Littorio* in March 1942: see John Winton, *Cunningham* (London, 1998), p. 262.

19. Olindo Malagodi, *Conversazioni della guerra (1914–1919)* (Milan, 1960), vol. 1, pp. 58, 199–200 ("i discoli e i deficienti").

20. Geloso AAR, quoted in Montanari, *Grecia*, vol. 1, p. 907; age: ibid., p. 905.

commander, General Enrico Frattini, had been the only general officer in the entire army willing to accept a command that involved jumping from aircraft in flight.[21]

Catastrophic failure in the Albanian mountains offered an occasion for wholesale housecleaning of the army's operational leadership. But inhibitions against washing dirty linen in front of the Germans and the Italian public, the brevity of the campaign, and the army's sclerotic promotion system combined to block renewal. During the first eleven battles of the Isonzo in 1915–17, Italy's supreme commander, Luigi Cadorna, had "torpedoed" unsuccessful or suspect subordinates with savage abandon. Commanders whom Cadorna had spared had in many cases fallen ill or died in battle. By 1916–17 a crude and often counterproductive process of selection had rejuvenated the army's operational leadership. The ductile Cavallero had served directly under Cadorna, but had not in this respect acquired the master's touch. Cavallero was delighted to eliminate actual or potential rivals but treated indulgently those who failed as combat leaders, clearing for future reemployment as a division or corps commander a former Badoglio aide who had fled to the rear while his division disintegrated in the face of Greek probing attacks.[22]

Other than Badoglio, whom Mussolini designated as scapegoat for the Greek fiasco, the only prominent army victims of battlefield defeat were Graziani, who suffered a nervous breakdown and pleaded piteously for his own relief, and Soddu, who panicked during the Greek counteroffensive of November–December 1940. Mussolini had Graziani investigated with a view to court-martial; nothing came of it. The marshal's immediate successor in North Africa, Italo Gariboldi, showed little energy or aptitude, but nevertheless went on to preside inertly over

21.   Marco Di Giovanni, *I paracadutisti italiani: Volontari, miti e memoria della seconda guerra mondiale* (Gorizia, 1991), p. 132.

22.   Ceva, *Le forze armate*, pp. 357–58; for Cavallero, General Ottavio Bollea, and the collapse of the "Wolves of Tuscany" (January 1941) see Knox, *Mussolini*, pp. 258–59 and notes.

the disintegration of 8th Army in Russia.[23] Roatta and Ambrosio traded places as army chief of staff and commander of 2nd Army in Yugoslavia. Division and corps commanders showed similar stability, except for Sebastiano Visconti Prasca, who commanded the failed invasion of Greece at the outset, and those killed or captured in Africa and Russia. In North Africa, war, fatigue, and disease took their toll, but Cavallero was hard-pressed to ensure – as he felt compelled to direct Ambrosio explicitly as late as September 1942 – that general officer replacements be "up to operational requirements, not [simply] chosen from the seniority list."[24]

The promotion system, in sharp contrast to its German counterpart, added a further layer of resistance to any renewal of the officer corps.[25] In theory the *Regio Esercito* promised swift promotion to "merit in war." In practice, selectivity was low, seniority and connections counted heavily, and Mussolini unlike Hitler never took a grip on officer policy. Cavallero's reaction to Hitler's decrees of autumn–winter 1942 promoting all combat commanders – without regard for age, seniority, education, or social provenance – to the substantive rank appropriate to their battlefield duties was a dismayed "for us this would be a bit excessive [un pò forte]," and a listing of the bureaucratic obstacles facing general officer promotions. What little selectivity the *Regio*

23. The official historians, after heaping deserved praise on his predecessor in Russia, Giovanni Messe, say of Gariboldi only that his command activity "had without doubt very narrow limits" due to German interference (USE, *Le operazioni delle unità italiane al fronte russo* [Rome, 1977], 507–08, 510); Gariboldi's inertia in North Africa: Roatta to Cavallero, 10 July 1941, in *Africa*, 2:279–80.

24. The division, corps, and army commanders of June 1941 show remarkable continuity with those of June 1940 (order of battle lists, Ceva, *Le forze armate*, pp. 492–95, 501–05); Cavallero, *Diario 1940–1943*, pp. 489–90.

25. For the *Wehrmacht*'s 1942–45 promotion system and its consequences, see Knox, *Common Destiny*, Chapter 5, and "1 October 1942: Adolf Hitler, *Wehrmacht* Officer Policy, and Social Revolution."

Esercito's system possessed appears to have operated perversely: Messe complained fiercely and repeatedly from Tunisia that desk warriors in Rome were receiving promotion ahead of his battle-tested division commanders.[26]

Severe and interlocking defects of force structure and performance that derived primarily from the army's already described vision of war further compounded its operational inadequacies. Operational knowledge and foresight about the enemy through intelligence were not a high priority of the army's staffs, although they were also not entirely lacking. The army's *Servizio Informazioni Militare*, rechristened *Servizio Informazioni dell'Esercito* in a 1941 reorganization of intelligence by Cavallero, achieved two major operational coups in the course of the war. In April 1941 it used its expertise with cyphers to disorganize with bogus orders a dangerous Yugoslav advance against the poorly defended rear of the Italian forces in Albania. And throughout the first half of 1942 decrypts of U.S. Army messages from Cairo gave Rommel and Cavallero vital information about British 8th Army's forces and intentions.[27] Signals intelligence units specializing in traffic analysis and low-level British army and RAF cyphers also provided valuable operational and tactical intelligence throughout the North African campaign.

Air reconnaissance was as vital as signals intelligence to the planning and conduct of army operations, but the air reconnaissance units assigned to the army were initially equipped with biplanes proven in Ethiopia but unable to coexist in the same sky with modern fighters. Strategic reconnaissance was almost nonexistent at the outset, a situation the air

---

26. The exemplary remarks of Montanari in *Africa*, 4:574–76 suggest that close study of the army's interwar and wartime promotion policies is overdue; Messe: 4:636, 661.

27. See "The Contribution of 'S.I.M.' to the Second Counteroffensive of [sic] Cyrenaica (21 January–5 February 1942)," and "The Contribution of the Information [sic] Service to the May–June 1942 Offensive in North Africa," NARA RG 457/1035; also De Risio, *Servizi segreti*, pp. 111–12.

commander in North Africa rightly viewed as "an unpardonable error." SM79 bombers and twin-engined monoplanes of less than stunning performance – the Caproni Ca311 and later variants – replaced the biplanes. But not until December 1941 did the first MC202s with Kodak automatic cameras provide the constantly updated photo mosaics needed to plan the Malta landing.[28] In joint theaters such as North Africa, the Luftwaffe inevitably carried the weight of the air reconnaissance effort.

Intelligence and reconnaissance can only find the enemy and estimate his strength and intentions. The operations that follow require coordinated movement to ensure surprise, and thus depend absolutely upon swift and secure communications. The *Reichswehr* leadership had therefore decided in the late 1920s that it would develop the swiftest, most flexible, and most secure operational and tactical communications systems in the world.[29] The resulting techniques and systems helped ensure Germany's early victories, even if German arrogance in assuming that ENIGMA machine cryptography was unbreakable contributed much to Germany's subsequent defeats in 1942–45. The Italian army followed its allies only hesitantly, and entered and fought the conflict of 1940–43 with communications inadequate for static warfare. Shortages of telephone wire crippled even its 1915–18 land-line systems in the final defensive battles in Tunisia.[30] Radio communications between divisions, corps, and higher headquarters depended upon equipment that functioned, if at all, only when stationary and after a lengthy set-up process, and was largely useless in the Russian winter. Army communications security was relatively weak. Especially after October 1940, Cairo read much of the army's lower-grade operational traffic and an increasing amount of higher-level

28. Felice Porro, "La Quinta Squadra Aerea in Libia (10 giugno 1940–5 febbraio 1941)," *Rivista Aeronautica*, 1948 no. 8, p. 487; Arena, *Aeronautica*, vol. 1, pp. 93, 581–82; vol. 3, pp. 366, 392.

29. See James S. Corum, *The Roots of Blitzkrieg: Hans von Seeckt and German Military Reform* (Lawrence, Kansas, 1992), pp. 107–08.

30. *Africa*, 4:453.

material, including information that allowed General Richard O'Connor to cut off the remnants of Graziani's 10th Army at Beda Fomm in early February 1941. Cairo likewise read virtually all high-level army traffic in East Africa in winter–spring 1941, including the viceroy's daily situation reports to Rome, a circumstance that speeded markedly the dismantling of Italy's empire. Communications security improved thereafter, but the army's ultimate adoption of ENIGMA cypher machines rendered high-level Italian communications in Tunisia largely transparent to the Western powers.[31]

The army's operational concepts and structure were unserviceable at the outset, and scarcely improved thereafter. In North Africa, the theater in which (as an eloquent *Comando Supremo* memorandum put it in early 1941) "our flag is committed before all the world," Italian forces enjoyed a ratio of motor vehicles to men of almost 1 : 21 on 1 June 1940. By early 1942 that ratio had dropped only insignificantly, to 1 : 19, while Rommel's forces enjoyed a ratio of one vehicle to 3.6 men. Infantry divisions and corps, the *Regio Esercito*'s basic operational units, could neither move at more than walking pace nor hope realistically to attack their British counterparts, even after discounting the 2.5 : 1 manpower advantage of the British three-brigade division over the Italian *divisione binaria* (Table 5.1).[32]

The Italian motorized infantry division was similarly equipped; Gàmbara had to explain patiently to the Germans that the *Trieste*, unlike a German light division, could only fight on foot and was at the mercy of "any idiot armored car" when mounted in its defenseless trucks.[33] The virtual absence of effective anti-aircraft defense except for a few modern

31. Bastico AAR, February 1943, NARA T-821/9/000232; Alessandro Massignani, *Alpini e tedeschi sul Don* (Novale di Valdagno, 1991), pp. 114–19; security: F. H. Hinsley, *British Intelligence in the Second World War* (London, 1979–90), vol. 1, pp. 378–81; vol. 2, pp. 294, 588–89, 599.

32. Quotation: Montezemolo memorandum, 5 July 1941, Ceva, *Le forze armate*, p. 591; base figures for ratios: *Africa*, 1:463, 3:104.

33. *Africa*, 2:628.

Table 5.1. *Italian and British infantry divisions, North Africa*
(table of organization strength; actual combat strength was invariably lower)

Italian infantry division type A.S.42		British infantry division, 1941–42
7,000	Officers and men	17,300
72	Anti-tank rifles	444
146	Automatic rifles	819
92	Machine guns	48
–	Light mortars	162
18	81mm/3″ mortars	56
60	Field guns	72
72	Anti-tank guns	136
16	Light anti-aircraft guns	48
142	Trucks	1,999
35	Other vehicles	268
–	Trailers	197
72	Artillery tractors	159
147	Motorcycles	1,064
–	Tracked ammunition carriers	256
–	Armored cars	6

Source: Adapted from Mario Montanari, *Le operazioni in Africa Settentrionale* (Rome, 1984–93), vol. 3, p. 707.

20 mm cannon meant that occasional flights of British fighter-bombers could paralyze whole Italian divisions; RAF attacks reduced Graziani almost to incoherence in August 1940.[34]

The Italian armored division was similarly uncompetitive, especially considering that the Italian M14 main battle tank had half the weight and a fraction of the firepower and off-road speed of the Grant and Sherman tanks that British units in the desert received in increasing numbers in 1942 (Table 5.2).

The *Ariete* had been even more deficient when originally deployed to North Africa in February–March 1941; initially its only tanks had been a

34. Knox, *Mussolini*, p. 163 (Graziani diary, ACS).

Table 5.2. *Italian and British armored divisions, North Africa*
(table of organization strength; actual combat strength was invariably lower)

Italian armored division (Ariete)		British armored division, 1942
8,600	Officers and men	13,235
18	Anti-tank rifles	348
900	Machine guns	868
–	Light mortars	60
9	81mm/3″ mortars	18
70	Field guns	64
61	Anti-tank guns[35]	219
34	Light anti-aircraft guns	88
918	Trucks	1,415
205	Other vehicles	374
–	Trailers	134
54	Artillery tractors	53
504	Motorcycles	956
–	Tracked ammunition carriers	151
–	Other armored vehicles	37
40	Armored cars	60
189	Tanks	280

Source: Adapted from Mario Montanari, *Le operazioni in Africa Settentrionale* (Rome, 1984–93), vol. 3, p. 710.

doomed regiment of 3.5-ton L3 tankettes, and it received no armored cars until spring 1942. Yet Graziani's successor, Gariboldi, had indignantly rejected Rommel's well-meant March 1941 suggestion that the North African command attach additional vehicles, artillery and support units to the division to give it the mobility and firepower needed to fight alongside German units. The army staff had established the division's table of organization and equipment, and that – except for the addition of M13 medium tank battalions to supplement the useless L3s – was that.[36]

35. The source's implausible figure of 250 Italian anti-tank guns has been adjusted downward by subtracting the 47 mm main guns of the *Ariete*'s tanks.
36. Gariboldi letter, printed in *Africa*, 2:29–30.

Not even the airborne operations that became possible by 1942 – despite a perceptible lack of enthusiasm within the army leadership – offered much prospect of operational movement. The *Comando Supremo* estimated in 1941 that dropping the entire paratroop division (then being formed, and eventually baptized *Folgore*) in a single lift would require sixteen months' production of transport aircraft, not including production to compensate for the predictable aircraft losses in the meantime.[37]

Much of the penury that hampered Italian operations was deliberate: in an effort to render the *divisione binaria* "slim" and "agile," Pariani and his successors had invented and implemented a theory of theater logistics found in no other army. A centralized *Intendenza*, equipped with the lion's share of the few trucks the army staff saw fit to provide, would replenish corps, divisions and even regiments *from the rear forward* on a daily basis. In 1940–43, fear of logistical abandonment consequently rooted to the spot all division and corps commanders who faced the enemy. Even immobility might not ensure the uninterrupted resupply without which their units, lacking organic transport and reserves of food, ammunition, and water, would disintegrate. The slightest movement might, and usually did, disrupt the supply chain. Nor did the highly effective German system of replenishment through divisional truck columns operating from the front back inspire emulation.[38] Cavallero was not even content with an *Intendenza* centralized dysfunctionally under the theater commander: as described, he placed the supply of forward units in North Africa under his own immediate authority in August 1942.[39]

37. Di Giovanni, *I paracadutisti italiani*, p. 94.

38. See Montanari's ironic comments on the army's quest for "*snello*" and "*agile*" units (*Africa*, 3:709), and the devastating analysis of Botti in "La logistica dei poveri," pp. 425–32, and "Problemi logistici," pp. 301–03; for the contrast with the German system, Mancinelli, *Dal fronte dell'Africa settentrionale*, pp. 46–47.

39. *Africa*, 3:537–41.

The army's logistical system frequently failed even on its own terms. Central vehicle maintenance depots in North Africa and elsewhere often functioned barely or not at all, and contributed to restricting what little operational reach Italian ground forces might have possessed. As late as spring 1942 neither armored units nor *Intendenza* possessed trailers or specialized vehicles for the recovery and forward repair of immobilized armored vehicles. Unserviceable rates for trucks and other vehicles in North Africa approached 40 percent for much of the campaign. The multiplicity of types issued to units – in the forces in Russia alone, seventeen different species of light truck and thirty of heavy – taxed drivers and technicians, and made it almost impossible to ensure an adequate flow of spare parts.[40] The war ministry also failed to provide the units in Russia with low-temperature lubricants, necessary even in North Italian winters, for vehicles and weapons. The army's physical immobility and operational paralysis were powerfully over-determined.

The navy escaped paralysis only in part, despite the inherent mobility of its major units. It suffered from five major deficiencies at the operational level. First, its command structure and style were static, overcentralized, and inflexible. The navy staff war room in Rome maintained tight control of operational and even tactical detail: nature and timing of operations, the routes the fleet was to follow, and the assignment of aircraft, surface forces, and submarines to the fleet commander. When the fleet was at sea, *Supermarina* frequently invaded even the tactical prerogatives of its commander by countermanding dispositions or ordering

---

40.   See the sad tale of bureaucratic dysfunction in 1941–42 with regard to vehicle maintenance at all levels from the army staff downward in *Africa*, 3:864–65; vehicle totals/unserviceable, 1:170, note 185 (8 November 1940: 37 percent of 5,273); 2:17–19 (20 February 1941: 26 percent of 5,000); 2:440 (15 November 1941: 38.8 percent unserviceable); 3:104, 106; Ceva, *La condotta italiana*, p. 71 (17 July 1941: 36 percent of the entire army's 47,500 motor vehicles unserviceable); types in Russia: Ceva, "Industria bellica ed esercito," p. 247.

changes of course.[41] The process of selection for high naval command reinforced this rigidity. The navy chose surface fleet commanders from the late 1920s onward through judgments of "comparative merit" rather than seniority, but the essence of the system was a control of the chief of staff over appointments as absolute as – and congruent with – his control over fleet operations. Cavagnari's dismissal after Taranto did not appreciably modify a system that contrasted sharply with the respect that British naval custom, formed in the days of sail, accorded to the judgment of the man on the spot.

The navy's second major operational deficiency was its complete lack of preparation at the tactical level for night combat, an omission that contrasted markedly with both Japanese and British – although not U.S. Navy – practice, and severely restricted both fleet and convoy operations even before the arrival of radar. Third, the navy lacked in 1940 and developed only slowly thereafter the ability to integrate – with the highly specialized daylight-only battle fleet that had absorbed most of its budget – the inexpensive and fuel-efficient weapons of coastal warfare that had made immense strides in the interwar period: mines, land-based torpedo-bombers and dive-bombers, light surface forces, submarines, and its own neglected secret weapon, the *maiali*. Fourth, the navy was almost completely unprepared at all levels, including that of operations, for the convoy war that became its main task after Taranto and Matapan. Finally, the navy's lack of amphibious doctrine, experience, and equipment made the naval aspects of the Malta landing operation prepared in spring–summer 1942 a work of embarrassed improvisation.

Naval intelligence focused narrowly on enemy communications, movements, and order of battle. Within these limits, and despite the absence of the rudimentary mechanical or electronic computers used in Britain and the United States, it served the navy well. Agents in Spain usually provided Rome with notice within four hours of fleet

---

41. For a particularly noteworthy case (31 August 1940), see Knox, *Mussolini*, p. 149.

and convoy departures from Gibraltar; efforts at Alexandria were less successful, and the British briefly concealed the sinking of the *Queen Elizabeth* and *Valiant* in December 1941. Traffic analysis and decrypts provided advance warning of British operations from the very outset of the war; *Supermarina*, with some German help, had a remarkably clear picture of British dispositions and movements before Punta Stilo.[42]

The air reconnaissance needed to confirm signals intelligence and locate the enemy for attack was however almost wholly lacking at the outset, and severely deficient thereafter. The air force had throughout the interwar period fought fiercely – as an attempt to subordinate it to the navy – all efforts to promote among its bomber forces the specialized crew training and equipment needed for maritime reconnaissance and strike missions. The navy itself, as described, had ensured that it entered the war without the aircraft carriers needed to provide the fleet with effective onboard reconnaissance. Its few catapulted float-planes were limited in range and speed, and provided only sporadic tactical coverage. For longer ranges, the navy made do with the Cant Z501 amphibian ("an archaeological artifact," in the words of Cavagnari's deputy), the Z506 and FIAT RS14 float-planes, and – despite fierce air force defense of its assets – Cant Z1007 and SM79 land-based bombers. But the Royal Navy's radar-directed carrier-based fighters regularly shot down all such aircraft

42. For a useful description of naval intelligence organization and capabilities, see Admiral (Franco) Maugeri, "The Italian S.I.S. Prior to the Armistice," (undated but autumn 1944), NARA RG 457/145; on the effectiveness of Italian and German surveillance of Gibraltar, see also "Norme Generali...," 1 October 1941, *Direttive Superaereo*, 1/2:751, and Hinsley, *British Intelligence*, vol. 2, pp. 719–21. For Punta Stilo, see the 8 July entry in Roatta to Graziani, 140, 9 July 1940, ACS, Carte Graziani, bundle 42; in addition, Mario De Monte, *Uomini ombra* (Rome, 1955), pp. 30–34; Jack Greene and Massignani, *The Naval War in the Mediterranean, 1940–1943* (London, 1998), pp. 68–69, and Weichold to Oberkommando der Marine, B. Nr. Gkos. 55/40, 10 July 1940, German Naval Records, file PG 32211 (NARA T-1022/1773).

long before they could sight British surface forces.[43] The arrival in autumn 1941 of a few Re2000 fighters adapted for maritime reconnaissance remedied only partially one of the navy's most galling operational weaknesses. Picket submarines also on occasion provided warning of British movements, but the Royal Navy's sonar-equipped escorts, anti-submarine aircraft, radio direction-finding techniques, and signals intelligence exacted a high price.

Navy operational communications, although still erratic and poorly organized, were far superior to those of the army.[44] But *Supermarina*'s overcentralization of command made such communications success as the navy achieved a decidedly mixed blessing. And in the fateful area of communications security the navy suffered a series of undetected defeats with devastating impact, especially on the North African convoy war. British command of the navy's operational cyphers led to the sinking or capture of numerous Italian submarines, some of them with code books intact, in the first weeks of the war. The navy improved its cypher security markedly after mid-July 1940, and thereafter Italian high-level naval communications largely resisted British attack except for the ENIGMA machine cyphers used on German insistence when operations required high-speed secure transmission. The British cracked one such source of ULTRA intelligence in September 1940, in time for Matapan, and a second cypher system used for shipping control in summer 1941. From that point onward, losses on the Libyan run rose dramatically whenever British forces were strong enough to make use of advance warning of convoy and ship departures. The Italian submarine effort continued to suffer from ULTRA disclosures, and the ENIGMA machines of the Luftwaffe, Rommel's headquarters, and the German

43. For the initial situation, see *Direttive Superaereo*, 1/1:177, 179–82, and especially Navy staff memorandum, 10 November 1940, ibid., 380–81; Z501: Admiral Somigli in Greene and Massignani, *Naval War*, p. 94.

44. See the harrowing technical description in USMM, *L'organizzazione*, vol. 1, pp. 169–72.

commands in Greece also did their part in broadcasting the navy's operational intentions to Cairo and London, while the unsuspecting Italians and Germans mounted periodic witch-hunts for presumed traitors.[45]

The navy's reconnaissance and communications difficulties were minor compared to its crippling lack of air defense fighters and maritime strike aircraft. By early 1941, both fleet and convoy operations required air cover against British carrier-based and land-based reconnaissance and torpedo aircraft throughout daylight hours. By late 1941, British aircraft-mounted search radars and ULTRA made night cover increasingly necessary. Air force day cover was nonexistent at the outset, since Pricolo flatly refused to contemplate fighter escorts for the fleet except "in wholly exceptional cases." Despite incessant requests by *Supermarina*, fighter escort often proved impractical thereafter, for British aircraft improved in performance, striking power, and numbers more rapidly than the *Regia Aeronautica* could counter. Even in mid-1942 and with German help, the air force found it impossible to maintain four fighters continuously over a surface force or convoy in the central Mediterranean – at a time when the British had at least 150 combat-ready bombers and fighters on Malta.[46] In the Axis attack on the last great Malta convoy (Operation PEDESTAL) in August 1942, the Italian and German air forces preferred to use their few available long-range fighters to protect their own bombers rather than the navy's surface ships. Yet even when provided with air support the major surface units were a problematic

---

45. Hinsley, *British Intelligence*, vol. 1, pp. 205–06, 210, 404; vol. 2, pp. 22 and note, 281, 283–87, 320–25, 329–30, 335, 339, 347, 349, 351, 397, 402, 422–24, 490, 495, 611, 613, and, in general, Santoni, *Il vero traditore* (Milan, 1981); witch-hunts: Rintelen, *Mussolini als Bundesgenosse*, pp. 154–55.

46. Pricolo to Cavagnari, 23 July 1940, *Direttive Superaereo*, 1/1:174; Mattesini, *Mezzo agosto*, pp. 138, 270–71, 277, 540; the final air force offer of 20 fighters to cover the navy's planned cruiser sortie during fifteen hours of daylight meant no more than a wholly inadequate two to three fighters on station at a time.

operational instrument: their inability to fight at night repeatedly impelled *Supermarina* to order them homeward in late afternoon.

Attempts to use air strikes in cooperation with the fleet got off to a disastrous start in the July 1940 battle off Calabria. The air force bombed both British and Italian naval units heavily, impartially, and ineffectually; the Italian main fleet downed an Italian SM79 bomber. Decentralizing air support requests to the naval communications centers and air commands in the islands and South led to chaos during an inconclusive sortie by the battleships *Vittorio Veneto* and *Cesare* against the British Gibraltar squadron in late November 1940. The only link between the air force and navy commands on Sardinia was a "telephone line that, [even] when it [was] working, [did] not permit clear communication." In February 1941, while battleships of the British Gibraltar force shelled Genoa with impunity, confusion prevented notification of the fleet commander at sea, who continued to look for the enemy west of Sardinia. A few hours later, inaccurate air reconnaissance reports caused the fleet to alter course abruptly away from the British.

Coordination had not improved by March 1941; the navy and air force improvised at the last moment the liaison arrangements for the fleet sortie that led to the Matapan disaster; the crucial air units based on the Dodecanese did not receive their communications instructions until after the operation. The Luftwaffe, by contrast, presciently sent an air liaison team equipped with its own radios to join the Italian flagship.[47] Air-sea cooperation improved after Matapan, although the absence throughout the war of a joint air force-navy operations center and planning staff still led to confusion, duplication of effort, and navy complaints of insufficient air cover. Subsequent air attacks on British fleet

47. Arena, *Aeronautica*, vol. 1, p. 456; Pricolo to Cavagnari (communications annex), 23 July 1940; Air staff AAR for navy staff, 20 December 1940, both in *Direttive Superaereo*, 1/1:175–76, 391–92; Genoa: Knox, *Mussolini*, pp. 125–26; USMM, *Azioni navali*, pp. 339–60, 367–68; Santoro, *L'aeronautica*, vol. 1, pp. 274–83; Matapan: Greene and Massignani, *Naval War*, p. 154.

units and convoys were only loosely integrated with the invariably unsuccessful attempts of Italian battleship and cruiser battlegroups to close with outnumbered British forces.

The navy and air force nevertheless learned slowly: overall operational performance in the Malta convoy battles of June and August 1942, even after discounting the vital German contribution, was a noteworthy improvement over the first phases of the war. Navy efforts to use mines and submarine ambushes in support of fleet movements were however generally unsuccessful; the navy staff sought throughout the war to block the Sicily channel to east-west British traffic with minefields. But only the belated arrival of improved Italian mines and rare German generosity with modern deep-water mines made possible successes such as the virtual destruction in December 1941 of "Force K," the British Malta surface squadron that had ravaged the North African convoys. The *Regia Marina*'s mine effort was a major missed opportunity.[48] The large submarine force, in which the navy had placed high hopes, was an even greater disappointment. Submerged daylight ambush in front of British ports and on the margins of planned fleet actions exposed the boats to British anti-submarine aircraft and escorts, and *Supermarina*'s insistence on keeping the submarines under separate command rather than assigning them to the surface fleet made coordination with fleet operations difficult.

The navy had given some thought to surface and submarine warfare, but was almost wholly unprepared for convoy operations. Like its Japanese counterpart and ally, and in part for similar reasons – its exclusive focus on the battle fleet – it lacked at the outset and was slow to acquire early warning radar, convoy air cover, anti-submarine aircraft, sonar, effective depth charges, and ships conceived as anti-submarine and anti-aircraft escorts.[49] Most of the twenty-nine corvettes the navy

---

48. Bernotti, *Cinquant'anni nella Marina militare*, p. 244; USMM, *L'organizzazione*, vol. 1, pp. 113–20; USMM, *La guerra di mine* (Rome, 1966), pp. 14–15, 203–22.

49. For the inability of all but a few Japanese naval officers to imagine the relentless U.S. Navy submarine campaign that throttled the Japanese

actually completed became available only in 1943, as final defeat in North Africa largely ended the convoy war.[50] These self-imposed handicaps forced the navy to sacrifice most of its destroyers to hold the supply lines to North Africa, Albania, and the Dodecanese open. Luftwaffe help and the use of battleships as escorts was also vital in winter 1941–42: in November, before Kesselring began punishing Malta, the British sank over three-fifths of the tonnage that the *Regia Marina* shipped. Once German airpower and the "battleship convoys" overcame that crisis, losses were proportionally low until the final months of 1942, although concentrated cripplingly on tankers and on ships carrying ammunition and vehicles. Only in spring 1943 did the tonnage lost on the Tunisian run reach a prohibitive 31 percent in April and 72 percent in May – but even there the navy's overall record from November 1942 to May 1943 was 71 percent of cargoes delivered. In aggregate terms, 83 percent of the 2.68 million tons of cargo shipped to North Africa arrived safely – although that total, and especially the supplies of fuel, ammunition, and vehicles actually received by the front-line units, was ultimately far less than the Axis forces required to face the increasingly massive Anglo-American build-up.[51]

Malta's resistance achieved one thing beyond dispute: it converted the *Regia Marina* to amphibious operations, even in the face of the risk of a fleet action should the British Gibraltar squadron sortie to rescue the island fortress. A decade of shunning landing craft and army cooperation meant

economy – because the Imperial Japanese Navy itself disdained commerce warfare – and Japan's consequent failure to develop convoy and anti-submarine warfare techniques, see Evans and Peattie, *Kaigun*, pp. 434–41, 483–86.

50. Cavallero, *Diario 1940–1943*, ed. Giovanni Bucciante (Rome, 1984), p. 313; USMM, *L'organizzazione*, vol. 1, pp. 135–49; vol. 2, pp. 116–18, 121–22.

51. On ULTRA, see especially Santoni, *Il vero traditore*; shipping statistics: USMM, *La difesa del traffico con l'Albania, La Grecia e l'Egeo* (Rome, 1965), p. 47; USMM, *Dati statistici* (Rome, 1972), pp. 127, 129, 134–35, 144; *Africa*, 4:569.

months of frenetic improvisation in winter–spring 1942. The navy's landing flotilla was a bizarre patchwork of minesweepers, small merchant ships and tankers, tugs, self-propelled barges, armored motor launches, motor sailors, and ferries from as far away as Venice. The state railways provided diesel engines for the barges, and the navy conscripted power ladders from Italy's fire departments for the assault on Malta's cliffs.

The navy nevertheless lacked experience with opposed landings on any scale, much less one involving two seaborne and one airborne army corps. The inevitable complexity of the naval plan, the need for extensive night movement under radio silence, the coordination and support of two main landing sites and several subsidiary ones, the likelihood that (as in Sicily in July 1943 and Normandy in June 1944) the air forces would deliver the paratroops far from their designated drop zones, the pervasiveness and strength of the British fortifications, and the central uncertainty about the reaction of the British Gibraltar squadron, suggest an Axis Dieppe – or with supreme good fortune a Tarawa – in the making.[52]

The navy's final operational deficiency was defensible bases. Geography and the navy's spending priorities had prevented the creation of a Mediterranean Scapa Flow, a single well-fortified base from which Cavagnari's battleships could command the Sicily Channel. Major fleet units consequently wandered throughout the war between Taranto, Naples, and La Spezia. The Taranto disaster of November 1940 was conspicuous primarily because the British put three battleships out of action simultaneously through their own skill and the poorly planned and even more poorly implemented Italian defensive measures. Yet air attacks on Naples, La Spezia, La Maddalena, and other key Italian bases – especially after the arrival of large American air forces in late

---

52. For a useful summary of the planning, see Mariano Gabriele, "L'operazione 'C 3' (1942)," in Rainero and Biagini, eds., *1942*, pp. 409–34, and his *Operazione C3: Malta* (Rome, 1965); also DRZW 6:588–94. The operational and tactical skills the three services had so far shown do not justify the retrospective optimism about the outcome found in some of the literature.

1942 – also damaged the battleships *Cesare*, *Littorio*, and *Vittorio Veneto*, and sank or damaged cruisers, lesser warships, and merchant ships at a rate beyond the ability of Italian shipyards to replace or repair. Italy's only relatively secure bases lay in the upper Adriatic, far from the North African convoy routes or the vulnerable beaches of Sicily.

Doctrinal vacuum and industry's failure to develop a heavy bomber rendered the *Regia Aeronautica* largely incapable of independent operations. Pricolo and his successor, Rino Corso Fougier, inevitably insisted that avoiding dispersal of effort demanded that they control everything that flew, but their inability to achieve decisive results through air action alone led to piecemeal surrender to the incessant demands of navy and army. Reconnaissance in support of air operations was as inadequate as air force efforts on behalf of the other services. Air intelligence was more enterprising, although its history is poorly understood. By 1941 it had developed an extensive intercept service targeted at RAF communications in the Mediterranean, and – with some German help – some rudimentary electronic warfare activities around Malta. It may also have realized the hopelessness of Italy's position ahead of its army and navy counterparts, precisely because Italy's inferiority in the air was so great after late 1942. Fougier informed Ambrosio even before the fall of Tunisia that the air war in the Mediterranean was irremediably lost and that Italy's cities were "perhaps about to see, by an irony of fate, the realization of Douhet's vision" by the U.S. Army Air Force.[53]

Air force operational communications were remarkably transparent to British decryption: from the first month of the war through spring 1941, except for a few intervals after cypher changes, the British read up to 80 percent of the air force's high-grade communications. The RAF gained a remarkably complete picture of the air force order of battle, basing arrangements, and operations in North Africa, which contributed

---

53. On the air intelligence organization and electronic warfare, see Arena, *Aeronautica*, vol. 1, pp. 163–65, 200–03; vol. 2, pp. 633–34. Spring 1943 assessment: Fougier to Ambrosio, 15 April 1943, *Direttive Superaereo*, 2/2:705.

powerfully to its success in forcing the *Regia Aeronautica* onto the defensive.[54] Once the Germans arrived, Italian communications became less useful to Cairo – for the Luftwaffe carried the weight of operations with an effectiveness at the tactical level that made it difficult for the British to exploit their equally thorough reading of *Luftwaffe* ENIGMA communications.

Realizing Douhet's vision on its own account was from the beginning far beyond the *Regia Aeronautica*'s reach. The air staff's initial war-planning document, drafted in March 1940, confessed sheepishly that the absence of bombsights and bombs needed to hit and sink heavily armored ships meant that surprise blows against Bizerte, Toulon, Malta, Gibraltar, or Alexandria were not in prospect. Nor did the air force develop anything resembling a campaign plan for the coming Mediterranean war.[55] The air staff did briefly attempt independent air operations against France in June 1940; the results were operationally and strategically negligible despite considerable wear and tear on aircraft and crews. Thereafter the air staff mounted sporadic long-distance raids on Gibraltar, Haifa, and even an oil refinery at Bahrein. But high-altitude night bombardments did little damage, while Alexandria harbor proved too shallow and too well-defended to offer profitable targets for the few torpedo-bombers available in 1940.

In North Africa, the RAF's system of forward staging fields, fed from bases in the Nile delta outside Italian range, made it impossible for the *Regia Aeronautica* to convert its initial numerical superiority into air superiority at the operational level. The RAF was as determined to seize the initiative as the British navy and army, and it struck repeatedly and savagely at Italian airfields and forward ground units before withdrawing out of range. Italian air operations in North Africa swiftly degenerated into an improvised and largely ineffectual defense until the Luftwaffe arrived.[56]

---

54. Hinsley, *British Intelligence*, vol. 1, pp. 212–14, 375–77.
55. Air staff memorandum, 1 April 1940, *Direttive Superaereo*, 1/1:92–103.
56. Pricolo to Mussolini, September 1940, *Direttive Superaereo*, 1/1:242–48, especially 247–48.

In the Greek war Pricolo initially planned an air effort to "defeat the enemy air forces," "counter enemy naval action," and "assist ground operations on Greek territory and the occupation of Corfù."[57] But neither the Greek air force nor the navy were threats worthy of much attention, while the army soon needed rescue from its Greek counterpart. The air staff had to improvise, amid wretched visibility and without air-ground radio communications, both airdrops of food and munitions in the snow-capped Albanian mountains and ground support missions using fighters and even bombers. In the process, Mussolini's bloodcurdling if thoroughly impractical orders that the *Regia Aeronautica* "[sow] panic everywhere" and raze to the ground "all [Greek] urban centers of over 10,000 population" fell by the wayside.[58]

Albania was the only theater in which the *Regia Aeronautica* achieved a degree of air superiority. The closest it came thereafter to independent campaigns were its efforts to suppress Malta while the Luftwaffe was otherwise engaged. Its effectiveness at that task is perhaps best summarized by a Maltese reaction to the departure of Kesselring's forces for the eastern Mediterranean and Russia in May 1942: "We felt that our prayers had been answered. God had sent back the Italians."[59]

A further form of support for ground operations was air transport, a mission the air force had despised and resisted until spring 1940, when it formed its first transport units. Then disaster in Albania forced it to accept German help in the form of a Luftwaffe transport wing. The Germans' Junkers Ju52s, the conversion of over 100 obsolete Italian bombers, and increased production of SM82 transports allowed the

---

57. Pricolo to subordinate commands, B-02038, 25 October 1940, NARA T-821/ 127/000250–54.

58. Mussolini to the chiefs of staff, 10 November 1940, VCSMG 1939–43, 4:247.

59. Quoted in Greene and Massignani, *Naval War*, p. 224; see also the comparative analysis of *Regia Aeronautica* and Luftwaffe efforts against Malta to spring 1941 in Mattesini, *Il contributo del 'X Fliegerkorps'*, pp. 271–73.

Axis to airlift to Albania almost 70,000 troops, stripped of their heavy equipment and vehicles, and evacuate 25,000 wounded and frostbite cases. Graziani's simultaneous defeat in North Africa necessitated a second massive airlift – continued over the following two years – of all the necessities of war, "from torpedoes to women, from artillery ammunition to mail, from cannon to bocce games."[60] Large-scale airborne operations were and remained impossible without German help; the air force never accumulated enough SM82s to drop more than three battalions of paratroops at a time, and only the Germans could provide troop-carrying gliders.[61]

A final and often crippling air force operational weakness was its basing and logistical arrangements. The full exploitation of airpower's inherent mobility requires both mobile and fixed bases lavishly provided with specialized technicians, equipment, air defense, and motor transport. The *Regia Aeronautica's* initial backwardness is perhaps best measured by the carping in spring 1941 of its officers at the "not inconsiderable squandering of fuel and funds" by the allegedly "heavy" ground and base defense organization that Luftwaffe X *Fliegerkorps* installed in Sicily.[62]

The *Regia Aeronautica's* own ground organization, although far more motorized than the army, correspondingly lacked the sheer numbers of trucks and specialized vehicles required for full mobility, especially in the North African wastes. The first retreat from Cyrenaica in winter 1940–41

60. Quotation: memorandum by the *Comando Supremo* air representative, 27 August 1941, in Santoro, *L'aeronautica*, vol. 2, p. 225; on women as an alleged "necessity of war," see also the brief but carefully documented note of Giorgio Rochat, "Sulle 'case' militari nella II guerra mondiale," *Storia militare* n. 3 (December, 1993), pp. 48–49.

61. Air staff memorandum on Malta operation, 19 April 1942, *Direttive Superaereo*, 2/1:171.

62. Quarantelli (acting chief, air force military police) to Air Ministry, 19 June 1941, and the scathing comments of Mattesini, *Il contributo del 'X Fliegerkorps'*, pp. 461–63, 270–71.

was particularly catastrophic, with the loss of huge stocks of munitions, fuel, and immobilized but repairable aircraft; by the second great withdrawal, in December 1941, the North African air force command was far better prepared for movement. The air force's permanent bases in North Africa, the Dodecanese, and southern Italy in many cases lacked hard runways and taxiways. Those in Albania and Cyrenaica regularly turned into swamps with the autumn and winter rains, grounding all aircraft. Protected dispersal sites were initially largely unknown. Maintenance, as in the case of the army, tended toward overcentralization, using large fixed installations vulnerable to RAF attack rather than the small mobile workshops through which the British serviced their dispersal airfields. The air force's operational immobility derived from many of the same attitudes and material causes as that of navy and army.

6

TACTICS

Tactics is the art of battlefield destruction of the enemy; its essence is the concentration of strength against enemy weakness in space and time. Tactical success, like that at the operational level, requires seasoned and daring leadership, creative freedom for subordinates, foresight, coordination, movement and surprise, firepower, and support. The three services displayed varying degrees of tactical inadequacy. The army's recruitment, training, and promotion policies; tactical intelligence and reconnaissance; tactical communications; ability to engage the enemy in a coordinated manner; and logistical support of its combat units were all moderately to severely deficient.

Part of the inheritance of the *Regio Esercito* hierarchy was a congenital inability to create effective fighting units. Fear of regional mutinies and the Liberal state's hope that military service would "make Italians" had from the mid-1870s dictated the recruitment of each regiment from several different regions and its stationing in yet another region.[1] Only the Alpine divisions, in which each battalion derived from the close-knit mountain communities of a particular valley, were exempt. Neither the battlefield disadvantages of national recruitment in a society fractured by

1.　　See Rochat, "Strutture dell'esercito dell'Italia liberale: i reggimenti di fanteria e bersaglieri," in his *L'esercito italiano in pace e in guerra*, pp. 41–73.

Tunisia, 1943: the Italian 47mm antitank gun, obsolescent in 1940 and never superseded; the consequences of its lack of a splinter shield are apparent (U.S. National Archives 208-260-DD).

dialects, nor the enormously slow and cumbersome mobilization system that resulted, nor the obvious success of the German and British armies in creating strikingly cohesive regiments and battalions through regional recruitment led to revision of what by the 1940s had become time-hallowed dogma.

Relentless individual and unit training might have redeemed the performance of units thrown together from disparate human materials. The obvious alternatives or complements to such training were ideological fanaticism on the one hand, and on the other the disciplinary terror that the Italian high command of 1915–18 and the *Wehrmacht* of 1941–45 practiced enthusiastically. But terror and fanaticism were not in the 1940–43 *Regio Esercito*'s repertoire, despite occasional threats – on one notable occasion at Rommel's fierce insistence – to court-martial those guilty of "abandonment of positions in the face of the enemy."[2]

The army's higher leadership did not discover the connection between training and military performance until 1941. Pariani sent a senior commander off to Libya in 1937 with the remarkable injunction not to do "too much training." An eminent staff officer, in a well-known postwar work otherwise devoted to defending the wartime record of the armed forces, wrote of "the [army's] widespread assumption that in battle, intuition and individual valor counted for more than training."[3] With the unique exception of the paratroops of the *Folgore* division, whose brief but supremely professional resistance at El Alamein testified to the wisdom of their commanders and the effects of a year and a half of tactical training, no Italian ground unit in the Second World War entered combat as well-prepared as corresponding units of the British or U.S. armies, much less

---

2. DRZW 6:670; *Africa*, 3:464-65, 950–51 (Gioda [X Corps] to division commanders, 18 July 1942).

3. Mario Caracciolo di Feroleto, *E poi? La tragedia dell'esercito italiano* (Rome, 1946), p. 43; Emilio Faldella, *L'Italia e la seconda guerra mondiale* (Bologna, 1960), p. 114; on prewar training see also Roatta, *Otto milioni di baionette*, pp. 37–41.

those of Italy's German ally. On-the-job training was the norm, and even elite units did not escape: tank battalions of the *Ariete* division routinely received as replacements drivers and gunners who had never driven a tank, or had fired at most three rounds with the 47 mm main gun.[4] Even commanders who understood the imperative necessity of training were helpless in the face of the army's force structure megalomania, which so diluted the officer corps' store of experience and talent that much of the training actually done was of little use.[5]

The same combination of megalomania and neglect presided over the army's training of its junior leaders. In peacetime, the hierarchy deliberately limited the intake of regulars in order to provide the privileged few with decorous careers. In wartime, as in other armies, the immense majority of junior officers were reservists: 90 percent of all lieutenants and two-thirds of all captains as of March 1942.[6] But unlike other armies, the *Regio Esercito* made virtually no attempt to select its reserve officers for military aptitude or to train them to acceptable standards of tactical or technical competence. Well over 90 percent of officer candidates normally received commissions after courses that the authorities themselves recognized as wholly inadequate. University reserve officer training employed instructors who – in the words of a senior commander – were on occasion "so incompetent as to give rise to criticism and comments among the officer candidates." Selection, insofar as it existed, merely eliminated those who were physically unfit. Overage retreads from earlier wars, the army's principal source of captains and majors, had even less training in modern warfare than the green lieutenants, and often collapsed in the face of the physical and psychological rigors

---

4.   Enrico Serra, *Tempi duri: Guerra e Resistenza* (Bologna, 1996), p. 122; see also *Africa*, 2:792–93; Ceva and Curami, *Meccanizzazione*, vol. 1, p. 309.

5.   See particularly the almost despairing circulars on unit training and readiness issued in 1942–43 by the commander of 5th Army (garrison units in central Italy and Sardinia), Caracciolo di Feroleto: NARA T-821/86/000872ff.

6.   Figures: Rochat, "Gli uomini alle armi," Table E.4, p. 287.

of combat. Worse still, according to one retired general whose opinion the *Comando Supremo* found worthy of respect, junior regular officers in too many cases "allowed themselves to be attracted by choice to the quietism of sedentary functions" in the army's immense bureaucracies.[7]

The army hierarchy's deliberate stunting of its NCOs deprived combat units of the experienced leaders that might have compensated for the inadequacies of the junior officers. The NCO corps was calculatedly small (only 41,200 NCOs and technical specialists to 56,500 officers in June 1940) and long-service NCOs served primarily in unit administration.[8] The army's promotion system, although less static at the lower ranks – due to greater battlefield attrition – than for general officers, also offered little motivation to the competent. NCOs, in particular, could not aspire to become officers, as in the *Wehrmacht* or even the U.S. Army; battlefield commissions were apparently unknown to the *Regio Esercito*.

These forces were not the only impediments to the creation and maintenance of well-led and cohesive units. Strategic improvisation in attacking Greece begot organizational-tactical improvisation. As a result of the demobilization that Mussolini had ordered and Badoglio approved in early October 1940, the army staff found itself by November shipping

7.   Rochat, "Gli ufficiali di complemento," pp. 616, 621–23 (data for 1940, with excerpts from the school commanders' reports); Roatta, *Otto milioni di baionette*, pp. 32–33; OTC instructors: Caracciolo (5th Army) to subordinate commands, 19 January 1942, NARA T-821/86/001029; "funzioni sedentarie": Bongiovanni to Mussolini, "Vincere la guerra," 15 March 1941, p. 32 (NARA T-821/249/000412); *Africa*, 3:876–77 (retreads: 2:812); and in general, Sullivan, "The Primacy of Politics: The Influence of Civil-Military Relations on Italian Army and Fascist Militia Junior Officer Selection and Training, 1918–1940," in Elliott V. Converse III, ed., *Forging the Sword: Selecting, Educating, and Training Cadets and Junior Officers in the Modern World* (Chicago, 1998), pp. 65–81.

8.   Montanari, *Alla vigilia*, p. 220.

to Albania units hastily filled out with partially trained reservists and untrained recruits; the regime and perhaps the army staff as well had apparently lacked the moral courage to recall the trained reservists whom the army had just released. The Albanian command threw these units into line a battalion at a time, as they disembarked, often without their supporting weapons, communications, or supply echelons. Cavallero, who was ultimately responsible as theater commander, put it unhappily as late as March 1941: "we are making a tossed salad!" Under these conditions, units blessed with particularly inept commanders collapsed; the cases of the "Wolves of Tuscany" and Bari divisions were especially conspicuous.[9]

In addition – and throughout the war – the caste mentality of the officer corps itself precluded a relationship of trust with the lower orders. Officers had by right personal servants, better uniforms and equipment, more leave, and above all more and better food and drink than their enlisted men – an issue that Kesselring raised several times with Cavallero without significant result.[10] General officers often viewed the troops with a patronizing self-sufficiency that sometimes cost lives – including their own, as in the case of General Federico Ferrari Orsi, who walked into a minefield at El Alamein after apparently ignoring an enlisted man's warning.[11] The exceptions were above all the officers of the Alpine troops and of elite units such as the *Folgore*, where common danger, specialization, and esprit de corps created a bond between ranks

9. Roatta, *Otto milioni di baionette*, p. 131, and the more nuanced Roatta to *Comando Supremo*, 13 November 1940, in Biagini and Frattolillo, eds., *Diario Storico del Comando Supremo*, vol. 2/2, pp. 161–62; "Stiamo facendo un'insalata!" and Bari: Montanari, *Grecia*, vol. 1, pp. 724, 282, 293–94, 308; "Wolves of Tuscany": Knox, *Mussolini*, pp. 258–59, and the Albanian Command file, NARA T-821/210/000080ff.

10. Kesselring, *Memoirs*, pp. 107–108.

11. See Raffaele Doronzo, *Folgore! . . . e si moriva: Diario di un paracadutista* (Milan, 1978), pp. 93–94, and Cavallero, *Comando Supremo*, pp. 346, 333.

that overcame the officer corps' hierarchical mentality. One *Folgore*
recruit noted almost with wonder: "if we have to jump off a four meter
wall, the senior ranks jump first, and then we jump." The usual sort of
junior officers, "full of exaggerated dignity and bluster," did not survive
in such an atmosphere.[12]

After the initial defeats, and at the urging of Mussolini himself, the
army staff polled subordinate units for their views on adopting a common
ration and distribution system for officers and men, at least in the field.[13]
The replies received at 2nd Army, at that point occupying Yugoslavia,
have survived. Most corps commanders took a favorable view for logistical rather than leadership reasons, but "the mass of the officers" was
apparently far from delighted.[14] One commander insisted that officers
were simply not capable of functioning on the normal enlisted ration of a
mess tin slopped full of pasta or crude minestrone: "the officers' mess
relaxes [*ristora*] and puts the officer in the physical and psychological
conditions necessary for the accomplishment of his far from easy task ...
there must be some differentiation – for the purpose of the officers'
morale."[15] The suppression of officers' field messes might also produce
"excessive familiarity [*domestichezza*] and consequent loss of prestige," as
well as a loss of "collaboration and comradeship" among unit officers.[16]
Finally, the new system, if extended to garrison, might lead to "diminu-
tion of the already tenuous authority of the young subalterns, as a
consequence of the suppression of formal distinctions."[17] The fierceness

12. Doronzo, *Folgore!*, pp. 12, 33.
13. Cavallero, *Diario 1940–1943*, p. 211; Scuero (War Ministry) to major
    commands; Scuero to Ambrosio (2nd Army), 26 July 1941, NARA T-821/
    395/000034–36, 000041.
14. Corpo d'Armata Celere (Ferrari Orsi) to 2nd Army, 28 August 1941, ibid.,
    000014–17.
15. XI Corps (Robotti) to 2nd Army, 26 August 1941, ibid., 000018–20.
16. VI Corps (Dalmazzo) to 2nd Army, 24 August 1941, ibid., 000023–25.
17. V Corps (Balocco) to 2nd Army, 24 August 1941, ibid., 000026–27.

of the officer corps' defense of these "formal distinctions" suggests the extent of its doubts about its own ability to lead.

The defeats of winter 1940–41 led the army staff to diagnose belatedly the army's vices in leadership and training. In an emphatic circular that made no reference to his own heavy responsibility for the deficiencies that recent disasters had revealed, Roatta listed yawning gaps in the professional accomplishments of Italy's junior leaders and troops. Junior officers suffered from:

1. insufficient capacity for command (lack of authority, timidity in ordering and demanding, uncertainty in addressing troops),
2. inadequate knowledge of the mechanical side of weapons,
3. limited knowledge of small-unit tactics,
4. rudimentary knowledge of communications equipment and organization,
5. insufficient knowledge of how to read topographic maps, and little understanding of the compass,
6. insufficient knowledge of field fortification,
7. inadequate conditioning for long marches, [and]
8. total administrative ignorance.

NCOs were correspondingly deficient, and showed an "almost total absence of initiative." The troops themselves tended to act only in response to direct orders, were poorly acquainted with their individual weapons and with siting and digging foxholes, and were prone to "*extreme emotional reactions* to threats, real or assumed, to their flanks or rear." Roatta closed with an astonishing exhortation that demonstrates – by the fact that he felt the need to utter it – the extent of the army's professional destitution: "Instructors must keep in mind that battles are not only won on the battlefield, in the face of the enemy, but also in the barracks, on the firing ranges, and in field exercises."[18]

18. All from Annex 2 to Roatta circular, 4100, 15 March 1941, NARA T-821/130/ 000870–72 (emphasis in original).

Roatta's remedies were reasonable ones, given competent instructors: much practice in platoon and company tactics "using a variety of simple tactical situations, close to the real thing." Cavallero, evidently converted to the necessity for training by his hard winter in command in Albania, took a hand in June 1941, and personally ordered the creation of training battalions for the junior leaders of units destined for early combat. Roatta's implementing order was a compound of common sense (as much live-fire and anti-tank training as possible) and bluster: "education [*la cultura*] counts for nothing." *La cultura* might indeed count for nothing until it was time to navigate in the desert or adjust mortar or artillery fire. Italian units in North Africa prized enemy vehicle compasses, but even in *Ariete* their effective use was a skill that few tank commanders possessed.[19]

The consequences of the army's discovery of training in spring–summer 1941 are hard to establish with precision. But with the conspicuous exception of the armored or motorized units and of the *Folgore*, which attracted large numbers of career officers, some of distinguished lineage, the average infantry battalion in North Africa in 1942 still had one or two regular officers at best, with corresponding shortages of experienced NCOs. The reserve officers, in the guarded words of a division commander at El Alamein, were willing to learn but suffered from "notable deficiencies in professional preparation." The result was inevitably the overtaxing of the few regulars, and repeated crises that a corps commander on the El Alamein front summed up scathingly to his division commanders: "the lack of will to defend to the end, if attacked, is widespread among our soldiers, and is beyond doubt a result of the faults of our cadres."[20]

19. Cavallero to Roatta, 8 June 1941; Roatta to major commands, 15 June 1941, in Ceva, *La condotta italiana*, pp. 151–52, 161–64; Bizzi report, March 1942, in Ceva and Curami, *Meccanizzazione*, vol. 2, p. 340 (also NARA T-821/250/000100ff.); Serra, *Tempi duri*, p. 139.

20. Fabris AAR, April 1943, NARA T-821/355/000644–55; Bastico AAR, February 1943, T-821/9/000226–27; Gioda to division commanders, 18 July 1942, *Africa*, 3:950.

A final built-in deficiency in training that the army never even attempted to remedy was what the very perceptive attaché in Berlin, in reporting the disintegration of 8th Army in Russia, described scornfully as "the principle that service support personnel do not fight." Italian support and headquarters units, unlike German ones, did not train as infantry and normally made no attempt to establish all-around defensive perimeters to ward off enemy raids. In North Africa this principle proved dangerous. In Russia it proved fatal: during the retreat from the Don, Soviet armor patrols attacked the main Italian logistical base at Kantemirovka and routed both service troops and thousands of infantry undergoing reorganization.[21]

A further limit on the army's tactical effectiveness was its inability to avoid surprise and to inflict it on the enemy through intelligence and reconnaissance. Even the *Ariete* was short of two-way voice radios for its tanks until spring 1942. The equipment it did eventually receive broke down at intervals from the shaking received during movement and battle. The continuing weakness of communications at regimental level and above deprived signals intelligence and air reconnaissance of much of their timeliness. An on-the-spot investigation into armored vehicles and tactics in North Africa made at *Comando Supremo* request in winter–spring 1941–42, at the height of the *Ariete*'s relative success, gives the measure of the tactical blindness (in the literal sense) that attended the most effective Italian offensive actions of the war:

> our troops ... lacking both speedy armored cars with which to locate the
> enemy and air reconnaissance ... end up steering [toward the enemy] more or
> less randomly, using above all what evidence there is of the direction of
> incoming artillery fire, which however emanates from extremely mobile
> [British] batteries spread over a wide front.

21. Ceva, *Le forze armate*, p. 564 note; Mancinelli, *Dal fronte dell'Africa settentrionale*,
     p. 65.

Not until late spring 1942 did *Ariete* finally receive a short-lived reconnaissance battalion with forty radio-equipped armored cars.[22] Italian
infantry divisions for their part had to rely on foot patrols for direct
information about the enemy. But no activity in war requires more of
the junior leaders whose selection and training the army had so neglected;
the paratroops of the *Folgore* and some Alpine divisions were the only
units consistently capable of effective patrolling.

The overall key to the army's offensive tactics in 1940–43 was neither
movement nor surprise but the *Regio Esercito's* time-honored faith in
numbers. A British analyst writing in late 1940 or early 1941 noted:

> The principal characteristic of Italian tactics in both theaters, Libya and East
> Africa, has been rigidity. They have remained attached to one principle, the
> concentration of the greatest possible mass for every task that faces them. In
> the attack they deploy this mass in line and rely solely on weight of numbers
> to clear the way.

If stalled, Italian units sought to regain momentum by committing their
reserves frontally to reinforce failure. Even when Italian commanders
planned to flank their opponents, as in the 1940 offensives against
British Somaliland and Egypt, deficiencies in training, land navigation,
off-road mobility, and logistics made maneuver impractical, and left
frontal attack as the sole option.[23]

Tactical rigidity stemmed in part from the already described deficiencies in junior leadership and unit training that rendered Italian infantry
incapable of infiltrating enemy positions in small semi-independent
groups – the German method of 1917–18 that became the basis of

---

22. Bizzi report, March 1942, in Ceva and Curami, *Meccanizzazione*, vol. 2, p. 344
     (see also vol. 1, p. 310); *Africa*, 3:198–99.

23. Ceva, *La condotta italiana*, pp. 190–92 (my retranslation); Nasi AAR, 20 August
     1940, printed in Luigi Goglia, "La guerra in Africa nel 1940," in Rainero and
     Biagini, eds., 1940, pp. 186–87; *Africa* 1:99–106, 110.

small-unit tactics for the remainder of the century.[24] But in a larger sense rigidity was the consequence of the deliberate choice of numbers over machines that persisted to the bitter end in 1943. Only in North Africa did a new tactical style, improvised and poorly understood by the hierarchy, emerge. Despite what Bastico rightly described as the "brutal qualitative and quantitative inferiority" of its equipment, *Ariete* developed some limited ability to move at night, to find and attack enemy flanks and rear, to use deception by feinting withdrawal or creating clouds of dust to bluff the superior British into pulling back. The effective range of the 47 mm main tank gun against British armor of around 600 meters severely constrained Italian commanders. The *Ariete* armored battalion in the attack tended to make a headlong dash at the enemy at the M13's lamentable cross-country top speed of roughly 13 kilometers per hour, to bring the range down to 400 meters or less before British artillery and tank guns could perforate too many Italian tanks. Closer ranges also made best use of the M13's limited ammunition supply; as in other forms of firefight, the side that ran out first suffered deep embarrassment.[25] The arrival in spring 1942 of FIAT-Ansaldo 75 mm assault guns on an M14 chassis allowed the *Ariete* and the newly arrived *Littorio* division a somewhat wider tactical repertoire, until British deployment of U.S. medium tanks negated that small advantage.

In the desert, even the best Italian infantry was capable only of static defense and was poorly equipped even for that. But in hilly or mountainous terrain, and despite all their deficiencies in cadres and armament, Italian infantry units often fought remarkably well, as demonstrated by

---

24. See the lament of Cavallero after the failed March 1941 counteroffensive in Albania: Knox, *Mussolini*, p. 260, and Montanari, *Grecia*, vol. 1, pp. 656–57, 664, 667–69, 680–83.

25. Quotation: Bastico AAR, February 1943, NARA T-821/9/000226; on *Ariete* tactics, see particularly Oderisio Piscicelli-Taeggi, *Diario di un combattente in Africa settentrionale* (Bari, 1946), pp. 34–42, and Bizzi report, March 1942, in Ceva and Curami, *Meccanizzazione*, vol. 2, pp. 344–45.

their dogged stand at Keren in East Africa throughout February and March 1941, Cavallero's laboriously constructed but ultimately impenetrable "wall" against the Greeks in Albania, and the often excellent performance of improvised Italian units in the final battles in Tunisia. Even in the desert, infantry units such as the paratroops of the *Folgore* and the improvised unit of volunteers that became the *"Giovani Fascisti"* division fought in a manner that inspired German respect.

And the army – for all its manifold faults – at least had a conception of the integration of arms denied to its British adversaries, who as late as El Alamein attempted to funnel two corps – one infantry, one armored – simultaneously through a narrow attack corridor without effective coordination between them.[26] The Italian mobile units that accompanied Rommel in his desert peregrinations learned far more quickly than the British the lesson that armor, artillery, and infantry must function as a team both operationally and tactically. The German example was decisive, but Italian doctrine, precisely because its authors had never heard of the work of the British all-tank theorists, was already predisposed toward integration. Army doctrine inevitably proclaimed the absolute primacy of the infantry, "the decisive element of combat; if it advances, all advance, if it gives way, all give way." But it also stressed the obvious necessity for infantry–artillery cooperation. Armor, which the army saw as a supporting weapon until 1941 and even thereafter, was similarly linked to the infantry.[27] On the battlefield itself, weak communications, inadequate training, and the army's 1914–18 artillery inevitably limited the effectiveness of all-arms cooperation; on the offensive, Italian artillery frequently could not cover or talk to its infantry. Yet the commander of the *Ariete* in its final desperate stand at El Alamein could plausibly claim that Italian artillery, with its emphasis on centralized direction, had in

---

26. On this well-known episode, which reflects so poorly on Montgomery, see the balanced comments of Montanari (*Africa*, 3:832–33).

27. See especially the survey of army doctrine in Montanari, *Alla vigilia*, pp. 252–74 (quotation: p. 262).

Montgomery's set-piece 1918-style battle cooperated with other arms more effectively than had the decentralized German gunners.[28]

The army would also have gladly used close air support: in June–July 1940 its forward units had frantically demanded SM79 sorties to ward off British armored cars. But the failure of the air force and of industry to develop effective ground attack aircraft until 1942 and the absence throughout of voice radio or even of adequate smoke grenade signals and recognition panels linking Italian (but apparently not German) ground units with Italian aircraft overhead made close support of the kind practiced by the RAF for British 8th Army a utopian aspiration.[29]

Finally, the logistical support the army provided to its line units was as inconsistent with tactical success as were its training and tactical methods. Combat units in all theaters, once committed, were perpetually short of fuel, ammunition, water, food, vehicles, weapons, and even manpower. But the army hierarchy was not finished. The troops' rations, even when they arrived, were by universal testimony execrable in quality and notably inferior in quantity to the rations of enemy or ally; they contained even fewer calories than the barely adequate Italian rations of the First World War. The army's mobile kitchens consisted of primitive wood-burning devices dating from 1907–09 that were as unsuited to treeless North Africa or the Russian steppes as they were difficult to load and transport. Armored and motorized units might improvise mess vehicles in imitation of the motorized field kitchens and portable gasoline stoves of their German allies. But Italian infantrymen in their holes in the desert, when they ate at all, ate cold canned goods and hardtack.[30]

The services most vital to troop morale after food – medical care and evacuation, mail delivery, home leave, and rotation out of combat – were

28. Arena AAR, 13 December 1942, NARA T-821/31/000011–12; also (rhetorically) Messe AAR on Enfidaville, 30 April 1943, *Africa*, 4:760, 765.

29. See especially *Africa*, 3:613 (July 1942).

30. Rations: Ceva, *Le forze armate*, p. 269; Botti, "La logistica dei poveri," pp. 432–33; Serra, *Tempi duri*, p. 122; Cavallero, *Diario 1940–1943*, p. 448.

likewise frighteningly deficient. The army began the Greek campaign
with two ambulance platoons in all Albania, although improvised air
evacuation did good service thereafter for wounded who were lucky
enough to reach the airfields alive. Field medical services were ineffectual throughout the war; Italian units in North Africa were perhaps better
at field sanitation than their German allies, but both lived amid clouds of
flies and suffered inordinately from dysentery and hepatitis. The army's
mail service was from the outset wholly inadequate, despite a stream of
complaints from combat units and frequent mention in the morale reports
that the military police drafted for the hierarchy. Leave was infrequent,
and until autumn 1942, despite the German example of tours of duty of
twelve months or less, the *Regio Esercito* required that its enlisted men
serve thirty-four months in North Africa before rotation. The troops
inevitably came to regard themselves, as Bastico put it in early 1943, as
"sentenced to remain 'until consumed.'" They were not wrong.

Issue clothing and personal equipment ranged from the inferior to the
unusable: enlisted uniforms came unsewed and some units received boots
with "cardboard" soles that disintegrated in snow and mud. The war
ministry gratuitously rejected requests from units in Russia for felt *valenki*
to replace the hobnailed alpine boots that invariably caused frostbite. The
troops were also perpetually short of the small items that made the
difference between discomfort and despair: buttons, thread, needles,
razor blades, envelopes, writing paper, postcards, pencils, and rank and
unit badges. Finally, the self-contradictory and almost unimaginably
complex regulations governing unit administration and finance, which
the Italian state and its army had evolved as an ineffectual barrier to
corruption, exacted an enormous cost in wasted energy at company
and battalion level.[31]

31. Medical service, sanitation: De Risio, *Generali, servizi segreti e fascismo*, p. 84;
      Africa, 2:794–95; David Hunt, *A Don at War* (London, 1966), p. 135; for graphic
      description, Doronzo, *Folgore!*; mail: *Africa*, 1:96, 433, 3:996; leave and rotation:
      Africa, 1:433, 3:98, 339–40, 995, 4:574; Bastico AAR, February 1943, NARA

These dysfunctions for the most part derived neither from penury nor from technological backwardness, but rather from the attitudes of the higher officer corps. Roatta, for instance, made light of the accumulation of sixty tons of undelivered troop mail at Bologna in July 1940, ascribing complaints to the "pathological Italian characteristic of insisting on daily news of relatives about whom the average soldier, in normal circumstances, is merrily unconcerned."[32] Mail service did not improve thereafter because the hierarchy was unable to understand that caring for the troops might lead the troops to reciprocate – a concept Roatta might have absorbed during his prewar duty as attaché in Berlin, but had not.[33] The army's lack of cohesion and ultimate disintegration was mysterious primarily to its higher leadership.

The navy's tactics are far less easily understood than that of the army. The sources, perhaps symptomatically, rarely describe tactical concepts or training. Navy personnel selection and command style were nevertheless clearly implicated in the fleet's repeated failures. The 244,129 enlisted and 14,953 officer personnel of 1 August 1943 were an elite in comparative terms, with a high proportion of volunteers. Yet curious figures nevertheless achieved and retained positions of responsibility. Admiral Bruno Brivonesi, whom Cavagnari had allegedly judged unsuitable for command, remained in service with the Duce's acquiescence despite his condemnation by court-martial after an outgunned

T-821/9/000233; "cardboard" soles: testimony in Rex Trye, *Mussolini's Soldiers* (Shrewsbury, 1995), p. 29; disintegrating uniforms: Pricolo, *Ignavia contro eroismo* (Rome, 1946), p. 38; sundries: *Africa*, 4:576; administrative burdens: Botti, "La logistica dei poveri," pp. 425–26; on many of these issues, see also Sullivan, "The Italian Soldier in Combat," pp. 181–82.

32. 4 July entry, Roatta to Graziani, 140, 9 July 1940, ACS, Carte Graziani, bundle 42.

33. *Truppenführung*, paragraph 8: "[The leader] must . . . find the way to the hearts of his subordinates and earn their trust through . . . tireless attention to their welfare."

Malta surface force sank all seven ships in the convoy he was escorting in late 1941. And a submarine commander received accelerated promotion and Italy's highest decoration, the gold medal for valor, after claiming in 1942 that he had torpedoed and sank, on separate occasions, two non-existent U.S. battleships in the Atlantic. His misidentification of two aged cruisers and a corvette – none of which his torpedoes had hit – remained undiscovered until the 1960s.[34]

Command style at the top reflected British aggressiveness on the one hand and the restrictions imposed by *Supermarina* on the other. Successive fleet commanders responded with nerve-wracked passivity. Cavagnari entered the war determined for institutional reasons not to lose ships; that was the root cause of his attempts to control the fleet at sea from Rome. Then the fleet met the British at Punta Stilo, Taranto, and Matapan. Its commanders never recovered: even in the bleak spring of 1942, without battleships or carriers in the eastern Mediterranean, the British maintained their ascendancy in both surface action and submarine warfare.[35]

Supermarina was apparently content. Admiral Angelo Iachino, despite an increasingly apparent lack of resolve and three conspicuously unsuccessful operations after Matapan, remained fleet commander from December 1940 until 1943. In the first such action, Iachino wandered about indecisively with *Littorio* and *Vittorio Veneto* instead of intercepting the British Gibraltar squadron and a Malta resupply convoy in

34. Numbers: USMM, *L'organizzazione*, vol. 2, pp. 364, 346; Brivonesi: Ciano, 11 November 1941 and Greene and Massignani, *Naval War*, pp. 194–96; Giorgerini, *Matapan*, p. 526; for the bizarre case of Enzo Grossi of the *Barberigo* and his imaginary battleships, see Santoni, "The Italian Submarine Campaign," pp. 329–32.

35. See the comments of Admiral Somigli in Ciano, 13 December 1941 ("inferiority complex": English in original); of Ceva and Curami, *Meccanizzazione*, vol. 1, p. 292 ("ascendente psicologico degli ammiragli inglesi sui nostri"); and Giorgerini, *Matapan*, pp. 476 ("Ai vertici di comando ... questo animo [combattivo] non ci fu") and 467–68.

September 1941. He then withdrew swiftly at *Supermarina*'s orders even after the air force correctly reported that one of its aircraft had torpedoed the battleship *Nelson*.[36] In the two battles of the Sirte in December 1941 and March 1942, Iachino actually came within range of inferior British forces escorting convoys, but failed to close. On the second occasion, the admiral knew that the British had neither battleships nor aircraft carriers. Yet Admiral Philip Vian, with only light cruisers and destroyers, held off *Littorio*, two heavy cruisers, a light cruiser, and eight Italian destroyers for a long afternoon, losing not a single ship to Iachino's overwhelming preponderance of force. Lesser Italian admirals, apparently as a result of career rotations decreed by the high command and of the constantly diminishing number of available ships, rarely gained enough sea experience to act with confidence and skill. A unique exception was Admiral Alberto Da Zara, who led a successful light cruiser attack on a British convoy off Pantelleria in June 1942 – until *Supermarina* ordered him to break off and return to port.[37]

The counterpart to irresolution and passivity above was inadequate training below. The German naval attaché had commented in summer 1939 that *Regia Marina* training was "not at the same level as ours; difficult conditions of the kind we deliberately create in combat-type exercises are not sought." The repeated infuriating failures of rangefinding and main gun loading systems during the fleet's few surface actions were not merely technological. They also reflected training the navy had never attempted; the navy staff had assumed combat only occurred in calm weather, and therefore did not discover until 1942 that key electrical systems and rangefinders on its *Littorio*-class battleships had little or no waterproofing. Worse still, fleet units too large for convoy service

36. USMM, *Le azioni navali in Mediterraneo dal 1 aprile 1941 al 8 settembre 1943* (Rome, 1970) reports these events but avoids critical analysis.

37. "Questo amletico ammiraglio," personnel turbulence, Da Zara: Giorgerini, *Matapan*, pp. 495, 487, 525–26; also Greene and Massignani, *Naval War*, pp. 236–38.

normally remained in port after Matapan for lack of fuel and escorts.[38] Only the light forces and submarines proved more aggressive: as one high officer remarked bitterly after 1945, this was a war the admirals had left to the lieutenant commanders.[39] Increasingly severe combat attrition nevertheless inevitably diminished the light units' store of training and skill.

Tactical intelligence and reconnaissance, like that at the operational level, were limited in scope and timeliness. The battle fleet flagship normally carried an on-board decryption team that did good service. But the fleet's close-in tactical reconnaissance with catapulted float-planes and cruiser or destroyer squadrons did not usually provide Iachino or other surface commanders with a clear picture of the enemy. Ship recognition and reporting procedures were frequently inadequate, and unlike its British counterpart, the fleet was not equipped to recover float-planes at sea, which markedly limited their availability when most needed.

The surface tactical system of the fleet rested on the unexamined credo of Tsushima and Jutland: the supremacy of battleship and cruiser long guns at long range, without any of the qualifications introduced in the British, Japanese, and U.S. navies by the advent of naval airpower.[40] The system relied on the combination of arms: cruisers and destroyers acting as advance guards and flank screens, to find the enemy, make smokescreens, or launch diversionary torpedo attacks. But the inaccuracy

38. Löwisch to German navy high command, Nr. G. 1564, 16 August 1939, German Naval Records (NARA T-1022), file PG 33745. The ineptitude of German surface forces, most notably in the *Hipper-Lützow* and *Scharnhorst* fiascos of 1942–43, suggest that even German training failed to create conditions difficult enough. Italian gun system failures: Greene and Massignani, *Naval War*, pp. 151 (Matapan day action), 221–22 (Second Sirte).

39. Admiral Aldo Cocchia, quoted in Giorgerini, *Matapan*, p. 467.

40. It is noteworthy, for instance, that the navy with the most extreme fixation on the decisive exchange of gunfire (as exemplified by the 69,000-ton super-battleships *Yamato* and *Musashi*) should also by 1941 have created the world's largest and most effective carrier striking force.

of the big guns made the system largely useless in combat. And *Supermarina* made little effort either to improve accuracy or to develop a new tactical concept more suited to the battle fleet's weaknesses. Night battle, for which the British had begun to practice from the late 1920s as the Japanese battleship build-up faced them with inferiority at long range, was a possible recourse.[41] But Cavagnari had not only ruled it out doctrinally; he had also ensured that his fleet had neither flashless powder for the big guns nor adequate illumination rounds and night optics. After Matapan, the dawning consciousness that the British had operational radar devices impelled the navy staff to passivity, rather than spurring night, exercises. A second option was one the British had likewise frequently demonstrated, especially with the destroyers in which Sir Andrew Cunningham, who led the Mediterranean Fleet to victory at Punta Stilo, Taranto, and Matapan, had learned tactics: to close the range until it was difficult to miss. That was the method of Da Zara, who pulled off his unique success in the June 1942 action near Pantelleria by closing to under 5,000 meters.

Light units, submarines, and *maiali* were more successful. By late 1941 all had developed tactical systems that offered hope of damaging the enemy. Italian motor torpedo boats, along with their German counterparts, achieved striking night successes against convoys in the Sicily channel in 1942. Italian submariners, although less effective than their German or British counterparts in statistical terms, had learned enough by summer 1942 to make a considerable contribution to the Axis attack on the PEDESTAL convoy. The *maiali*, after a series of initial disasters that risked the loss of technological surprise, slipped past the Alexandria harbor defenses in December 1941 and paid Cunningham back for Taranto.

The convoy battles taxed the navy's tactical flexibility beyond its limit. The mission, despite prewar premonitions of its necessity, was one that

---

41. See Jon Tetsuro Sumida, "The Best Laid Plans: The Development of British Battle-Fleet Tactics, 1919–1942," *International History Review* 14:4 (1992), pp. 661–80; for the Japanese side, Evans and Peattie, *Kaigun*, pp. 250–62.

the navy staff had shunned until the outcome of Punta Stilo suggested that convoys were the least inglorious means of escaping the Duce's insistent pressure for battle. Yet thinking about convoy defense remained as low a priority as sonar (which the Germans first provided in 1941), effective depth-charges, and corvettes. The navy belatedly founded an anti-submarine school in 1941, but anti-submarine tactics – one of the few useful applications of probability theory to warfare – remained rudimentary. Convoy defense against surface forces meant night action, in which the immense superiority in training, experience, and rationally controlled aggressiveness of the British destroyer and cruiser captains were even more decisive than radar and ULTRA. Defending convoys against air attack proved still more difficult than against surface forces and submarines. Italian escorts routinely lacked the anti-aircraft firepower to break up torpedo- or dive-bomber attacks on their merchant vessels. The navy staff eventually commissioned anti-aircraft cruisers on the British pattern, but none were ready before September 1943. And anti-aircraft gun crew training and gunlaying equipment were less effective than that of enemy or ally – a complaint of which Hitler and Dönitz made much in their bid to seize control of the Italian navy in March 1943. The *Regia Marina* put the convoys through by sacrifice, not tactical skill.

Air force tactics are if anything even less well documented than those of the navy. As with the navy, officers and enlisted men were an elite. As with the navy, that fact alone did not guarantee their effectiveness. Pricolo purged the senior ranks of the air staff and ministry upon his appointment in November 1939, but high air force commands thereafter rotated among a restricted circle of generals.[42] Below that level, attrition from the inherent hazards of air transport and combat made possible some renewal in the course of the war. But the air force's system for

---

42. Compare the incumbents of air staff key positions, comandanti di squadra aerea, comandanti di Z.A.T., comandanti aeronautica zonale, and army and navy auxiliary aviation commanders for 1940 with those for 1942 in Arena, *Aeronautica*, vol. 1, pp. 151–58; vol. 3, pp. 18–22.

advanced officer schooling did not prepare its middle ranks to cope with the complexities of interservice cooperation. Nor did the air staff find it easy to fill mid-level command positions, which required flying skill, operational and tactical knowledge, and the ability to inspire others. Pricolo privately lamented in August 1940, after a number of officers had performed poorly in North Africa, that it was "far from easy to ensure that only officers fully up to their tasks receive[d] unit commands."[43]

Finally, the air force had failed to anticipate before the war the enormous combat attrition of crews – as well as of aircraft – that was coming. Its flight training schools, like those of the Luftwaffe, were already by autumn 1940 clearly inadequate to cope with losses unless the pace of operations slowed. By spring 1943, it was clear that the 800–900 pilots and proportionate numbers of crew and specialists the schools had turned out each year had not been anywhere near enough: "the air force, in the space of three years, ha[d] had to consume the greater – and often the best – part of its human capital, and ha[d] worn out the remainder." Between June 1940 and June 1942 the air force trained only 1920 pilots while losing perhaps a thousand.

The quality of training was also far from adequate. Fuel shortages, financial constraints, and a high accident rate bedeviled the initial pilot training course, which did not provide enough flying time to allow graduates to make an easy transition to front-line aircraft and techniques. Nor did the air force perceive until 1941 the need for operational training units where that transition might take place without burdening combat

---

43. Navy: USMM, *L'organizzazione*, vol. 1, pp. 279–80. Air force: Pricolo to Porro (air commander, North Africa), quoted in Knox, *Mussolini*, p. 24; also Felice Porro, "La Quinta Squadra Aerea in Libia (10 giugno 1940–5 febbraio 1941)," *Rivista Aeronautica*, 1948, no. 9, p. 533. Only the *Scuola di Applicazione della Regia Aeronautica* (Florence) provided advanced training for regular (but not reserve) line officers; on the inadequacies of its curriculum, see Arena, *Aeronautica*, vol. 1, p. 109.

units with on-the-job trainees.[44] Even pilots in line units did not fly enough at the outset, especially under adverse climatic conditions, to improve their proficiency; a survey conducted for Pricolo in 1940 determined that only 30 percent of the *Regia Aeronautica*'s 5,000-odd pilots had reached a standard of training the air force leadership judged adequate.

Tactical communications were lamentably inadequate throughout the war. Two-way voice radio was slow to arrive even for bombers, and not until early 1943 did it become standard equipment on Italy's front-line fighters.[45] Up to that point virtually all fighter pilots communicated by hand signals, with at best a receiving set for ground-controlled interception. Despite German help, the air defense radar and communications systems for the peninsula deployed in 1942–43 were little help in warding off RAF and USAAF attacks.

The air force's tactical system was a curious patchwork. Bombers were the dominant arm at the outset, and trained to fight in close defensive formations with simultaneous release of bomb loads on the objective. In combat, these tactics apparently served well in maximizing what little accuracy the primitive Italian bombsights and navigational aids provided.[46] The *Regia Aeronautica* also did not disdain the combination of arms: from the beginning it was less Douhetian than the USAAF. Combat in Spain had taught the need for fighter escort for the bombers.[47] From the first operations against France in 1940, air force commanders therefore attempted wherever possible to provide escorts, although Italian fighters

---

44. Pricolo to Mussolini, September 1940; quotation: Fougier to Ambrosio, 15 April 1943, *Direttive Superaereo*, 1/1:243, 2/2:699; figures: Santoro, *L'aeronautica*, vol. 2, pp. 470, 473 (fuel shortages: pp. 474–76); Arena, *Aeronautica*, vol. 2, pp. 563–67; for similar German difficulties, see Murray, *Luftwaffe*, pp. 254–55, 277–78, 302–3, 312.

45. Arena, *Aeronautica*, 4:635.

46. Santoro, *L'aeronautica*, vol. 2, p. 265, in part quoting British accounts.

47. LTC Bruno Montanari, *Appunti sull'impiego dei mezzi aerei* (Caserta, 1941/42), NARA T-821/461/000188, 000206.

throughout the war lacked the necessary range and firepower. By late 1941 the air force had also discovered the synchronization of level bombers, dive-bombers, and torpedo aircraft.[48]

Yet the air staff apparently placed little stress on surprise. Bomber units attacking well-defended targets such as Alexandria or Malta made little special effort to achieve it, even after the air force belatedly perceived in mid-1941 that the British had air defense radar. Pilots of the fighter-bombers that the air force belatedly acquired were more imaginative. In June 1942 two Re2001s, equipped with specially designed heavy bombs, joined the landing circuit of the British carrier *Victorious* to deliver a "brilliantly conceived and executed attack." Yet as so often in the history of the Italian armed forces, collective inadequacies in research and development cancelled out individual skill and valor. One bomb hit the carrier squarely, but its fuse had been sketchily tested, and it failed to explode.[49]

The tactics of the fighter force, which by 1943 made up two-thirds of the *Regia Aeronautica*'s front-line strength, rested initially on the prowess of the pilot as aerial matador: "*Vista, suerte . . . y al toro*," acquired in Spain, was the Italian equivalent of "tally-ho!" Thereafter the air force's pilots, as Lucio Ceva has put it, "rejected" the monoplane fighter. Low wing loading made the twin-machine-gun wood-and-fabric biplane more maneuverable, more suitable for aerobatic display and individual virtuosity than the soulless and alien aluminum monoplane. No other air force clung so stubbornly to its biplanes; even the Japanese naval fighter pilots, who prized maneuverability as much as their Italian air force counterparts, opted for the monoplane in 1934–37. Ultimately the total inadequacy of the FIAT CR42 biplane against Hurricanes and Spitfires forced change;

48. Peter C. Smith and Edwin Walker, *The Battles of the Malta Striking Forces* (Annapolis, MD, 1974), p. 91; also Santoro, *L'aeronautica*, vol. 2, pp. 380, 382, 391, 403–04.

49. Payne, *Red Duster, White Ensign*, p. 229; Arena, *Aeronautica*, vol. 3, pp. 463, 469–70, 715.

brilliance in aerobatic single combat was largely useless against high-speed formation attacks out of the sun, coordinated with two-way radio, by RAF fighters that possessed enormous advantages in speed, high-altitude performance, and firepower even over the *Regia Aeronautica*'s first monoplanes. The MC202, although undergunned, improved the fighter force's situation upon its arrival in the second half of 1941. But it was not until the first MC205s reached units in early 1943 that the *Regia Aeronautica*'s pilots had a machine capable of executing the tactics long practiced by their enemies and ally.[50]

The air force's support system was as inadequate tactically as it was operationally. Shortage of vehicles for transport of crew, water, fuel and ordnance limited dispersal of aircraft on the fields, and of units to satellite fields.[51] Unit maintenance and supply at the outset are best described by a pilot who deployed to Libya in 1940:

> The aircraft flew primarily because they were brand new, and also because our ground crews made the most unheard-of deals with other units, with mysterious Arab traders, and with the scavengers preying on wrecked Italian and British aircraft. . . . The same thing, the same system of improvisation, was followed for the mess, the aid station, and the other vital necessities of men in the desert. We had high losses; not from the enemy, but from equipment difficulties.[52]

Thereafter, even in Italy, Sicily, and Sardinia, the air force's ground organization and industrial backing proved unequal to the task of maintaining the high sortie rates that tactical as well as operational success required. Repeated shortages of torpedoes limited the effectiveness of the torpedo-bombers in 1941 and after, although the *Comando Supremo* had

50. See particularly Ceva, "Lo sviluppo degli aerei militari in Italia (1938–1940)," *Il Risorgimento* 35:1 (1983), p. 32; on the cult of the "pilot-hero," see also Alberto Rea, *L'Accademia Aeronautica* (Rome, 1977), pp. 134, 146.

51. Porro, "La Quinta Squadra Aerea in Libia," 6:356–57, 8:534.

52. Giuseppe D'Avanzo, *Ali e poltrone* (Rome, 1981), p. 348.

rightly given highest priority to their production. In the great Malta convoy battle of August 1942, the *Regia Aeronautica*'s swan song, it committed 500 torpedo-bombers, bombers, fighters, and reconnaissance aircraft only with extraordinary difficulty. Within six months the adversaries of the Axis had well over 4,000 aircraft operating in the Mediterranean theater alone.

CONCLUSION:
THE WEIGHT OF THE PAST

Most attempts to explain Fascist Italy's disastrous performance in the great war that it sought for twenty years have rested on two assertions and one comparison. The first assertion is that Mussolini and the Fascist regime engineered Italy's humiliation by deliberately creating a mere "facade" of military power. Intervention in June 1940 was in this reading nothing more than a gamble that German victories would dispense Italy from having to fight, and subsequent dissipation of effort allegedly resulted above all from the regime's domestic propaganda requirements. The second assertion is that for the vast majority of Italians the war of 1940–43 was "a war not felt" and therefore lethargically fought. The comparison is inevitably to the Great War, in which the armed forces and government allegedly performed with far greater competence, determination, and rationality, amid far greater elite and popular support for the war and its objectives.[1]

---

1. See most recently Rochat, "L'efficienza dell'esercito italiano nella grande guerra," *Italia contemporanea* 206 (1997), pp. 87–105, who argues (pp. 93–94) that the sole test of military effectiveness in 1914–18 was the ability to tolerate attrition, and that by that test the *Regio Esercito* performed no worse than the armies of allies or enemies.

The first defeats: troops from Italian 10th Army under British guard, Cyrenaica, January 1941 (U.S. National Archives 208-AA-310-P).

It should nevertheless be abundantly clear by this point that the humiliating inadequacy of Italian military performance in 1940–43 had sources far more complex than the alleged primacy of the regime's propaganda, and that those sources were reciprocally interrelated at a variety of levels. Parochialism, fragile military traditions, shortages of key technical skills; energy and raw material dependence; the regime's inability to mobilize effectively what resources existed; the incompetence and venality of industry; the deficiencies in military culture that prevented the armed forces from imagining, much less preparing for modern war; strategic myopia, dissipation of effort, passivity, logistical ineffectiveness, and dependence; and the armed forces' greater or lesser degrees of operational and tactical incapacity were so interwoven that separating them analytically is a thankless task.

Cultural limitations simultaneously affected matters as disparate as the technological and strategic insight of dictator and high command, and the ability of the services to find competent drivers and technicians. The army's defeats from 1848 onward and its failure to recruit and train talented leaders were historically intertwined and mutually reinforcing. The tolerance of armed forces and regime for industry's failures, the "atavistic intellectual narrowness" and astounding inefficiency of the service bureaucracies, and industry's unwillingness or inability to design or produce effective weapons fed upon one another. Such interrelationships are almost infinite in extent and complexity.

Comparisons to performance in the First World War are indeed revealing, although not in the way often supposed. What emerges is not a radical decline in effectiveness from 1918 to 1940 due to the pernicious influence of the Fascist regime that the armed forces had helped to create, but rather a continuity of radical deficiencies in military culture. As in its nine months' grace period in 1939–40, when the Italian army learned virtually nothing from Germany's destruction of Poland, the army had failed between autumn 1914 and May 1915 to draw useful operational or even tactical lessons from the trench fighting on the western front that its attachés closely observed.[2] Hostility to imagination and initiative was pervasive; as Cadorna's staff historical officer lamented to his diary in June 1917,

> We have to confess that the Austrian [tactical system] is a great deal more nimble, more elastic than ours ... the Austrian in his entire conception of warfare is less rigid than we are. It's odd, it may seem impossible, given our constant boasts about Latin geniality, but that's the way it is. [The Austrians] prove it every day ... .[3]

Italy's line units performed to their full potential only once, in the chaotic defensive battles on the Mt Grappa massif in late 1917, when communications breakdown freed the army's by-then experienced division, regimental, and battalion commanders to fight without constant interference from above.[4]

Care for the troops was as lamentable in 1915–18 as in 1940–43. Units languished for months in the mud and excrement of the trenches without rotation. Illness killed almost 30 percent of the roughly 500,000 dead of the *Regio Esercito*'s line units in 1915–18, whereas the German army, despite the privations inflicted by the Allied blockade, held its death rate from illness to under 10 percent. In the view from the trenches,

2. Compare Rochat, "La preparazione dell'esercito italiano nell'inverno 1914–15 in relazione alle informazioni disponibili sulla guerra di posizione," *Il Risorgimento* 13 (February, 1961), pp. 10–32, with Roatta to Servizio Informazioni Militare, 16 September, 16, 8, 19 October 1939, NARA T-821/108/000006–76; the army in 1939 concluded that the Germans had "pushed motorization to excess": Servizio Informazioni Militare, *L'occupazione della Polonia* (Rome, 1939), p. 16.

3. Angelo Gatti, *Caporetto: Dal diario di guerra inedito (maggio-dicembre 1917)*, ed. Alberto Monticone (Bologna, 1964), p. 140; similarly, pp. 154–56.

4. See the detailed comparison between Italian and German doctrine and training in 1914–17 in Mario Silvestri, *Caporetto* (Milan, 1984), pp. 38–111, and Silvestri's analysis of the Grappa fighting, ibid., Chapter 23.

the army hierarchy valued its troops less than its pack animals. Dead mules, noted a junior officer, cost money and therefore required "forms on top of forms, committees of inquiry. When a soldier dies, it's much simpler: a stroke through his name on the roster and a number on the morning report."[5]

Training in 1915–18 was if anything even less adequate than in 1940–43; Italy's company commanders, platoon leaders, squad leaders, and riflemen had learned on the job and perished in the attempt. The Germans and to some extent the Austro-Hungarians had used their specialized assault units as a pattern on which to train the rest of the army, with results seen in Ludendorff's spring 1918 offensives. The *Regio Esercito* designed its *Arditi*, its only units to receive regular live-fire tactical training, solely for swift raids, without the German emphasis on deep penetration as part of an operational design. And the Italian high command employed them not as a model but as a substitute for a line infantry always clumsy in the attack, and increasingly demoralized by repeated failures that resulted from rigid doctrine and ill-conceived operations.[6] Italian industry, despite more effective central direction in 1915–18 than that provided in 1940–43 by the Fascist regime, produced long runs of artillery pieces so poorly designed and sloppily manufactured that the army scrapped them at the end of the war and replaced them with captured enemy guns.[7] Italy's seemingly miraculous

5.   Paolo Caccia-Dominioni, quoted in Piero Melograni, *Storia politica della grande guerra 1915/1918* (Bari, 1969), p. 122, note 116; illness deaths: Virgilio Ilari, *Storia del servizio militare in Italia* (Rome, 1989–91), vol. 2, p. 444, and F. Bumm, ed., *Deutschlands Gesundheitsverhältnisse unter dem Einfluss des Weltkrieges* (Stuttgart, 1928), p. 166.

6.   Compare the story told in Bruce I. Gudmundsson, *Stormtroop Tactics: Innovation in the German Army, 1914–1918* (Westport, CT, 1989), with Rochat, *Gli arditi della Grande Guerra: Origini, battaglie e miti* (Gorizia, rev. ed., 1997), especially pp. 31–32.

7.   See especially Curami, "Commesse belliche," p. 59; Ceva and Curami, "Industria bellica e stato," pp. 326–28.

single-handed defeat of Austria-Hungary in 1917–18 after Russia's collapse derived above all from massive military-economic and financial assistance from the Western powers and from Austria-Hungary's own terminal decline.

The quality and extent of popular support for Italy's "fourth war of independence" in 1915–18 was likewise far from unambiguous. A violent minority below and government and king on high coerced the mass of the nation into a war wholly devoid of the righteous glow that suffused the German, French, and British efforts. The peasantry provided two-thirds of the infantry that suffered nine-tenths of the casualties in a "war of the *signori*" that it fought with resignation at best. Resignation was all the high command, with its distrust of spontaneity and hostility to initiative, desired. Cadorna's in-house expert on combat motivation, Father Agostino Gemelli, celebrated with singular obtuseness the character he ascribed to Italy's peasant soldiers, "crude, ignorant, [and] passive, [who] ... wholly succumbed ... to the influence of military life without rebellion, without resistance."[8] But when resignation was not enough and when cohesion enforced by terror broke down, as during the long retreat after the German-Austrian breakthrough at Caporetto in October 1917, the troops hailed the Pope, who had described the war as a "useless massacre," and in a few cases even cheered the advancing Germans for delivering them from war. The army gave up 294,000 prisoners, of whom only 4,170 were wounded, before rallying and barring the road to Venice and Milan. Yet although a key socialist leader broke with his party's hostility to the war effort and proclaimed that "On Mt Grappa lies the *Patria*," the solidity of both home and fighting fronts remained precarious.

The commitment of Italy's elites was indeed probably greater in 1915–18 than in 1940–43: unlike its Fascist successor the Liberal regime did not declare as a war aim the extirpation of the Italian *borghesia*.[9] But

8. Gemelli, *Il nostro soldato: Saggi di psicologia militare* (Milan, 1917), p. 101.
9. See Knox, *Mussolini*, especially pp. 9–14, 102, 289–90, and *Common Destiny*, Chapters 2–3 and p. 147.

even in the Great War, the warrior passion of that portion of the elite instrumental in ensuring military effectiveness was remarkably slight. The absence of the army regular officer corps from the 1915–18 battle-field registered in an overall death rate among its members of 7.7 percent. That was an *effort du sang* (only the French "blood effort" will serve) hardly more than half that of the general run of Italians mobilized, and less than a third that of Germany's regular officers, of whom a staggering 24.8 percent died in 1914–18.[10] The enormous disparity between the *Regio Esercito*'s disciplinary terrorism in 1915–18 and its virtual renuncia-tion of the firing squad in 1940–43 may be, as often asserted, evidence of burning conviction in the first instance and lack of it in the second. But other explanations are also plausible. Perhaps the army did evolve suffi-ciently after 1919 to see Cadorna's tactical moralism, his ascription of failure solely to cowardice or treason and his savage demands for ever more executions, as militarily unproductive. The initial catastrophes of 1940 and the armed forces' persistent and visible inferiority to enemies and ally thereafter in any event ruled out the conjoined use of ideology and terror as practiced by Nazis and Soviets. That solution was not merely wholly outside the royal officer corps' mental world; it also required for its application leaders consecrated by success – even Cadorna had his victories – within military institutions that retained some shreds of professional self-respect.

The troops themselves in any event did not necessarily show in 1940–43 the readiness to surrender of popular legend. Units in North Africa, Albania, and Russia held together in conditions – usually deriving from the army's logistical inadequacies – that would have caused soldiers of

10. Ilari, *Storia del servizio militare*, vol. 2, pp. 443, 446, and Constantin von Altrock, *Vom Sterben des deutschen Offizierkorps* (Berlin, 2nd rev. ed., 1922), pp. 64, 69. Altrock's figures cover a somewhat longer period (2 August 1914 to 10 January 1919) than Ilari's, but it is worth noting that German regular officers far outdistanced in death not merely their Italian counterparts, but also their own troops, of whom only 15.4 percent died.

the industrial democracies to quail.[11] With the exception of the Albanian retreat of 1940–41, where the disorganization resulting from hasty remobilization and chaotic shipment overseas was decisive, Italian collapse, like that of the French in 1940, normally resulted from surprise envelopment by enemy mobile forces. Graziani's desert débâcle, with its 130,000 prisoners out of a total force of 140–150,000, was nevertheless unique until the *Comando Supremo*'s dissolution and flight delivered over 600,000 prisoners into German hands in September 1943.[12] In Albania, the casualty figures from Mussolini's futile March 1941 offensive suggest that Italian troops were at least as willing to die in doomed frontal assaults as they had been in 1915–18: almost 25,000 casualties from two corps in six days, including 29 percent of the infantry and artillery strength of the lead corps.[13] In their ratio of dead and wounded to prisoners of war – a key indicator of commitment to the fight – Italian forces in North Africa rivaled their German allies from the beginning of the British offensive at El Alamein to the final collapse at Tunis: 1 dead or wounded to every 3.3 prisoners, against 1 dead or wounded to every 3 prisoners for the Germans.[14]

Two factors above all help explain the disparity between Italy's performance in the first and second rounds of the thirty years' war of 1914–45. First, the German Reich – the ally that Mussolini's imperial objectives imposed on Italy – not only lacked the raw materials, industrial capacity,

11. For life in North Africa with the *Ariete* armored division, see the diary of Serra, *Tempi duri*; for Albania, Gian Paolo Melzi d'Eril, *Inverno al caposaldo (Albania 1941)* (Milan, 1970) (my warmest thanks to Lucio Ceva for a copy of this perceptive brief memoir); for the Russian front, see especially Nuto Revelli, *Mai tardi: Diario di un alpino in Russia* (Turin, 1989).

12. Numbers: *Africa*, 1:443 note 5; Schreiber, "Gli internati militari in Germania," in Rainero, ed., *1943*, p. 531.

13. Montanari, *Grecia*, vol. 1, pp. 667, 669–70; see also p. 661.

14. Calculated from *Africa*, 4:550. It seems unlikely that the difference between the two allies is statistically significant.

and strategic insight to seize the world domination to which it aspired. It also proved unable to support its flagging ally in the style of the Western powers in 1915–18. Second, and most important, the war Italy entered in 1940 was more than a mere rematch. The terms of war had changed beyond the ability of Italy's military institutions to follow either materially or culturally. Coal, iron, grain, and loans from beyond Gibraltar had allowed Italy to develop swiftly in 1914/15–18: industrial production had swelled as a proportion of gross domestic product from 24 percent to 30 percent. FIAT had multiplied its vehicle production eightfold and its work force tenfold; an aircraft industry had sprung from nothing to produce 6,500 fighters, bombers, and observation aircraft in 1918 alone. Hydroelectric power generation had doubled. Yet battlefield realities on the Italian front had left intact the army hierarchy's illusion that peasants with rifles and mules were the ultimate weapon of war.[15] And in the ensuing long truce, however rapid its economic growth, Italy had changed more slowly than the external world. By 1940 society and armed forces faced a world revolutionized through the internal combustion engine. German success and French failure in mastering such revolutions was not new; Prussia's railroads had played the role in 1870 of the tank, aircraft, and truck engines that gave Germany its immense initial triumph in 1940. That victory in turn propelled into war, through Mussolini's ideological ambition, a society, regime, and armed forces that lacked the technological insight and organizational skills to compete even with their defeated neighbors.

The contribution to failure of dictator and regime was great, despite the inherited weight of an armed forces and industry stunted by parochialism and prey to institutional autism. Mussolini and his associates helped exacerbate an already pervasive reverence for demography, for the power of the human spirit, and for geopolitical fantasy over machinery. The regime added its own layer of fecklessness and bluster, a hostility

---

15. Sema, "La cultura dell'esercito," rightly stresses that the army's intellectual backwardness long antedated and was independent of Fascism.

to the very economic competition that might have helped it to forge a modern military instrument, and a "timidity in ordering and demanding" born of its compromise nature. Defeat was foreordained. But the full indecorousness of that defeat derived from social and institutional failings far larger than Fascism itself.

CHRONOLOGY

October–November 1914: Benito Mussolini, most prominent revolutionary leader of Italian Socialism, calls for war; the Socialist Party expels him; he founds a newspaper, *Il Popolo d'Italia*, dedicated to agitation for an Italian war against Austria-Hungary and Germany.

24 May 1915: Italy declares war on Austria-Hungary.

24 October 1917: a German and Austro-Hungarian offensive breaks through Italian lines on the Isonzo around Caporetto; in the long retreat the Italian army loses 294,000 prisoners.

November–December 1917: determined Italian resistance on Mt Grappa and along the Piave river halts German and Austro-Hungarian forces short of Venice and Milan.

24 October 1918: Italy's final offensive, later named for the town of Vittorio Veneto, begins as British and Italian forces cross the Piave.

3–4 November 1918: Armistice of Villa Giusti: Italy's victory is total – Austria-Hungary has disintegrated.

28 October 1922: King Victor Emmanuel III designates Mussolini as prime minister.

3 January 1925: Mussolini, with royal and military support, announces the silencing of the opposition and the imposition of dictatorship.

30 January 1933: Adolf Hitler becomes chancellor of Germany.

25 July 1934: Nazi Putsch in Vienna; murder of Engelbert Dollfuss, chancellor of Austria and Mussolini client; Italo-German estrangement.

7 January 1935: Mussolini and Pierre Laval, foreign minister of France, sign the Rome Agreements, which include an implicit understanding that France will not oppose Italy in Ethiopia.

3 October 1935: Italian forces attack Ethiopia.

6 January 1936: Mussolini suggests to the German ambassador that Germany make Austria "a German satellite."

9 May 1936: after Italian forces capture Addis Ababa, Mussolini proclaims the annexation of Ethiopia.

July–August 1936: Italy and Germany intervene against the Spanish Republic in the civil war launched by General Francisco Franco.

24 October 1936: Galeazzo Ciano, Mussolini's son-in-law and new foreign minister, visits Hitler at Berchtesgaden.

1 November 1936: Mussolini, in a speech in Milan, announces the existence of an "axis" between Rome and Berlin.

6 November 1937: Italy joins the German-Japanese "Anticomintern Pact," in reality directed against the Western powers.

11–13 March 1938: *Anschluss*. German occupies and annexes Austria.

3–9 May 1938: Hitler visits Rome, Naples, and Florence.

August–30 September 1938: the Czechoslovak crisis, provoked by Germany, leads to the Munich agreement; Germany gains the Czech border areas.

15 March 1939: Hitler seizes Prague, destroying the Munich agreement; Slovakia becomes a German satellite.

7 April 1939: Italy seizes Albania.

22 May 1939: Ciano and Ribbentrop sign the "Pact of Steel."

31 May 1939: Mussolini sends General Ugo Cavallero to Berlin bearing a memorandum expressing the view that Italy and Germany should delay the "inevitable" war with the Western powers until 1942–43; Hitler offers vague reassurances.

11–13 August 1939: Hitler informs Ciano that he intends war with Poland.

23–24 August 1939: the German-Soviet Pact divides Poland and Eastern Europe into German and Soviet spheres.

25 August 1939: Mussolini informs Germany that he cannot fight at present unless Germany provides 18 million metric tons of strategic raw materials as well as arms and munitions.

1 September 1939: Germany invades Poland; Italy declares its "nonbelligerence."

3 September 1939: Britain and France declare war on Germany.

7–8 February 1940: Mussolini refuses to sell war materiel to Britain.

1 March 1940: Britain halts German seaborne coal exports to Italy.

10–11 March 1940: Ribbentrop conveys to Rome Hitler's offer to meet Italy's coal needs.

13 March 1940: Italo-German coal agreement: Italy to receive one million tons per month (its full import requirement) from Germany by rail, bypassing the British blockade.

9 April 1940: Germany invades Denmark and Norway.

10 May 1940: Germany invades Belgium, the Netherlands, and France.

20 May 1940: German armored forces reach the Channel at Abbeville, cutting off the bulk of the French and British armies.

26 May–2 June 1940: the Royal Navy evacuates the British Expeditionary Force from Dunkirk.

10 June 1940: Italy declares war on Britain and France.

11 June 1940: RAF bombardment of Turin.

14 June 1940: Paris falls to German forces; French cruisers shell Genoa with impunity.

20–21 June 1940: abortive Italian offensive in the French Alps begins.

22–25 June 1940: Franco-German and Franco-Italian armistices.

3 July 1940: Churchill determines to hold the Mediterranean, despite Admiralty advice to the contrary; on order from London, the Royal Navy safeguards the North Atlantic naval balance with an attack on the French fleet at Mers-el-Kébir that sinks one battleship and cripples two more. The Italian navy fails to intervene.

4 July 1940: Italian forces occupy Kassala and Gallabat in the Sudan.

9 July 1940: fleet action off Calabria/Punta Stilo: Italian forces withdraw in disorder after the battleship *Warspite*, flagship of

Admiral Sir Andrew Cunningham of the Mediterranean Fleet, hits the *Cesare* at a range of 26 kilometers.

19 July 1940: battle of Capo Spada (western Crete): the Australian light cruiser *Sydney* and British destroyers sink the light cruiser *Colleoni* and drive off the *Bande Nere*.

3 August 1940: Italian forces invade British Somaliland; massively outnumbered, British forces withdraw by sea on 16–19 August.

15 August 1940: an Italian submarine torpedoes the obsolete Greek cruiser *Helli* in harbor without provocation or warning; Italian contingency planners are already considering an attack on Greece from Albania.

16 August 1940: RAF air raids on Turin and Milan.

August–September 1940: Battle of Britain; Germany fails to gain the air superiority required for cross-Channel invasion.

13 September 1940: after much prodding by Mussolini, Italian forces under Marshal Rodolfo Graziani invade Egypt and halt (18 September) at Sidi el Barrani, 80 kilometers inside the border.

27 September 1940: Germany, Italy, and Japan sign the Tripartite Pact ("Axis Alliance") in Berlin.

4 October 1940: Mussolini and Hitler meet at the Brenner; Hitler offers *Wehrmacht* units to spearhead Italy's drive on Egypt; Mussolini accepts German help in principle only for the final advance toward the Nile delta.

9–12 October 1940: powerful German forces enter Romania to secure the oilfields for Germany.

15 October 1940: Mussolini, in conference with his military advisers, orders the attack on Greece from Albania.

28 October 1940: Italy invades Greece; Hitler and Mussolini meet at Florence.

4 November 1940–January 1941: Greek counteroffensives drive the Italians back into Albania.

11–12 November 1940: British carrier aircraft sink the battleships *Cavour*, *Duilio*, and *Littorio* in Taranto harbor; *Cavour*, although refloated, is out of the war.

20–24 November 1940: Hungary, Romania, and Slovakia join the Tripartite Pact.

27 November 1940: naval encounter off Sardinia; despite superiority in battleships over the British Gibraltar squadron, Admiral Inigo Campioni breaks off action.

6 December 1940: Marshal Badoglio resigns as chief of general staff. Mussolini has already dispatched his successor, General Ugo Cavallero, to Albania to master the crisis there; General Alfredo Guzzoni, Cavallero's new deputy, serves as de facto chief of the high command until May 1941.

9 December 1940: Mussolini dismisses Admiral Domenico Cavagnari as navy chief of staff and Campioni as fleet commander; their replacements are Admirals Arturo Riccardi and Angelo Iachino.

9 December 1940–February 1941: the first British North African counter-offensive takes Cyrenaica and 130,000 Italian prisoners.

14 December 1940: RAF bombers from Malta severely damage the heavy cruiser *Pola* at Naples.

18 December 1940: Hitler secretly issues Führer Directive 21, Operation BARBAROSSA, for "the overthrow of Soviet Russia in a swift campaign even before the end of the war with England."

27 December 1940–9 January 1941: the Luftwaffe's X *Fliegerkorps* establishes itself at bases in Sicily, in the first of a series of German measures aimed at preventing Italian collapse.

8 January 1941: an RAF raid on Naples damages the battleship *Cesare*.

10 January 1941: X *Fliegerkorps* aircraft severely damage the British aircraft carrier *Illustrious* near Malta.

17 January 1941: Mussolini announces the mobilization of most senior figures of government and Fascist Party, including Ciano and Grandi, and assigns them to units in the Albanian theater in an eccentric effort to prove that the regime shares the risks and privations of the troops.

19 January 1941: British offensive against Italian East Africa begins, retaking Kassala.

19–21 January 1941: Mussolini visits Hitler at Berchtesgaden, and agrees to further German aid for Italy in the Mediterranean and North Africa.

29 January–27 March 1941: U.S.-British staff talks in Washington ("ABC-1") establish the fundamental principle of Anglo-American strategy: "Germany First"; in practical terms, given German invulnerability in northwest Europe until the U.S. Army is combat-ready and the Luftwaffe broken, the Anglo-American decision means "Italy First."

4–10 February 1941: Italian forces hold the British advance into Eritrea at Keren with a stiff defense and numerous counterattacks.

7 February 1941: the last remnants of Italian 10th Army, the force that had invaded Egypt, surrender at Beda Fomm.

9 February 1941: the British North African advance ends at El Agheila, on the border of Tripolitania, although the remaining Italian forces around Tripoli are incapable of offering serious resistance.

9 February 1941: the British Gibraltar squadron bombards Genoa without provoking significant Italian retaliation.

12 February 1941: General Italo Gariboldi replaces Marshal Graziani as theater commander; General Erwin Rommel, commander of the German expeditionary force later designated *Africa Korps*, arrives in Tripoli.

20 February 1941: British and German forces meet for the first time in the Libyan desert.

1–2 March 1941: Bulgaria joins the Tripartite Pact; German forces cross the Danube into Bulgaria on their way toward the Greek border.

7 March 1941: British ground troops begin landing in Greece.

9–14 March 1941: a major Italian offensive, demanded by Mussolini and planned by Cavallero, fails to break the Greek defenses in Albania.

11 March 1941: the U.S. Congress approves the Lend-Lease Bill, providing military-economic aid to Britain and all powers fighting the Axis.

24 March 1941: Rommel, against the express wishes of the German army staff, begins the first Axis offensive in North Africa; by 10–11 April

German and Italian forces have laid siege to Tobruk, the key port in eastern Cyrenaica.

25 March 1941: the Yugoslav government signs the Tripartite Pact in Vienna.

27 March 1941: a Serb coup removes the Yugoslav government; Hitler resolves to smash Yugoslavia.

27 March 1941: British forces finally break through the Italian defenses at Keren in Eritrea.

28 March 1941: battle of Cape Matapan: British Mediterranean forces under Admiral Cunningham damage *Vittorio Veneto* with an aerial torpedo, then sink the heavy cruisers *Pola*, *Fiume*, and *Zara* with gunfire in a night action.

6 April 1941: Germany bombs Belgrade and invades Yugoslavia and Greece; Addis Ababa falls to British troops.

11 April 1941: Italian 2nd Army under General Vittorio Ambrosio begins a hesitant advance from Trieste into Slovenia and southward along the Dalmatian Coast.

17 April 1941: Yugoslavia surrenders.

20 April 1941: Greek forces facing the Italians in northwest Greece surrender to *SS-Leibstandarte* Adolf Hitler.

29 April 1941: the last British troops evacuate the Greek mainland.

30 April–4 May 1941: a large-scale German attack on Tobruk fails to break the stalemate.

March–August 1941: Italian air force torpedo-bombers at last become operational in appreciable numbers.

6–12 May 1941: a British fast convoy forces the Sicily narrows and delivers tanks and Hurricane fighters to Egypt.

19 May 1941: the main Italian forces in East Africa under the Duke of Aosta surrender at Amba Alagi.

20 May–1 June 1941: German airborne invasion and conquest of Crete.

15–17 June 1941: Rommel handily defeats a British counteroffensive, Operation BATTLEAXE, aimed at relieving Tobruk.

22 June 1941: BARBAROSSA begins: Germany invades Soviet Russia.

12 July 1941: General Ettore Bastico replaces Gariboldi as Axis theater commander in North Africa.

21–27 July 1941: Operation SUBSTANCE, a major convoy operation, resupplies Malta.

26 July–1 August 1941: Americans, British and Dutch freeze Japanese foreign assets and cut off all petroleum supplies to Japan.

9–12 August 1941: Roosevelt and Churchill meet off Newfoundland; the resulting "Atlantic Charter" war aims statement is published on 14 August.

24–25 August 1941: the British Gibraltar squadron attacks Italian bases; *Vittorio Veneto* and *Littorio* sortie but fail to find the enemy.

6 September 1941: Japan decides in principle to go to war with the United States and Britain unless an (improbable) diplomatic solution is reached by early October.

24 September 1941: the first German U-boat enters the Mediterranean.

24–30 September 1941: Operation HALBERD, a major resupply of Malta; Admiral Iachino takes the Italian fleet to sea but fails to close with the British fleet or convoy.

September–November 1941: German preparations for industrialized mass killing of Jews and others in occupied Poland and Soviet Russia (the "Final Solution of the Jewish Question").

September 1941: British forces sink 28 percent of all supply tonnage bound for Libya.

2 October 1941: Operation TAIFUN, the final German drive on Moscow, begins.

October 1941: British forces sink 20 percent of all supply tonnage bound for Libya.

November 1941: British forces sink 62 percent of all supply tonnage bound for Libya.

8–9 November 1941: British light cruisers and destroyers based on Malta ("Force K") sink an entire Italian convoy of seven ships in a night action; the Italian support force under Admiral Bruno Brivonesi fails to engage effectively.

12–14 November 1941: additional Hurricanes flown to Malta; U-boats sink the British carrier *Ark Royal*.

18 November 1941–6 January 1942: Operation CRUSADER, the second major British offensive in North Africa, once more drives Axis forces back to Tripolitania.

25 November 1941: a U-boat sinks the British battleship *Barham* off Cyrenaica.

27–28 November 1941: Italy's last forces in East Africa surrender at Gondar.

30 November 1941: the Italian navy, faced with defeat in the North African convoy war, mounts the first "battleship convoy."

December 1941: the United States secretly decides to undertake an industrial-scale nuclear reactor and weapons project.

2 December 1941: Hitler orders *Luftflotte* 2 (Field Marshal Albert Kesselring) from Russia to the Mediterranean to master the convoy crisis.

6–11 December 1941: strategic turning-point of the war:

  6 December: Soviet counteroffensive around Moscow begins.

  7 December: Japan attacks the United States (Pearl Harbor, Luzon) and Britain (Malaya, Hong Kong).

  11 December: Germany and Italy declare war on the United States.

8 December 1941: Germany begins mass killings of Jews using gas.

10 December 1941: Japanese naval aircraft based on southern Indochina sink the battleships *Prince of Wales* and *Repulse*.

12–13 December 1941: night action off Tunisia: British destroyers meet and destroy two Italian light cruisers (*Da Barbiano, Di Giussano*) loaded with fuel for Tripoli.

13 December 1941: the Italian command cancels the second battleship convoy to Libya when British submarines torpedo two merchant ships and *Vittorio Veneto*.

16–17 December 1941: third Italian battleship convoy, and First Battle of the Sirte: Admiral Iachino, with battleships *Littorio, Cesare*, and *Doria*, fails to catch British cruiser forces under Admiral Philip Vian.

18 December 1941: Italian frogmen, operating *maiali*, sink the battleships *Valiant* and *Queen Elizabeth* in the shallow waters of Alexandria harbor; the same night, German deep-water contact mines laid by Italian cruisers cripple Force K.

December 1941: British forces sink only 18 percent of all supply tonnage bound for Libya: the Axis supply crisis is temporarily over.

20 January 1942: the "Wannsee Conference" (Berlin) establishes the bureaucratic framework for the deportation and murder of the Jews of Western and Central Europe.

21 January–4 February 1942: the second major Axis offensive in North Africa drives British forces back to the Gazala line west of Tobruk.

February–May 1942: the Luftwaffe's bombardment of Malta reaches its peak – then Germany returns the Luftwaffe forces to Russia or sends them eastward to support Rommel's drive on Egypt.

6 March 1942: the first Spitfire fighters reach Malta.

22 March 1942: Second Battle of the Sirte: Vian, with light cruisers and destroyers and a Malta convoy to protect, holds off *Littorio*, two heavy cruisers, a light cruiser, and eight destroyers.

20 April 1942: the U.S. carrier *Wasp*, operating from Gibraltar, launches Spitfires to reinforce Malta.

29 April–2 May 1942: Mussolini, Ciano, and Cavallero meet Hitler and Field Marshal Wilhelm Keitel at Klessheim, near Salzburg; the Germans decide to seize Tobruk before attempting the Malta landing (Operation C3/HERKULES).

9 May 1942: *Wasp* and *Eagle* launch further Spitfires to reinforce Malta.

26 May–7 July 1942: the third major Axis offensive in North Africa drives British 8th Army back to Tobruk, which falls on 20–21 June. Rommel hijacks Axis strategy and strikes eastward toward Alexandria, preempting any possibility of mounting the Malta operation. 8th Army ultimately halts Rommel at El Alamein, the last defensive position covering the Nile delta.

4–7 June 1942: Battle of Midway: the outnumbered U.S. Navy, exploiting its mastery of signals intelligence, smashes Japan's carrier striking force.

11–16 June 1942: Operations HARPOON and VIGOROUS (*"la battaglia di mezzo giugno"*) aim at resupplying Malta; Axis air forces, torpedo boats, submarines, and surface forces largely prevail, although a British submarine sinks the heavy cruiser *Trento*.

28 June 1942: Operation BLAU, the second great German offensive on the eastern front, begins; its objective is to seize the Caucasus oilfields and drive Soviet Russia from the war.

15–17, 21–22, and 27 July 1942: the first British counterattacks at El Alamein fail, but inflict severe losses on Axis forces.

11–13 August 1942: Operation PEDESTAL (*"la battaglia di mezzo agosto"*), the last great Malta convoy battle: a U-boat sinks the carrier *Eagle*, Italian torpedo boats attack the convoy with success, and only five merchant ships reach Malta. But one is a tanker with fuel for the island's striking forces.

31 August–4 September 1942: Battle of Alam Halfa: Rommel's final attempt to break the El Alamein defenses fails disastrously.

September 1942: Hitler's armies fail to take Stalingrad or the main Caucasus oilfields.

October 1942: heavy RAF bombardments of Genoa, Milan, and Turin.

23 October 1942: Montgomery, after accumulating a greater than 2:1 superiority in men, armored vehicles, and aircraft, launches a major counteroffensive at El Alamein.

4 November 1942: British forces break through at El Alamein; the Axis retreat to Tunisia begins; *Ariete*, *Trieste*, *Littorio*, and *Folgore* are largely destroyed.

8 November 1942: Operation TORCH: Anglo-American landings seize Morocco, Algeria, and control of the western Mediterranean.

9 November 1942: German forces begin landing by air in Tunisia.

11 November 1942: Germany and Italy occupy Vichy France.

19 November 1942: the Soviet counteroffensive around Stalingrad begins.

23 November 1942: the last Axis troops leave Cyrenaica.

December 1942: heavy RAF and USAAF bombardments of Naples, Palermo, and Taranto.

2 December 1942: the United States achieves the first man-made self-sustaining fission reaction at the University of Chicago.

4 December 1942: the first attack by the USAAF on the Italian mainland sinks the light cruiser *Attendolo* and damages the *Montecuccoli* in Naples harbor.

16–19 December 1942: the second phase of the Soviet counteroffensive around Stalingrad destroys Italian 8th Army.

18–19 December 1942: Ciano and Cavallero meet with Hitler at his eastern headquarters; Hitler insists that the Axis must fight on in Tunisia in order to deny the Mediterranean to the British and Americans.

14–24 January 1943: Churchill and Roosevelt meet at Casablanca and announce that they will force the Axis powers to surrender unconditionally.

30 January 1943: Mussolini dismisses Cavallero; Ambrosio becomes Fascist Italy's last chief of general staff.

31 January–3 February 1943: Italy decolonizes: the last Italian troops leave Libya; Bastico hands over the North African theater command to Rommel.

2 February 1943: final surrender of the Stalingrad pocket.

5 February 1943: Mussolini dismisses Ciano as foreign minister and assumes the position himself.

20 February 1943: General Giovanni Messe takes command of Italian 1st Army, controlling Italian and some German units in southeastern Tunisia.

February–April 1943: strikes in Turin, Milan, and elsewhere in north Italy expose the fragility of the Fascist regime.

14–15 March 1943: Hitler sends Admiral Karl Dönitz, commander-in-chief of the German navy, to Italy with instructions to impose German advisers and techniques on his Italian counterparts.

20–26 March 1943: British/New Zealand attacks on the Mareth line, held by Messe; he is ordered to retreat when U.S. forces under General George S. Patton threaten from the west.

4 April 1943: the Hungarian prime minister, Miklós Kállay, visits Rome and entreats Mussolini to persuade Hitler to make peace with Stalin.

7–10 April 1943: Mussolini, Ambrosio, and Bastianini (undersecretary for foreign affairs) meet Hitler at Klessheim; Hitler is adamant about continuing the war against Russia; German promises of further aid to Italy do not meet Italian needs and expectations.

10 April 1943: USAAF bombers sink the heavy cruiser *Trieste* off La Maddalena.

18–19 April 1943: Anglo-American "turkey shoot" of Axis air transports bound for Tunisia; further resupply becomes impossible.

13 May 1943: Marshal Messe surrenders the last Axis forces in Tunisia.

11 June 1943: the strong and well-fortified Italian garrison of Pantelleria, off Sicily, surrenders after Anglo-American bombardment, but before ground forces can land.

1 July 1943: Mihai Antonescu, the Romanian foreign minister, meets Mussolini in Rome and pleads with him to lead a bid by Germany's allies to leave the war; Mussolini is evasive.

5–12 July 1943: the German offensive around Kursk fails with heavy loss; the operational initiative in the East passes definitively to Soviet Russia.

10 July 1943: the Anglo-American invasion of Sicily begins.

19 July 1943: Mussolini meets Hitler at Feltre, and fails to make clear that Italy must leave the war; the USAAF commits over 500 bombers to a destructive daylight raid on Rome.

24–25 July 1943: after the Grand Council of Fascism, by majority vote, urges Mussolini to give up command of the armed forces, King Victor Emmanuel III dismisses Mussolini as prime minister and arrests him.

26 July 1943: Marshal Badoglio, head of the new government, announces that "the war continues"; Hitler orders intensified preparations to crush Italy before it can defect.

August 1943: intense Anglo-American air bombardment of Naples, Rome, Milan, Turin, Genoa, and Italian airfields, ports, and railroad facilities.

31 July–2 August 1943: The Badoglio government secretly decides to seek an armistice; the new foreign minister, Raffaele Guariglia, orders an approach to the British and Americans in Lisbon.

6 August 1943: Ribbentrop and Keitel meet with Guariglia and Ambrosio at Tarvisio on the Austrian border to exchange recriminations; Guariglia stresses that Italy has not approached the Western powers.

12 August 1943: Ambrosio sends his own representative, General Giuseppe Castellano, to approach the British and Americans in Lisbon.

19 August 1943: talks begin in Lisbon between Castellano and General Walter Bedell Smith, chief of staff to General Dwight D. Eisenhower, Anglo-American commander-in-chief in the Mediterranean.

31 August 1943: Castellano, having returned to Rome to report, flies to Sicily and is given Eisenhower's terms for Italy's surrender.

3 September 1943: Castellano, with Badoglio's authorization, secretly signs the "short armistice" in Sicily. British forces cross the Messina strait; Badoglio, in Rome, tells the German chargé d'affaires "we will fight [on] and never capitulate."

8–9 September 1943: Eisenhower announces the Italian armistice; Italy surrenders unconditionally; U.S. and British forces land at Salerno and Taranto. German forces seize Rome and disband the Italian armed forces in Italy, Southern France, and the Balkans against ineffectual resistance.

10 September 1943: the Italian fleet, minus some smaller units and the battleship *Roma*, sunk by a German glider bomb, surrenders at Malta to the British.

12 September 1943: German paratroops rescue Mussolini from the Badoglio forces and fly him to Munich.

27 September 1943: Mussolini constitutes in northern Italy the "Italian Social Republic" (RSI), a Fascist regime without the monarchy. In practice the German army and SS wield supreme authority throughout the RSI's ostensible territories, and – along with a variety of Fascist private armies – visit barbaric reprisals upon the

Italian civilian population while seeking to deport Italy's Jews to Auschwitz.

13 October 1943: the Italian monarchy and its government, from its provisional capital at Brindisi, declares war on Germany, proclaiming its "cobelligerence" alongside the Western powers and Soviet Russia.

8–11 January 1944: the RSI tries and shoots Galeazzo Ciano and other Fascist leaders who voted against Mussolini on 24–25 July 1943.

11–17 May 1944: U.S., Polish, British, and French North African forces finally break down and bypass the German defensive line anchored on Monte Cassino, which has held the Western powers since November–December.

4 June 1944: U.S. forces enter Rome.

6 June 1944: Operation OVERLORD: U.S.-British-Canadian landings in Normandy.

20 July 1944: failed assassination of Hitler by dissident officers; by chance Mussolini arrives at Führer Headquarters the same day, in time to congratulate Hitler on his seemingly providential escape.

25 August 1944: Paris falls to U.S. and French forces.

27–28 April 1945: Communist partisans capture Mussolini, shoot him "in the name of the Italian people," and exhibit his body and those of his entourage in central Milan.

29 April 1945: German forces in Italy surrender to the Americans and British.

30 April 1945: Hitler commits suicide in Berlin.

7–9 May 1945: Germany surrenders unconditionally to the Western powers and Soviet Russia.

BIBLIOGRAPHICAL NOTE

Despite a fifty years' undergrowth of memoirs and popular accounts, Fascist Italy at war remains poorly understood in comparison with its German ally. The best short introductions are Lucio Ceva, "Italy," in I. C. B. Dear and M. R. D. Foot, eds., *The Oxford Companion to the Second World War* (Oxford, 1995), pp. 580–603, and the relevant chapters of Ceva's *Le forze armate* (Turin, 1981). Among the few narrative histories, Giorgio Bocca, *Storia d'Italia nella guerra fascista* (Milan, 1969), still stands out. MacGregor Knox, *Mussolini Unleashed, 1939–1941: Politics and Strategy in Fascist Italy's Last War* (Cambridge, 1982), Ceva's *La condotta italiana della guerra: Cavallero e il Comando Supremo 1941/1942* (Milan, 1975), and Sir William Deakin, *The Brutal Friendship. Mussolini, Hitler and the Fall of Italian Fascism* (London, 1962), if read in sequence, offer an approximation of continuous coverage of warfare, high politics, and the German alliance. The anniversary conference works covering each successive year of the war, edited by Romain H. Rainero and Antonello Biagini, *L'Italia in guerra* (Rome and Gaeta, 1991–96), contain contributions uneven in quality but offering a useful cross-section of recent work. Finally, three diaries, by Galeazzo Ciano (*Diario 1937–1943* [Milan, 1980], also available in dated and inept English translations), Giuseppe Bottai (*Diario 1935–1944*, ed. Giordano Bruno Guerri [Milan, 1982]), and the industrialist Alberto Pirelli (*Taccuini 1922/1943* [Bologna, 1984]), offer striking insights into the thinking of dictator and inner circle.

For the internal politics of the regime and its process of collapse in 1942–43, Deakin's inimitable *The Brutal Friendship* is still vital. Readers with Italian may profitably consult the chapters on internal affairs of the late Renzo De Felice's gigantic *Mussolini l'alleato*, vol. 1, *L'Italia in guerra 1940–1943* (Turin, 1990), despite De Felice's bizarre interpretation of Fascist diplomacy and strategy, and his even odder reverence for Mussolini's devious associate and rival Dino Grandi.

The chief administrator of the war economy, Carlo Favagrossa, conveys his self-exculpation in his memoir title: "Why We Lost the War: Mussolini and War Production" (*Perché perdemmo la guerra: Mussolini e la produzione bellica* [Milan, 1946]). Umberto Spigo, *Premesse tecniche della disfatta* (Rome, 1945), another inside account, is more dispassionate. Angela Raspin, *The Italian War Economy, 1940–1943* (New York, 1986), ably surveys the older literature. Vera Zamagni, "Un'analisi macroeconomica degli effetti della guerra," in Zamagni, ed., *Come perdere la guerra e vincere la pace: L'economia italiana tra guerra e dopoguerra 1938–1947* (Bologna, 1997), pp. 13–54 (for an English version, with slightly different data, see Mark Harrison, ed., *The Economics of World War II* [Cambridge, 1998], pp. 177–221) provides fresh gross domestic product and war production data, along with eloquent commentary. Massimo Legnani, "Sul finanziamento della guerra fascista," in Gaetano Grassi and Legnani, eds., *L'Italia nella seconda guerra mondiale e nella Resistenza* (Milan, 1988), pp. 283–306 and Giuseppe Maione, *L'imperialismo straccione: classi sociali e finanza di guerra dall'impresa etiopica al conflitto mondiale (1935–1943)* (Bologna, 1979), tell the sorry tale of Fascist war finance. Fortunato Minniti, "Aspetti organizzativi del controllo sulla produzione bellica in Italia," *Clio*, 4/1977, pp. 305–40, well describes the administrative incoherence of the war economy.

On industry, Lucio Ceva and Andrea Curami, *Industria bellica anni trenta* (Milan, 1992) and *La meccanizzazione dell'esercito italiano dalle origini al 1943*, 2 vols. (Rome, 1989), are fundamental, although confined primarily to the deeds and misdeeds of the Ansaldo combine and its military interlocutors. Ceva's "Grande industria e guerra," and Curami's "Commesse belliche e approvvigionamenti di materie prime," in Rainero and Biagini, eds., *L'Italia in guerra: il primo anno – 1940* (Rome, 1991), pp. 33–53, 55–66, neatly summarize their authors' incisive and innovative analysis of the relationships between industry, armed forces, and regime.

A good starting point for understanding both the armed forces as a whole and the high command are Brian R. Sullivan, "The Italian Armed Forces, 1918–40," in Allan R. Millett and Williamson Murray, eds., *Military Effectiveness*, vol. 2, *The Interwar Period* (Boston, 1988), pp. 169–217; "The Italian Soldier in Combat, June 1940–September 1943: Myths, Realities and Explanations," in Paul Addison and Angus Calder, eds., *Time to Kill: The Soldier's Experience of War in the West, 1939–1945* (London, 1997), pp. 177–205; and "A Thirst for Glory: Mussolini, the Italian Military, and the Fascist Regime, 1922–1936" (dissertation, Columbia University, 1984). Biagini and Alessandro Gionfrida, eds., *Lo Stato Maggiore Generale tra le due guerre (verbali delle riunioni presiedute da Badoglio dal 1925 al 1937)* (Rome, 1997), and Biagini and Fernando Frattolillo, eds., *Verbali delle riunioni tenute dal capo di Stato Maggiore Generale*, 4 vols. (Rome, 1983–85), provide a more or less continuous, if hardly all-inclusive, set of minutes of meetings of the chiefs of staff and other key figures from 1925 to 1943. The *Diario storico del Comando Supremo* (Biagini and Frattolillo, eds., 5 vols. in 2 parts, through 31 December 1941 to date) (Rome, 1986–) is largely routine, but contains occasional nuggets despite the editors' unimaginative selection from the war diary's many appended documents, which are fortunately also available in part from the NARA T-821 microfilms. The two editions of Cavallero's private war diary and its document appendices, *Comando Supremo* (Bologna, 1948) and *Diario 1940–1943*, ed. Giovanni Bucciante (Rome, 1984), are more vital than the official diary, although drastically foreshortened for publication and intercut confusedly with the appended documents in the chaotic Bucciante edition, which should always be read in conjunction with the relevant volumes of *Verbali delle riunioni tenute dal capo di Stato Maggiore Generale*. Finally, Francesco Mattesini and Mario Cermelli, eds., *Le direttive tecnico-operative di Superaereo*, 2 vols. in 2 parts (Rome, 1992), offer much evidence on the high command in their exemplary collection of high-level air force documents.

Virgilio Ilari, *Storia del servizio militare in Italia*, 4 vols. (Rome, 1989–91); Giorgio Rochat, "Gli uomini alle armi 1940–1943," in his *L'esercito italiano in pace e in guerra* (Milan, 1991), pp. 262–304, and his "Una ricerca impossibile: Le perdite italiane nella seconda guerra mondiale," *Italia contemporanea* 201 (1995), pp. 687–700; and Dorello Ferrari, "La mobilitazione dell'esercito nella seconda guerra mondiale," *Storia contemporanea* 18:6 (1992), pp. 1001–46, ably assemble the fragmentary evidence on manpower mobilization and losses.

For the strategic issues, Klaus Schmider, "The Mediterranean in 1940–1941: Crossroads of Lost Opportunities?," *War and Society* (Australia) 15:2 (1997), pp. 19–41, eloquently fleshes out Andreas Hillgruber's thesis, advanced in *Hitlers Strategie: Politik und Kriegführung 1940–41* (Frankfurt a. M., 1965), of the global quasi-irrelevance of the Mediterranean theater. Knox, *Mussolini Unleashed*; Ceva, *La condotta italiana della guerra*; and the four massive volumes of General Mario Montanari's masterly history of the war in North Africa, *Le operazioni in Africa Settentrionale* (Rome, 1984–93), offer detailed coverage of Italian strategic decision making to spring 1943. They should be read in conjunction with the chiefs of staff minutes, *Comando Supremo* and Cavallero diaries, and similar sources noted above. Thereafter Deakin's *The Brutal Friendship* remains useful, and Elena Aga Rossi, *A Nation Collapses: The Italian Surrender of September 1943* (Cambridge, 2000) and *L'inganno reciproco: l'armistizio tra l'Italia e gli angloamericani del settembre 1943* (Rome, 1993), are illuminating, incisive, and brilliantly researched except for their relative neglect of German sources.

Antonio Sema, "La cultura dell'esercito," in *Cultura e società negli anni del fascismo* (Milan, 1987), pp. 91–116, and Mario Montanari, *L'esercito italiano alla vigilia della seconda guerra mondiale* (Rome, 1982), explain much about the army's misadventures. Montanari, *La Campagna di Grecia*, 3 vols. (Rome, 1980), his *Le operazioni in Africa settentrionale*, and Alberto Santoni, *Le operazioni in Sicilia e in Calabria (luglio–settembre 1943)* (Rome, 1983), document the persistence of army operational and tactical failings throughout the war. The works of Ferruccio Botti, especially "La logistica dei poveri: organizzazione dei rifornimenti e amministrazione dell'Esercito nel 1940," *Memorie storiche militari 1992* (Rome, 1994) and *La logistica dell'esercito italiano, 1831–1981*, vols. 3 and 4 (Rome, 1994–95), throw much new light on the army hierarchy's logistics of poverty. Giorgio Rochat, "Qualche dato sugli ufficiali di complemento dell'esercito nel 1940," *Ricerche storiche* 18:3 (1993), pp. 607–35, is most revealing on its failure in the selection and training of junior leaders.

For understanding of the army's – and armed forces' – most successful units, *Ariete, Folgore,* and *"Giovani Fascisti,"* see first of all Ceva, *Africa settentrionale 1940–1943* (Rome, 1982), which brilliantly sets the North African scene and surveys the memoir and diary literature. Enrico Serra, *Tempi duri: Guerra e Resistenza* (Bologna, 1996), and Oderisio Piscicelli-Taeggi, *Diario di un combattente in Africa settentrionale* (Bari, 1946), for the *Ariete;* Marco Di Giovanni, *I paracadutisti italiani: Volontari, miti e memoria della seconda guerra mondiale* (Gorizia, 1991), and Raffaele Doronzo, *Folgore! . . . e si moriva: Diario di un paracadutista* (Milan, 1978), for the paratroops; and Alpheo Pagin, *Mussolini's Boys: La battaglia di Bir el Gobi* (Milan, 1976) for the *"Giovani Fascisti"* are profoundly instructive on the view from the line units.

The navy is best approached initially through Jack Greene and Alessandro Massignani, *The Naval War in the Mediterranean 1940–1943* (London, 1998), which is well-documented on the Italian and German side. Giorgio Giorgerini, *Da Matapan al Golfo Persico: La Marina militare italiana dal fascismo alla Repubblica* (Milan, 1989) offers an often cutting analytical survey. Mattesini, *La battaglia di Punta Stilo* (Rome, 1990), *Il giallo di Matapan: Revisione di giudizi* (Rome, 1985), and *La battaglia aero-navale di mezzo agosto* (Rome, 1986), provides accounts of key engagements that notably improve on the navy's reticent official histories. Santoni, "The Italian Submarine Campaign," in Stephen Howarth and Derek Law, eds., *The Battle of the Atlantic 1939–1945* (Annapolis, 1994), pp. 323–44, throws light on the submarine effort as a whole. On the convoy war, Santoni, *Il vero traditore* (Milan, 1981) and F. H. Hinsley, *British Intelligence in the Second World War* (London, 1979–90), vols. 1 and 2, are essential. Mariano Gabriele, *Operazione C3: Malta* (Rome, 1965) remains the best work on the abortive Malta landing project, but see also his summary in Rainero and Biagini, eds., *L'Italia in guerra: il terzo anno – 1942* (Rome, 1993), pp. 409–34. Finally, Santoni and Mattesini, *La partecipazione tedesca alla guerra aeronavale nel Mediterraneo (1940–1945)* (Rome, 1980) offer a detailed and frank accounting of the relative effectiveness of Italian and German naval and air forces in the war at sea between 1940 and 1943.

The air force semi-official history by its wartime deputy chief, Giuseppe Santoro (*L'aeronautica italiana nella seconda guerra mondiale,* [Rome, 1957]), has stood up well. Its successor, Nino Arena, *La Regia Aeronautica 1939–1943,* 4 vols. (Rome, 1981–94), is lavishly illustrated and contains much new material, but conceptual and organizational chaos along with failure to fully exploit non-Italian sources limit its usefulness. Curami, "Piani e progetti dell'aeronautica italiana 1939–1943. Stato maggiore e industrie," *Italia contemporanea* 187 (1992), pp. 243–61, is carefully documented and merciless on air force procurement policy; see also his "I riflessi delle operazioni nello sviluppo della Regia Aeronautica," in Rainero and Biagini, eds., *L'Italia in guerra: Il secondo anno – 1941* (Gaeta, 1992), pp. 493–518. Mattesini, *L'attività aerea italo-tedesca nel Mediterraneo: Il contributo del 'X Fliegerkorps' gennaio–maggio 1941* (Rome, 1995) documents the effectiveness of the Luftwaffe's initial Mediterranean foray in winter–spring 1941 and the Italian air force's reaction. Santoni and Mattesini's *La partecipazione tedesca alla guerra aeronavale nel Mediterraneo,* as indicated, also assesses the relative effectiveness of German and Italian air forces against maritime targets throughout the war. Finally, Achille Rastelli, "I bombardamenti aerei nella seconda guerra mondiale: Milano e la provincia," *Italia contemporanea* 195 (1995), pp. 309–42, offers a beautifully researched analysis, complete with American and British target photographs, of the costs of *Regia Aeronautica* and Luftwaffe inability to defend Italy's airspace.

INDEX